SEEK ON!

Susan Merritt

Strategic Book Group

Copyright © 2011

All rights reserved—Susan Merritt

No part of this book may be reproduced or transmitted in any form or by any means, graphic, electronic, or mechanical, including photocopying, recording, taping, or by any information storage retrieval system, without the permission, in writing, from the publisher.

Strategic Book Group
P.O. Box 333
Durham CT 06422
www.StrategicBookClub.com

ISBN: 978-1-60911-337-7

Book Design: Suzanne Kelly

DEDICATION

There would be no book, website, or who knows how many saved lives during the Vietnam conflict without the service of my heroes, the Combat Tracker Teams. In addition, had I not had the unbelievable miracle of finding my Better Half after a thirty year "hiatus," I would not be able to relate their history and work—to the best of my ability. This book is a history and story of how this came to be and the "boys" who did it. I have listened to my guys, their instructors, and have amassed file cartons of documents over the years and this is the result. I have an "A Team" consisting of Dick Baumer, John E. Dotson, Don Hendricks, Jim "Frenchy" La Farlette, Mike Landers, Dave Layne, Estel Matt, Vic Sokeland and Chuck Steward. These veteran Trackers have read and helped me out as I bumbled my way through this. Thank you, Guys, I could not have done it without you! Of course, my Frank was by my side throughout, although we differed at times and I claimed "author's privilege" and he would say, "Make damned sure no one thinks I said that!" Here you are, Beloved, you DID NOT say it, I did! In truth, any errors are mine and mine alone. To my dear veteran Trackers, Thank You for your honorable service! This one is for you!

And to my family: First Generation—Ed, Lizz and Cate; Second Generation—Samantha, Eryck, Kiera, Bethany, Owen, Ian, Al, Thias, Maggie and Rozzle; and Third Generation—Madi; you make every day a good one. Thank you!

TABLE OF CONTENTS

Prologue vii
Chapter 1   British Jungle Warfare School 1
Chapter 2   Deep in the Jungle 10
Chapter 3   School Days 1967 16
Chapter 4   Reflections 1990s 25
Chapter 5   In the Dogs' House 33
Chapter 6   Till Death Us Do Part 49
Chapter 7   Deployment Vietnam—1967 59
Chapter 8   Workin' It Out—Deployment 1967 69
Chapter 9   Return of the Tracker 1998 79
Chapter 10 Indian Country 1967 86
Chapter 11 Good News/Bad News 95
Chapter 12 An Officer's Reflections 1999 118
Chapter 13 An Old Dog Teaching New Tricks 127
Chapter 14 Reflections New Zealand 2000 139
Chapter 15 Major Rewards 147
Chapter 16 Passing The Torch 158
Chapter 17 Together Again 166
Appendix 173

PROLOGUE

June 16–18, 2000—New Orleans, LA

The City of New Orleans is hostess to many diverse conventions, national meetings and worldwide events. The Lower Garden District of New Orleans boasts a plethora of renovated and restored historical homes and businesses. On any given day, tourists stroll along Magazine Street enjoying the ambiance of this unique city. They walk and gaze into 150-year-old windows. They find a new perception of Magazine Street-the "Street of Dreams." People came to New Orleans from all parts of the globe and had equally diverse reasons for being there.

In mid-June 2000, a different kind of veterans' group was drawing together after years of separation. Most were staying in the old Victorian Foundling Home-St. Vincent's Asylum. More than a few proffered pithy humor about being lodged in a former unwed mother's home and the phrase, "You old bastard!" had new meaning. They made quite a picture as they walked the old streets of New Orleans. Some walked with stiffened gait and others bore different but less obvious physical scars of warfare.

Gathering together was this very diverse group of men. They, along with some of their immediate families, had been anticipating the event with great emotion. There had been some limited contact with one another over the last few months and years, but this was a physical reunion. There were also men present who had taught these veterans back in the late 1960s. They had flown in from all parts of the world to see with their own eyes, that the "lessons learnt" had meant survival. These former Instructors were representing the cadre of the famous British Jungle Warfare School in Johore Bahru, Malaysia. The

School had been the breeding ground for some of the most respected soldiers in history-the famous Special Air Service 22 R. The Instructors were members of the NZ SAS, the Royal Army Veterinary Corps' own Combat Tracker Team veterans-turned-trainers-#2 War Dog Training Unit. In addition, they were a part of the clan. This Family assembled because of a terrible war over thirty years ago. Gathered with the living were the spirits of those who had given their lives in that time. Each name was paid homage, each life honored and tribute given in the telling of stories of their lives.

Some of the guys brought wives, sweethearts and kids—each man chose the nearest to him to share this momentous occasion. After all, this was a reunion of kinfolk. In many cases, the brotherhood had traveled from all parts of the country. There were men from every year of that war, and there were both officers and enlisted men. Former support personnel who remembered this group wanted to be with their old friends. There was a delegate from the Viet Nam Archives at Texas Tech. He was attending so that the history of this unusual military specialty remained unforgotten. Every individual Team had representatives; and so were the instructor cadres who taught them the unorthodox, but highly successful, methodology to deal with guerilla warfare. There were tributes sent from Australia, New Zealand, England, Scotland and various war veterans and their groups from the US. Unlike the persistent myth that came from the War that "No one could find the elusive enemy," these men did indeed "find and fix the enemy."

There had been School graduation photos of the groups of men here, as well as photos of the Schools themselves. The returning Trackers came back into civilian or military life without the praise and open acknowledgment they deserved—and until now, had not had contact with the "Family." This secrecy was not due to an ongoing program of CTT in the Army, but because the British had participated in the foundation of the specialty despite their pledge of neutrality. In the past, some tried to join US Veterans' groups-but whenever they told anyone about their experiences, disbelief was the response.

Although many of these men were virtual strangers to one another, they were still brothers.

For this was the first Reunion of the Family known as the Combat Tracker Teams of the Vietnam War. Even in their wildest dreams, none could have envisioned that this would really happen. Then again, the nature of the missions and how the Teams went about it were not only classified, but also hidden well behind miles of red tape. Even so, they were not known as "Trackers" for nothing and they had started to find one another. Men that had fought as a single entity in 1967 through 1972 had been cruelly isolated from one another by the secrecy surrounding their service and the sequestering of their records as Teams.

We created a Website just for the Trackers to find one another and to be able to share their experiences with the only other people in the world who would understand. This internet-meeting place built up to an incredibly emotional "gathering of the tribe." They had all felt a renewed desire growing strong within each of them to find the brothers they had last seen in Vietnam. The British and New Zealand Instructors had wanted to find their former students for years. The official Ministry of Defence response was that the British Army had *never* been involved with the war in Viet Nam. However, the instructors and their students were still as attuned to one another as they had been then. The was a great intensity of feeling about this need to reunite, to breathe a long sigh of relief as they were able to talk of things they had accomplished, and to *heal* at last. Separately, they had all come to the same conclusion. The time had come to see one another. They needed to speak, to see, to laugh and to cry with those who were their "second selves" so long ago.

Some special team members couldn't possibly have survived, because their life spans were not the same as the soldiers who accompanied them in their hunt for the enemy. These were the amazing Labrador retrievers whom the British trained so well for tracking down men. The photos brought to the Reunion showed every one of the four-legged warriors who had accompanied the Teams. It was tangible-the Labs were there too. Not much is widely known about these military canines and their soldiers. These were typical working dogs, which would good-naturedly protect their people every time they went out on a Mission. This brotherhood had loved their Labs, even if some would have driven a saint to drink.

The family was finally coming home, and as they had started, they were again one indivisible element. These men who had trained together as boys, then deployed as Teams of men over 25 years ago still had as strong a union as that which had been forged during their arduous training, and immovably bonded in the swamps and jungles of Vietnam. Teams were not a frequent designation in the U. S. Army at any time, but in this conflict, extremely rare. The Combat Tracker Teams were "Teams" throughout the war and united to the point that the "Team" was a single entity. It was not a case of five men and a dog rather it was a "fist" with one purpose, one mission and one goal: "Find and fix the elusive enemy." Even after the authorization as Infantry Platoon Combat Tracker or Infantry Detachment Combat Tracker, the individual teams were the smaller elements that comprised the larger unit.

It seemed amazing to watch how a man trained by American Instructors at Fort Gordon, Georgia in the later years, and completely understand a man trained by the British Army, RAVC, British military and NZ SAS at BJWS or a man who trained in country at the DTD or OJT. There was not a missed step. The conversations flowed freely for the first time since that war. This was a release of feelings, experiences and more, that none had ever been able to share with other Veterans, and in many cases, not even their own families. There was a collective sigh of relief and an infusion of peace.

There were so many stories that allowed everyone to "catch up" on the events of the others' lives. There were comparisons made to actions and idiosyncrasies of then and now. The mutual judgment was, "You haven't changed a bit!" "Still crazy after all these years," was another refrain. There was the same enjoyment of one another's' triumphs throughout the intervening years, as they had experienced in some of the "wilder" escapades that only young men in the military may create. There were tears shed for the loss of years since they had been with one another and a resolve that *nothing* would stand in their way again.

The work that these individuals had done on a daily basis during their service was no less than heroic. They would tell anyone who asked, "I did my job." Every day, they had truly lived the Biblical ethic written in the New Testament in John 15:13, "Greater love hath no man than this, that a man lay down his life for his friends."

The Trackers were finally coming home. It was as if the clock had stopped back then in South East Asia-and the second hand started its sweep again in New Orleans.

CHAPTER ONE

British Jungle Warfare School, Johore Bahru, Malaysia 1967

The group of Americans was sitting in the area designated for lectures in one of the buildings at the British Jungle Warfare School. They were a diverse group: young guys like Steve Cradick from Indiana, Dave Layne and Perry Callaway from Texas, James "Frenchy" La Farlette from Oklahoma, Mike Landers from Missouri and Tom Presley from Tennessee. Others were obviously experienced Senior Non-Commissioned Officers (Sr. NCOs), Joe "Nick" Nicholson, Neil Couch, Don Eveland, Roger Cool, Gary Ward and Howard Schetrompf, who looked like they had seen and done everything despite the fact that they were not wearing uniforms of any kind. Then, there were the more "street savvy" guys who came from both of the American coasts—the New York/New Jersey Metro area Frank Merritt or Juan "Poncho" Alvarez y Navarez or the California cool guys like Bill Reed and John E. Dotson. They all had one thing in common, they had no idea what was to come. These "students" were all part of a great new "experiment" that was about to commence. There were American Lieutenants who would be going through the School as well, but they not being treated to these events and were given different briefings. They were First and Second Lieutenants both University graduates and "mustangs" (jumped up from enlistment ranks) backgrounds, men like Don Best, Ron Reed, Steve Williams, Jim Myrick, Don Hendricks, Don Campbell and Ron Hudson.

Some of the young men felt that by being there, they had "dodged a bullet." The thought was that by volunteering for this new special ops training and deployment, maybe they would get a pass out of Viet Nam for their entire tour! Some of the boys who had not been farther away from home than the county seat thought they had come to paradise—they could not have imagined anything like Malaysia in their wildest dreams. Frank and John E. were slightly older and they had seen at least one prior tour in Vietnam. They had been Sentry Dog Handlers at the First Cavalry Division, and wanted to get into this new program because they would be engaging the enemy—not just patrolling inside the perimeter. The whole idea, the little that they gleaned from all sorts of sources, was what fighting this war should be in their minds. They extended their tours to be a part of this. Then, there were Sergeants Couch and Nicholson who had seen service in Korea, and had done many "interesting" things before signing up for this. Like most of the Senior NCOs, they were "lifers" (career Army). There were about sixty male Americans of different backgrounds and Army grades gathered to learn about this new infantry "thing." These career Army guys actually had smiles on their faces—and these really green newbies were watching them carefully.

Without any more time to think about anything, a Senior Non-Commissioned Officer of a very different Armed Force flung the door open—and he did not look like an American to anyone in the room. He was wearing a completely unfamiliar British uniform consisting of shorts and shirt and had knee-high socks with something like a plaid tab on them! He had no distinguishable insignia that the boys could identify and when he told the audience to stand up—they were not even sure what he was saying! As this hard-bitten warrior stood by the door, a man strode in carrying a swagger stick. Nevertheless, even without a defining uniform, it was obvious that this was an officer of rank, and quite possibly, a gentleman. They did not know what his rank was as identifying badges or patches were unobtrusive and now, none of the Americans could decipher the shoulder board insignias that would tell them. The welcoming address included some startling comments. He stated to the Americans that the problem with the United States Army is that it was too much like the Russian and German Armies—that there was a focus on rank rather than on knowledge. The BJWS' spokesman summed up his point of view by saying, "When you entered this School, I already knew everything that you know. When you leave our School, you will know everything that I know. You see, on a Mission, if the lieutenant is killed, the sergeant must take over; if the sergeant is killed, the corporal must take over; if the corporal is killed, the private must take over. The Mission must be completed." This put the equality of the team concept on the table at the very beginning. Couch and Nicholson looked at each other and grinned. They could not believe what they had heard! An outfit where doing your job right was what counted. Bringing your team together and nailing the enemy! It's probably fortunate that this same Officer did not enlighten his audience about the 50 mile in one week trek, fending off the Gurkhas (the superb Nepalese "mercenary" warriors who had been part of the English Royal military for almost two hundred years) and NZ SAS (New Zealand Special Air Service) members posing as the "enemy" as the final exam. (Most of them would have gone back to Vietnam at that, even if they had to swim!) At the time of that final exam, however, they did just that. Had they not been able to do so, they would be exiting unceremoniously from the program long before that time. The last words that the British Officer said were, "Whilst you are here at JWS you are also subject to British Military discipline." There was no further explanation given and the newly arrived students thought, "Just what the hell does that mean?" The clock began ticking. The world that these trainees had once known just changed forever

The newest trainees had volunteered for the program from the reception center in Viet Nam after their arrival from CONUS (Continental United States). Layne was like a sheep into Tent City B where they herded him to different places offering various "marvelous" opportunities for their tours of duty in Viet Nam. One of these was "months of training out of Vietnam for a new specialty that was right up there with Special Forces and the like, *plus* it has dogs!" This sounded like a real good idea to many of the new soldiers who had just arrived into what they euphemistically described as "hell." The noise, heat, smell and overwhelming oppressiveness of Viet Nam could push a newly arrived soldier to contemplate different choices offered by the various groups. There was still a great deal of patriotism in these young Americans and they thought that this war was righteous. Every man who entered the Combat Tracker program was a volunteer.

There were other potential Tracker trainees found within the ranks of serving Army personnel. These were the Non-Commissioned Officers, (Sergeants), trained and blooded in Korea and earlier tours in Viet Nam who were "warriors born." Sergeants Couch and Nicholson had fought in some tough places and they thought this was going to be a good program for them to enter. Some of the enlisted men were also joining up from within the ranks of the serving Army. Combat veterans Mitch Scott and Roy Burchfield had time in service when they heard about the program. They were given enough information about the program to be interested and to put "ear to the ground" to find out from the "grapevine" more than was officially out there. What they learned was that this program was going to teach them how to track those damned enemies who kept disappearing on them after every encounter. The Americans had the guns, the ammo, the airpower, the arty (artillery), the support—they just could not figure out where the hell these little bastards went! This new specialty was supposed to be the answer to that—and they wanted in from the beginning. They passed the word on to others like themselves. They were Staff Sergeant Chris Hodge, Sergeant First Class Hugh Lamb, Staff Sergeant Gary Ward, Sergeant Moses K. "Pappy" Nahinu, Sergeant Dan Tharp, Sergeant Don Eveland, Sergeant Roger Cool, Sergeant Grant Golden and Sergeant James P. Moore in the first Provisional classes at the School and in the teams and they all were "gung ho" non-coms.

Others were serving currently and were already working with canines in other specialties. "Pappy" Majors had long been a part of the canine program in the Army, wanted to do more. As he understood it, this specialty would teach them to pursue the enemy aggressively instead of passive response.

The guys who had previous time in country had been there long enough to see that there was a terrible imbalance between the terrorist tactics of the enemy and the regular military field responses of the American and Allied military. Reggie Maxham, Ralph Clemings, Bill Cannon, Dotson and Merritt had all observed it—from the time one of Merritt's high-school friends had been KIA in bombing while guarding personnel in a hotel in Saigon to shared knowledge of the horror and ferocity of the VC raids on villages in the Central Highlands and elsewhere in Vietnam. They wanted to do more than just wait for a chance to respond. Besides, their former Sr. NCOICs had put their ear to the ground and told them that this was the program for them. Whatever this new thing was, it sounded like something they really wanted to get in on at the ground floor.

All of these trainee candidates had come to Malaysia on "maroon" passports—State Department issued. These had been issued showing that the holder being "abroad on an Official Assignment for the United States Government." In fact, a vehicle with escort picked up the selected trainees took them to Saigon, where they purchased civilian shirts. In short order, they were whisked off to the back door of the U. S. Embassy and photographed for their official State Department passports. They were to bring nothing with them from the U. S. Army and then given one hundred dollars each to buy "civvies." They were to use British uniforms and gear while at the School. All of them found this very cool—they had all seen or read about James Bond and all of this made them think that they might be meeting with "Q" next! It was an extremely exciting beginning, to say the least. The new guys were strutting around in sunglasses and turtlenecks, trying to be as impressive as hell. Moreover, even if they were totally in the dark as to what would happen next, it was something they would never forget for the rest of their lives.

The groups of new Tracker candidates flew in on regular and military air transport from Viet Nam to Singapore to begin their awesome transition. They sure were surprised that there were flights on Pan Am and others with seemingly normal passengers and crew—although they thought that the stewardesses were somewhat "long in the tooth"! On landing, there was an official from the School. They gathered like tourists and sat in somewhat unusual vehicles called "lorries" for the trip to their new adventures at Johor Bahru.

As they came across the Causeway from S'pore (as Singapore was called by the locals), Johor Bahru looked like an arched panorama in front of them with towers and buildings in the middle and shoreline on the side. It was a truly amazing sight to the young men who had never left the States before their Basic Training and Advanced Individual Training (AIT). It was, as these kids said, "mind blowing!" They poked at one another and stared and their mouths were so far open that they would have caught every fly in the air. They looked like kids from the inner parts of the most rural areas of America at the State Fair for the first time in their lives seeing the Bearded Lady.

Here in front of them was typical, bustling Asian commerce; obvious English heritage in some landscape and buildings; Buddhist, Hindu, Muslim Temples and Mosques and Christian Churches! They saw the Grand Palace and the Royal Abu Bakar Museum, the foundation stone of which the royal family created in 1864.

Once out of the city and into the school, all of the Americans had impressions of their new environs. Malaysia was a federated country established in 1963. It was a former colony of the British Crown and granted independence in 1957. The difference in the way that England released her colonies vis-à-vis the other European countries was vast. The British worked with their colonies to ensure their well-being and helped them become strong as they achieved self-sufficiency. Historically, the other former countries that had owned colonies, had not enjoyed good relations with the indigenous peoples and the process of severing the colonial status was usually violent, or at the least, embittered. Because of the British way of doing business, it was highly common to have a continuing presence of military—or military assistance from the British on the soil of a former colony. This was the case at this time in Malaysia. In addition, it was because of the insurgencies of the past decade that the British had foiled—again unlike the other former colonial powers.

The highly secret connection that was made to have the Americans schooled at BJWS had to be accomplished with the greatest discretion. The United Kingdom as a member of the Geneva Conference of 1954 had to maintain a stance of neutrality, if not condemnation toward America's involvement in the War. It certainly would not do to have the world aware that the same Great Britain was instrumental in training US students to fight against the North Vietnamese Communist efforts to annex South Victnam.

To say that the Yanks had landed was an understatement. To say that they were somewhat flabbergasted was also an understatement. To be able to rub shoulders with some of the elite warriors of the UK was "something else!" The rest of the American military troops serving in the war would not, in all probability, cross paths with a British Combat Tracker or a man in the Royal Army Veterinary Corps, let alone a Special Air Service soldier, in their entire lifetimes. At the School, all manner of British military specialists were present as students, instructors or serving personnel. It was a very different world from any they had ever experienced or would ever know.

The American trainees selected for the Combat Tracker program were going into a schooling that would turn them out as soldiers capable of aggressively pursuing the fleeing enemy in Viet Nam. This meant that they would be going into areas at top speed in a manner never imagined by line troop commanders. All the Americans were going to become warriors of the highest caliber. They would have to be able to read signs (a sign is something left by the quarry like excrement, or a piece of human detritus, cigarette butt, etc.) and/or spoor (spoor is a footprint, or disturbed foliage, natural environmental disturbance by the quarry), "bread crumbs" left by a fleeing unit or man in an environment antithetical to anything they would ever have known "at home." But, perhaps ever more dangerous for the team, was to be able to track down the escaping VC (Viet Cong or Viet Cong Regulars) or NVA (North Vietnamese Army) and *not* be annihilated by their own "friendly" support, or by the gunships called in by someone behind them that didn't realize the team had survived the track. Unlike the rest of the world's finest trained warriors, these American students did not have up to two years to attain the needed skills. They had a limited amount of time, perhaps two to six months and it was into the jaws they went.

Meanwhile, the trainee candidates went to their new accommodations. Those who trained as visual trackers (VT) were under the aegis of a New Zealand Special Air Service (NZSAS) Squad. This Squad had just come in from another tour of duty. This new set of orders was different from any other: to train the first eight teams of the new Program. They escorted their new American trainees met up with others who had begun their training a few weeks earlier. Young men from across America who hadn't failed any of the thorny field exercises to date; George McDonald, Larry Snitgen, Dennis Beuke, Elmer Mahurin, Mike Sisco, Bob Brede, James Boyer, Arnold Johnson, George Koon, Jerry Quinn, Larry Hadzima, Rodney Asino, Joe Farmer, Kent Near, Willie Cox, Jeff Dejewski, to name but a few of the sixty or so who were in the School at the time. During the training, a training manual was supposed to evolve. After the first eight Provisional teams had been stood up for duty, it was believed that there would be enough American Sr. NCOICs and Officers who would then be able to begin training under BJWS cadre to take over the instruction for the specialty in the future. However, this was the era of the Kiwis and they were passionate about being sure that their "Yanks" would graduate with every skill needed to excel as Combat Trackers. Moreover, they were determined to do that if it killed them!

As an insight to the manner in which the BJWS Instructors regarded their trainees' schooling, they made the training as difficult and realistic as possible. Some of these Instructors felt that their young Americans were on "suicide missions" and it was their contention that if they threw everything at the students, they would never be overwhelmed when in the actual War. To simulate combat situations, Gurkhas played the "enemy" as

Seek On!

directed by the NZSAS Instruction Staff. More than one US Trooper could be heard cursing vehemently as the "enemy" would pop up in a mock ambush, pointing and laughing at the students, with the infuriating refrain, "Ha! Ha! All dead!" The frustration of the trainees was so intense it was tangible. The credo was "Train Hard, Fight Easy."[1]

---

[1] This motto is found on the wall of the Headquarters of SAS21R in London, England

CHAPTER TWO

Deep in the Jungle—mid 1950s

Lieutenant F. Huia Woods and his team flew through the dense, triple-canopy jungle like ghosts. They were so stealthy that not even the leaves of the prolific foliage moved more than they would have under natural conditions. These men and the little, black Labrador retriever sped through this terrain with unheard-of speed. They were on a blood trail left by the Communist Terrorists who had just launched an ambush killing and wounding innocent villagers in an inner area of Malaya. The "insurgents" were brutal and determined to wrest the emerging colonial country from its path to freedom and self-rule by using fear tactics and terrorizing the poor people who quailed as their women, children and headsmen were tortured and maimed in front of them. There was no conscience in the hearts of the terrorists, only a determination to destroy whatever it took to achieve their goals. It was a classic case of asymmetric warfare. However, the British were not above donning the "ghillie" suit and fighting back and then some on the enemy's terms.

The British were equally resolute that their former colonies would stand up in peace and freedom as they achieved their statehood. In addition, to ensure this, the UK backed their promise with force. The resident High Commissioners called in armed forces from the Ministry of Defence as soon as the situation began to become ominous in the late 1940s.

Initially, the UK, as with the rest of the Allies who had just finished defeating the Axis powers in World War II, was busily taking their massive war machine apart persuaded that it was obsolete, that war was a thing of the past. Nevertheless, history always repeats itself and there was a new horror on the rise. The new face of evil was Communism but it was the same imperialism just dressed up in different clothing.

There had been too much demand on the manpower of the Allied forces for troops to be able to populate to these former colonies in World War II with military. As part of the defense of the former client states of the United Kingdom, great stores of war materiel and other necessary goods went to these colonies for sustenance and storage during the war. These supplies arrived in as much abundance as feasible for them to defend themselves in the horror of that Great War. As a result, there were still supplies and military wares remaining in large amounts after the war. The Communists—in the form of insurgents and terrorists—raided the holding areas and stripped as much of these as they could steal for their upcoming assault against the fledgling, free states. This was occurring in all of South East Asia's former colonies—whether British, French, Dutch or Portuguese. The difference was that the Brits would *not* let their areas fall into the maw of despotism.

Lieutenant Woods was by education a schoolteacher, but he was also a New Zealander with a particular skill that did not fit in a proper classroom. He had proven himself to be one of the foremost jungle trackers in the world. Moreover, he had proven so in jungle tracking competitions against the Australian aborigine, Gurkha, Iban and Dyak (former headhunters) from Sarawak and Borneo as well as other Malayan aboriginal tribesmen who were competing in their own "backyard"! Huia was simply the best.[2] He became the recognized expert in jungle tracking and made a remarkable comment: if he added a Tracker dog to the visual tracking team, he added speed to the track to find the quarry. In addition, a man could not follow a track with the accuracy of a dog's sense of smell—and certainly, not as with the speed the dog brought to the track.

---

[2] *http://www.britains-smallwars.com/malaya/Frank/ops.html*, Frank Burdett-#330522, 1st Battalion NZ Regiment

Susan Merritt

On this mission, Huia and his team were determined to find and "fix" those who had sprung the ambush. Little did the quarry know that they had absolutely no chance of outrunning Huia's team on that final day. The constant physical exertion and moisture in the air was keeping the enemy's wounds from drying. The heat of the day was increasing and even though they thought they had gained enough distance on their pursuers, this day, they could not cheat their fate. No one would find the remains, and hopefully, in what was left of their "kits," there would be some "Intel" of interest. Other than that, there was very damned little of value to these lives. These terrorists would understand that there would be a price to pay.

It is important to understand the history of the New Zealand SAS to the extent that it was an integral part of the U. S. Army's Combat Tracker Team program. The Kiwis were world renowned for their warrior abilities. New Zealanders had proven to be enormously ingenious during WWII along with the Australians in their assistance to defeat the Japanese. They were involved in all of the Asian campaigns that the UK had fought and had brought their enormous skills to great advantage. The New Zealand contingent became a Squadron of the re-established SAS on 7 June 1955. For a man to be able to be a part of the legendary New Zealand Special Air Service, it was not enough to have one or two special skills. He had to have the entire range: Counter-revolutionary warfare; Airborne credentials; Sea training; Reconnaissance; Indigenous recruitment and training; Search and Rescue in Combat of hostages. These renowned soldiers were the best New Zealand had to offer—and Captain Huia Woods was one of the finest of their breed.

The NZSAS brought to the SAS22R a rich heritage of tracking skills unequaled then or now. They taught tracking to the SAS and to other Special Forces of allied countries. It is something that seems second nature to them and something that they had to offer to the British Jungle Warfare School and to a group of young American trainees.

In 1966, General William Childs Westmoreland chose this same Huia Woods to create this program for him at BJWS. The

General heard too many times the refrain, "They are melting into the jungle!" His line commanders had not dealt with this type of "terrorist/guerilla" tactics and it surely had not been a course in Advanced Individual Training back in CONUS. The French had been ignobly defeated by it—even the vaunted French Foreign Legion. In fact, that is why the Americans were there in Vietnam to protect the Republic of South Vietnam from Communism coming from the north. At the end of the disaster, Vietnam was like so many other countries with Communist infiltrators. With no better solution, two countries were made from one in 1954 and the Geneva Conference convened to define the two states. One Communist and one free, they had lived in an unhappy tandem since then and the United States had been involved in the success or failure of the Republic of Viet Nam in the South from its beginning at the last pen stroke of the Conference.

The idea that the British had used their special ops' anti-terrorist tactics in Malaysia and won was a very important lesson for nations to follow. The future General, Donn Starry, then a Lt. Colonel, was sent to British Jungle Warfare School to assess the various programs and training. An advisory group met to discuss the potential of the Tracker program: the Commandant of BJWS; Major Huia Woods; Captain Donald Hall-Smith, commanding officer of the Royal Army Veterinary personnel in the area; Lt. Albie Kiwi, NZSAS; Colonel Hill, Chief of Operations (G3) USARV; and then Captain William Welch (who would be tasked with oversight for this and other K9 projects, i.e. Scout). The US personnel returned to General Westmoreland with a favorable review, and the rest, as they say, is history.[3]

The Visual Tracking training and final "marry up" for the Teams would be carried out by the BJWS cadre. Initially, Huia's own protégée Lieutenant Albie Kiwi and a six-man NZSAS squad just back from Borneo would be the trainers for the first eight teams. The Visual and final weeks of team training continued and concluded by the JWS staff throughout the contracts with the US Army. However, they would install Army Officers

---
[3] Personal E-mail from William Welch to Sue Merritt, 18 July 2007

and Sr. NCOs as instructors as soon as possible to "Americanize" the Program. The inclusion would begin as early as the training for teams 9 through 14 and onward. On the K9 side, the Royal Army Veterinary Corps' (RAVC) #2 War Dog Training Unit (#2WDTU) would be the instructors for the Handlers and would supply the dogs. After the Lab and Handler team were proficient, they would go to the Team group for a three-week blending of the entire team.

The RAVC #2 WDTU was another group of Combat Tracker Team veterans. These warriors had also worked throughout the world in ten man/two dog teams. They were as highly skilled in their way as their allies, the Kiwis, were in theirs. These CTTs were highly secretive in nature and work. They worked in the "Recce" mode—where they would be tasked on a mission that might put them deep in enemy territory for weeks at a time with few supplies from base. One of the intrepid Trackers was a Scot who had been a great hunter and cook of any number of things during his tours. Sometimes, he was known to "purloin" catches of others—and since his culinary specialty was stew—who could identify what that main ingredient was, or where it came from? Someone who was missing some prized food would stop by and ask, "Hardie, have you been here all day?" Bright eyes looked back at the questioner, "Oh, aye! Been cooking here all day!" In addition, as the other marched away, our Scot would be smiling to himself, thinking about how deft he had been, filching his prize that would feed his whole team nicely, thank you!

The Instructors from the #2 WDTU were incredible "dog men" who could take a young dog and create a war dog capable of avoiding trip wires; punji pits; booby traps; ambushes and always pursuing the quarry to the end of the track. The challenge for them was teaching their young Yank trainees to listen to their dogs and to them. They knew that it was a matter of teaching the human trainees to let the dog do what he did innately—and for the trainee to learn how to interpret the actions. It was not easy to bring boys around to that way of thinking after they had been taught that they were supposed to impose their will on all canines. They thought that these young men had a lot of

Seek On!

promise—and were, in fact, very much like the young British lads they were used to training. It did worry them that there was so little time. Like their counterparts in the BJWS cadre, they opened their hearts to the young men who came in to become Trackers. To a man, they believed the boys were on "suicide missions"—and they were determined to give them every tool, every trick of the trade in their vast arsenal of experience to balance the equation in their favor. They had years of experience in jungle warfare to bring to these lads—and they would find a way to do it.

Each of the instructors that had been chosen for this new program had a wealth of experience that was far and beyond what the regular AIT (Advanced Infantry Training) School had to offer. They were not known to the world, in fact, they were very careful not to curry favor with the public affairs people. The less said about their skills, the better. They were capable of incredible military successes in fields that were far off the beaten path. They were men who valued courage and honor and loyalty and they were very impressed with these Americans who had volunteered to learn how to thwart the asymmetric warfare style that the enemy was employing against a vastly superior force. That these trainees would step up despite the fact that they were probably looking at a death sentence impressed them and that they would do this so that they could to help the soldiers behind them was all the instructors needed to know about the students' intentions. Now, did they have the formidable strength, the intellect, the eyesight, the agility, the inner strength and that obscure "X factor"?

CHAPTER THREE

School Days 1967

One of the main objectives for preparing these American troops with these skills was so they would be able to reestablish contact with the enemy. (According to the students, that meant that when those bloody bastards set up ambushes that didn't just kill a bunch of innocent young kids from home, but usually mutilate and maim the shit out of them, and then ooze off into the jungle—Tracker Teams were going to catch them and bring them some old-fashioned American-style justice.)The second function would be able to tell if there had been recent enemy activity in a given area. (They were going to spy on them-to bring the war to them—instead of playing "catch up"!) The third use was to be able to find captured friendly personnel. (This one needs no explanation in the boys' terms.)

One of the new skills that they would attain would be "jungle craft." Rather than feeling disoriented in the environment of Vietnam, these graduates would feel "at home" in this very different milieu. They would-be empowered by virtue of this instruction to deal with the enemy on their terms. The alien geography of South Vietnam would be natural to them-in fact, more so than the North Vietnamese. In the normal duration of one year in Vietnam, the average U. S. soldier was at a disadvantage because of his total unfamiliarity with his surroundings. The "total immersion" offered by BJWS gave its trainees a higher degree of comfort within these unusual confines. It was a different approach for all of these men. It was a typical part of special ops' training, but normally the trainees were given many months to obtain the skills necessary. These initiates in the arcane arts of special warfare had a matter of weeks. By the time of the "marry-up" of Visual Team and Dog and Handler training, many would fall by the wayside before the final exam and be sent back to line units. The attrition rate for students who could not "make the grade" was between 35% and 75%. Mike Landers was in the group that had started with 73 men-and finished with 23.[4] There was no such thing as a "second chance." There was latitude in other ways. Unlike the civil rights problems in the US, there was no culture barrier in the program. There were native Americans, Afro-Americans, white Americans, Hispanic-Americans, Asian-Americans, Cajuns, Catholics, Protestants, Jews, agnostics and atheists. All that mattered was this, if you didn't keep up every time, you were out and back to a line unit in 'Nam. No one could afford to have a soldier who could not hack the max. However, this is how the instructors had been trained—and it was how they lived to tell the tale. They did everything that their students did and then some. The only difference was that the instructors' training had been two years[5] in duration to attain membership in their respective regiments and they were unwavering in their determination that their students would not be at a loss despite the lack of training time.

After the first day's end when they men looked around and decided that they had indeed survived, the next day brought new and "exciting" surprises. The "basha" was introduced to them. It was sort of a cross between a hammock and a cocoon. They were taught that the placement of these exotic sleeping devices was very important, indeed. A mistake in that decision could mean nighttime difficulties with the opposition force and other problems—not the least of which was being checked out by some of the large and small predators that roamed the jungle or being investigated by any of the numerous snakes indigenous to the area. It was also strongly advised to learn not to move or snore in sleep—that made a definite "tell" for anyone in the

---

[4] Mike Landers, CTT #6 and 66th IPCT-Instructor Ft. Gordon, GA
[5] *NZSAS—1ST AMONG EQUALS*, YOUTUBE Series

area, although this was secondary to placement as the jungle was incredibly noisy at night. One of the other new rules was, "Always 'basha' up in a place difficult to get to at dusk, and impossible to sneak into at night." That made for some sleeping accommodations that were never thought of before by the young trainees like Elmer Mahurin and Dennis Beuke. This was not the Hilton, for sure!

In addition, at the end of the second training day, the Visual trainees were treated to an evening in the Jungle. They found a secluded spot, and some of the native pathfinders and Trackers of the School would come back to the camp with them. Before setting up their bashas for the night's sleep, they had yet to have their evening's meal. It was then that improvisational culinary skills were brought to bear. The Gurkhas, who were part of the training team when not playing the role of the enemy, really liked these big kids called "Yanks." In an effort to bridge the ethnic gap of the groups, the "happy little psychopaths"[6] presented the trainees with delicacies of the Jungle-this might include fish caught with "thunder flashes," frogs, lizards, bugs, monkeys, bats, or snakes. It was said of the time, "If it walked, crawled, flew or swam-we ate it."[7] Sometimes they would smoke the meats that were procured for that dinner's menu. If they were unlucky about catching up with their dinner on an evening, they always had the British rations to fall back on: tea, sweet biscuits and a "meat bar"—that none of the Americans could figure out how to eat. Dick had the idea that their Kiwi Instructors had stacked the deck. He firmly believed that instead of having to set up the night bashas, the New Zealand SAS veterans had places where they had stashed their bashas-making it much easier for them at the end of the day.[8] The truth was, however, that the Kiwis actually did everything along with their trainees and it was not that they took shortcuts-it was just that they were the experts.

---

[6] Ray "Jock" Hardie's name for the Gurkhas whom he supported financially and in every other way during his life.
[7] Don Hendricks, Lt. and Commander, CTT #13 and 61st IPCT
[8] Dick, BJWS 1967

The men had to learn to use their "sixth sense."[9] In a world where not knowing what was happening around you, that little feeling could literally be a matter of life or death. If a trainee could not experience that intangible signal, he would not be long in the course. It was that important an issue. The feeling of "something is going to happen" expressed itself in many different ways—it could be a feeling that could not be explained, or as in the French word, a "frisson," a quiver or thrill of something that you experience and know to be a sign of something. This "X Factor" was a quality that was encouraged by all of the instructors in both of the training groups. Along with the regular training received as Visual and K9 Tracker Handlers, a heightening of the senses to an ultimate level was supported. This arcane human ability was still within the men, layers of civilization had to be removed so that they could access it. The way to do that was to acclimatize them into an environment that all but their most primitive genetic memories had forgotten. This return to the most primeval abilities of humanity—to the time when a shift in the air pressure could signify an impending event—would be another ability that the new Trackers would have that would save their lives in combat. It was, to say the least, an interesting concept for a group of very serious warriors to believe in absolutely.

"Bushcraft" was a way of seeing things in the field out of the ken of most people. The logic behind each lesson became very clear and the consequences of not learning them evident. The "Jungle Telegraph" was one of the first lessons at school. As Dick commented, "No matter how steep the embankment, you could not touch any trees to prevent you from falling or to pull yourself up. The top of the trees' motion was the tip off to the Kiwi's troops."[10]

The days were also filled with adventure. There were "flashers" (light charges of explosives) placed in areas to teach the Trackers what to avoid. The NZSAS instructors were so determined to make the training realistic that even they went overboard. It seems that one of Instructors had decided to place explosives around the base of a large palm tree. That tree was

---

[9] Chet Ellingson, Ft. Gordon-78th IDCT
[10] Dick, BJWS 1967-CTT #13

adjacent to the trail that the group of students would pass on the track. The instructor went at his mission with great enthusiasm, happily humming "The Battle of New Orleans"[11] that Frenchy La Farlette insisted on playing over and over at top volume on a 45 RPM record player to remind the Brits of events that they would much rather forget. The intrepid trainer climbed the tree and waited for his students to come to the spot. In his determination to teach the lads well, he had overdone the explosives a bit, and when the trainees came around to the spot much earlier than he had anticipated, he "command detonated" the charges-blowing up both the tree and himself! The zealous instructor had not been hurt by his "unplanned flight"-unless you include a bruised ego. He became known as the "Flying Kiwi"—but *never* within his or the other instructors' hearing!

The new trackers-to-be were taught to see everything without seemingly looking at anything. This seems to be a contradiction in terms, but in fact, was one of the secrets of their craft. They had the ability to see things with their peripheral vision; to see what *wasn't* in place that should be; what leaves were moving that shouldn't be—and they processed this in fractions of seconds. They could take in the entire vista surrounding them, where their fellow soldiers would focus on a specific spot. It was as if they could see through everything around them in order to find what they were looking for as a point of reference. It was uncanny—and to many, it was downright "spooky." This ability was something that was partially innate and partially taught. There were components that the soldier had to have to be able to do this, like being able to see printed holographic images immediately. Nevertheless, in these cases, it was as if camouflage did not exist or if there was a man hunkered in a rice paddy, he will be visible. Most Visual Trackers can go to a green grassy area with clover and pick up four-leafed variant out of the ground with ease! They were the human beings who could literally find the needle in the haystack! Classes could be given on the tech-

---

[11] "The Battle of New Orleans" by Johnny Horton, 1959—a song celebrating the defeat of the superb British troops at the hands of a group of American Southern "Good Ol' Boys"!

nique to any number of people, but a miniscule few will have the innate abilities to be able put the principles to use successfully. It is based on understandable principles—but the application is the rub. Once again, this borders on an ancient ability that we once had but have lost in layers of era of "civilization." This was another asset for the Trackers' arsenal—and brought them closer to the dealing with non-conventional enemies.

One of the most important things that had to be accomplished was "speed" while running on the track with the heavy packs of supplies. You were not going to catch the "elusive enemy" if you could not move like the wind. The daily physical training was geared so that it would become second nature for the novice trackers to feel comfortable in their new Jungle world. The trick to that part of the war craft was to be so at ease in the environment that you could move fast enough to overtake the enemy, and quiet enough so that he did not know you were coming. It completely demoralized the young Americans to see the barrel-chested NZSAS Sgt. Ben Morunga running *backward* with them, as they were killing themselves just to reach the barracks without dying. To give an idea of the difficulty of the course, "It was some of the hardest training I've ever been through. I've been through airborne school, commando school, Korean SF School, LRRP schools, 7th Army LRRPs and all and I believe this was one of the toughest schools I had ever encountered," is the way Neil Couch stated it.[12] All of the physical training and total immersion into the jungles shifted the men's attitude toward the new environment completely. They made it their home and were very comfortable in those surroundings. If they were not, they would not survive.

The Trainees were also "fitted out" like proper British recruits. Don Hendricks, CO of CTT 13 remembered, "We were issued British PT boots-which looked like green high-top basketball shoes and all too small for large American feet. They lasted for about five days of PT and Jungle training, and would then rot off the trainees' feet. However much the boots were

---

[12] Neil Couch, Sr. NCOIC—BJWS 1967-CTT #8–1/9th Cav, 77thIDCT, US Army Retired

scorned; it was not the same thing with the scarf, the slouch hat and the British "parang" (jungle machete like knife). The scarf was made of what appeared to be a camouflaged mesh mosquito netting. The scarf could be put over the head-and the wearer would seem to disappear."[13] Dick added that, "Usually the trainees had two of these 'scarves'. They would wash one while using the other-drying the second scarf on the back of their packs—'BJWS Wash and Wear'. The slouch hats became standard with the US Trackers, as did the parangs. Most of the rest of the standard equipment was substituted by American items."

The differences in the Dog Handler and Visual Tracker side of the Instruction were sharply defined. While the Handlers had a longer time to make the transition from trooper to Tracker, the Visual group was given a complete course of Jungle Survival in a month's less time. According to Don Hendricks, "We started our first day of Physical Training with our Instructor commanding us to, 'Lightly on your toes, right wheel, go!' As we all stared at one another, we were thinking that an 'English to English' dictionary might be in order. Could not figure out what he was trying to say. It became apparent when he directed us with sign language. He was telling us to 'Double-time, column right, March'. We had no clue that he had been speaking English!"[14] The students-both officer and enlisted also said that their Sergeants "were the hardest Drill Instructors (DI) than any ever encountered in any service of any military anywhere or at any time in history." The Instructors were delighted!

At the school weekend, the young Americans would swim and relax at the NAAFI (Navy, Army Air Force Institute) drinking "'Alf and 'alfs." These unusual British recipes used beer as a base and included fruit juices or a mixture of stout and light beers. The NZ SAS Instructors were heard going about buying "aw case aw piss" (a case of beer). Out of school, the staff and students interacted and became friends. Little did they know that the friendships and bonds wrought at BJWS would become enduring for the rest of their lives though many years would

---

[13] Don Hendricks, BJWS 1967—Commander CTT 13–61st IPCT
[14] Ibid

pass before they would reunite. They had surpassed a relation of teacher and student and become family. The adventures that they shared during the school days became stuff of legends—and not to be retold in front of children!

The irresistible lure of throwing one another into the swimming pool by the NAAFI was one of the most innocent diversions. The emotional and physical demands on the students made for some interesting events. One of the tales told literally "out of school" involved some of the trainees who were "Airborne" qualified. At afternoon tea one day, two of the airborne soldiers had been explaining about the Airborne Divisions in the United States Army. They were telling one of their Instructors, George Yeandle of the #2 WDTU, how tough and how highly qualified you had to be to become Airborne. Then Yeandle, himself a highly decorated combat veteran, replied, "It's my experience that the US Airborne was stubborn and thick-headed." The trainees agreed, but with the proviso that the Airborne men always obeyed their orders to a "T." The British Sergeant said that he could respect that-and promptly ordered the more outspoken of the two recruits to run headfirst into a nearby tree. Looking puzzled at first, the "parachutist" that he had stepped in it and to save what little "face" he had left, had to obey the order. He got up and ran headfirst into the tree causing his face and nose to bleed profusely. He ended up on the ground, bleeding and dazed. The Sergeant just shook his head. The other airborne trooper, not to be outdone, also ran headfirst into the tree! This was the last straw for the British Sergeant-he was rolling on the ground in gales of laughter, and saying something about the "stupid, bloody, fucking Yanks!"

There were other cultural lessons to be "learnt" as well. Close to the JWS' main entrance was a small wooden shack. This diminutive, crude structure was divided into two equal parts. One-half was occupied by the local tailor. He offered the students necessary "kit" for a proper basha: loose fitting, two-piece pajama-like outfits with elastic at the waist, ankles and wrists. This was important to keep one's body as protected as possible from all harmful "critters" when sleeping in the jungle. All of the gear was fashioned from salvaged, black parachute silk. The British mantra was, "The jungle is your friend! The jungle is your home!" A man might as well be as comfortable as possible and support the local economy while at home with his friend.

The other half of this small shack was the only redeeming feature for the Yank students' stomachs. This was the local version of a "fast food joint." Most of the Americans could not abide the British Mess Hall's offerings and this strange form of Johore Bahru "deli" was a real hit. A guy could purchase a sliced hardboiled egg sandwich on white bread, fresh fruit and other delicacies. There were many of the trainees who lived on that fare throughout their time at the school.

The interesting thing about this "outpost of normalcy" was that the two vendors could not abide each other. One of them was from Pakistan and a devout Muslim, and the other was a Hindu from India. They could not be more diametrically opposed. Because of the size of the shack, they were always in very close proximity with each other and they simply could not leave discussions about politics and religion alone. When the students arrived back to camp after an exhausting day of Field Training Exercise (FTX) they were looking for fast food or gear from the tailor, but were treated to something unexpected—a down and out verbal "pissing match" between the two former natives of the subcontinent. None of the students could understand a word that the combatants screeched at each other, but spitting on the ground was a sure sign that harmony was disturbed in any language. In the end, all was reconciled and the opponents withdrew to their respective sides of the shack where they awaited the next day and a repetition of this bellicose performance.

Interestingly at this stage in the game, some of the Visual trainees had no idea that a canine and handler would be joining them. The comment overheard on the first day of the merging members into a Team, "What the hell's that dog doing here?" Other classes were informed about this addition, and told further that the dog would definitely get their "egos" back into perspective. "It worked, too, damn dog like to have killed me!"[15]

---

[15] Don Hendricks, Commander CTT #13–61st IPCT

CHAPTER FOUR

Reflections 1990s

Thirty-some years after the first Teams had graduated from BJWS, the desire to reconnect with those who had shared such important events in their lives overcame the fear of doing so. Some of the men began to search seriously for their former team members. Mike Landers had reached out to find most of his team and was trying to locate other guys who were at BJWS with them. John Dupla, who had come in to one of the Teams as a replacement in September 1967 was also doing what he could with Steve Cradick. It was a difficult decision for many of these vets. There were many "lessons learned" in their lives, which had only made the bond of the "Brotherhood of Trackers" more compelling. Part of the reticence in looking for one another was the apprehension that maybe what they had thought was an unquestionable loyalty and, yes, love for one another had only been a dream. One feeling that was universal within the community of veteran Trackers was that maybe as individuals they had not done enough. Everyone was so driven in his specialty that each also had inner doubts about his own performance. Some thought that maybe they had dreamed the whole thing! In addition, since official documents never referred to the Combat Tracker Teams-maybe the whole thing did not exist.

As a matter of fact, even as early as when the veteran Trackers returned to CONUS, some would wonder if they had really gone through the war as Trackers. Dave Layne related an incident that happened at Fort Hood after his return to "the World." This incident took place early 1968, when those who had been members of the first Provisional Teams had completed their tours and had returned to the States. Layne had been in the mess hall and was looking around. He saw a fellow BJWS graduate who had finished the training course with him. They had not seen each other since school at Johore Bahru. He walked over to the other Tracker who said, "Well I'll be damned, how are you?" They proceeded to eat together and talk a bit. Then a strange silence overtook both of them. The other Tracker asked, "What was it that we did over there? Nobody in this entire Goddamn Army will ever believe it...and I am not sure right now if I even believe it... Did we do it? Were we at those places?" Dave did not even have an answer. Sometimes, he still calls his fellow BJWS graduate-and the question always comes up, "Did we do all that?" Layne does not really know what to say. The assignment was so difficult on his schoolmate that it has affected his entire life. Moreover, he still does not have an answer for that question.[16] The graduates had individual plaques and other significant things from the School, but nothing on their formal records.

It was in the early 1990s that some of the Veteran Trackers started to request updates of their DD 214s (Abbreviated Service Record and Discharge Document). They were informed that there were no records of any U. S. Army personnel going to the British Jungle Warfare School in Malaysia. There were records of the Teams authorized as Infantry Platoon Combat Tracker (IPCT) or Infantry Detachment Combat Tracker (IDCT). There were no records regarding Combat Tracker Teams #1-#14 (Provisional CTTs). It was as if the Provisional teams never existed.

Some of the Trackers became career Army. The one complaint that they all voiced was there was never again the feeling of "esprit de corps" that they had experienced as Trackers. Their future assignments were placements as Drill Instructors, Sr. NCOICs as well as Officers in Special Ops and Military Intelligence. However, there was always something "missing"

---

[16] Dave Layne—BJWS Track Layer, Green Dog Handler, CTT# 2, Current Combat Tracker Team Trainer

Please refer to Chart A—Teams and Affiliated Regiments/Brigades

after their tours of duty with the teams. In addition, wearing the Combat Tracker Team tab was not permissible, as it was an unauthorized tab.(The same held true for the graduates of the Panama Jungle Warfare School.)Since the Army did not recognize it, they could never wear it with dress uniforms or fatigues. Most of the Trackers never discussed their experiences of combat. Some described it as if the clock had stopped when they separated from their teams for the last time in whatever manner.

It had consequences on all of those who were a part of the teams. In addition, that applied to every Tracker from every "era" of CTT. It didn't matter where they had been trained: BJWS; Fort Gordon, GA; the "School" at the Dog Training Detachment at Ben Hoa, RVN; or On the Job Training (OJT)—a Tracker by any other training was a Tracker. No matter how they came into the specialty—once they had been a part of the Team and had become one of the "Family," they were forever bonded. They were able to see first-hand what they and the other men were capable of, and the almost unlimited abilities that they possessed. In the years that followed, the team members who remained in service felt that they had become "dinosaurs" in the Army of the 1980s. Interestingly enough, some of the veteran trackers became involved with SWAT and other police special canine units in the mid-90s and more are instructing today. It was an unimaginable concept for most of the men to think that the specialty was disposed of like so much trash.

Despite their unusually difficult problems with reintegrating into a vastly different America from the one they had left, they assimilated well. The warriors who fought on the very edge of the spectrum of combat action were not, mostly, the stereotypical "Vietnam Vet" that was scorned by the public. Quite a few went into helping others; working with the Vietnam Veterans of America (VVA), the Disabled American Veterans (DAV), counselors and sponsors for VA processes. Others became American Legion Officers, Honor Guards for veteran funerals. Some stayed with the canines assisting in search and rescue and police efforts, training search and rescue dogs, training Leader Dogs, breeding and raising Labrador retrievers and other breeds of dogs, training therapy dogs. Some became men of the cloth—Priests, Deacons, Bishops, Preachers, and Laymen who work to help their fellows. Many of these Tracker veterans have earned respect for their work with the community and their generosity toward their fellow man. They do these things without the need or desire for recognition. For men had who walked fearlessly into the "valley of the shadow of death," they returned, alone and unacknowledged, and went on to become good, solid Americans. Those who stayed in the Army had some difficulty in achieving rank, as Tracker was not an asset on their curriculum vitae. Those who had remained in the Army usually entered into other Special Ops work. They also taught their tracking skills as part of training in those specialties.

In the beginning, in an effort to fill the void left from the intensity of their experiences as Trackers in the War, some of the vets went to the veterans' groups; Vietnam Veterans of America, Veterans of Foreign Wars, or the American Legion to have a place where they could relate to other vets and let some of the common war events come out. However, too often, the Tracker got questions about his Vietnam War experiences. There came the inevitable kicker, "Which outfit did you serve with?" The men would reply, "Combat Tracker Team," with the affiliated Division. When the inevitable explanation was given by the veteran Tracker, the kindest response to that was, "What the hell are you talking about?" The worst response was, "Bull shit!"

At a VVA meeting in Virginia, a former member of the Fifth Special Forces Group (SF) asked about the "Team" designation, the veteran Tracker explained about the training they had received and that they were indeed officially "Team" members. The former SF vet blustered and carried on, saying, "There were no other Teams authorized by the United States military in Vietnam except Special Forces and S. E. A. L.s." The Tracker was unusually patient in trying to educate this sterling example of bullheaded stupidity. He told the former SF member about BJWS in Malaysia, and many of the missions that the Trackers had successfully performed "in-country." The former Special Forces member was unmoved. "You're lying," he said, "You can't possibly have gone to BJWS-you're not jump qualified, you're not Ranger qualified, so it's just not possible!" The Tracker could not produce the records and documents that would have attested to all that he had explained. It was a very difficult time for veteran Trackers.

On one occasion in 1993, Frank Merritt and John Dupla[17] went to Fort Hood for the reflagging of the First of the Ninth Regiment of the First Cavalry Division (1/9th). They were wearing Combat Tracker insignia. The 1/9th had been the reconnaissance for the First Air Cavalry Division (Air Mobile) during the Vietnam War. The insignia "flashes" and t-shirt designations not only proclaimed Combat Tracker Team, but also included the emblem from the British Jungle Warfare School. This ceremony was an incident that had both recognition and rejection for the Trackers.

The veteran Trackers "crashed" a Cav Long Range Reconnaissance Patrol (LRRP) Group in their hospitality ("hostility") suite. Again, the questions came at them about training and qualifications. One former LRRP member was vehement in saying that that the LRRPs were more highly qualified and trained than any damned Tracker. A "lively debate" ensued as the two representatives of their respective specialties argued on. Finally, when they had both exhausted the "bona fides" of each aspect of their groups' credentials, one of the Trackers asked the former LRRP for his Military Operational Skill (MOS) code. The querulous LRRP responded, "Eleven Bravo, (11-B Rifleman) of course!" The Tracker just smiled and said, "We were eleven Foxtrot, (11-F Infantry Ops and Intelligence Specialist)." At that, the LRRP's eyes lit with recognition, and there was an apology on his lips. The later teams were 11-B, but the first few years that the Trackers deployed after BJWS training, the majority carried an 11-F MOS designation.[18]

---

[17] Merritt and Dupla were both assigned to CTT #7–Provisional Team with the First Cavalry Division (Air Mobile), 1/9th HHQ. Merritt had been on the first Tracker team attached to the Cav, and Dupla had arrived in September 1967 as a replacement.
[18] Ibid

Susan Merritt

The former Commanding Officer of the 1/9th from the Trackers time in Vietnam was also at this ceremony. He had taken part in it as a tribute to his service with the Cav. He was Colonel Robert S. Nevins, and he certainly did recognize his Trackers. In fact, he went over to them to let them know he remembered their work for the 1/9th with appreciation. Col. Nevins was a great commander in the field and showed his concern for his men and all under his command. In fact, to tell stories out of school, Col. Nevins found his Trackers and the Labs to be so impressive, that he "decorated" the dogs for their valor. Someone in the "higher-higher" of the system had caught this, and Bob Nevins was reprimanded for giving medals to the dogs. As an aside, it was understood by all that he found another way to do it-and said that they were worthy of the awards, and that was that.

Another chance meeting at this ceremony was when one of the "chopper" pilots stopped the Trackers and asked about what they were and what they had done. The Trackers responded with a synopsis of their training and deployment. The Cav pilot said he had been in the battles at Ia Drang, and said that had there been Trackers to define the enemy's positions; there would have been a lot fewer casualties. His exact question was, "Oh man, where were you when we needed you?" In addition, of course, the Trackers were not in country until after Battle of Ia Drang is a matter of history.

The 1990s were a time when the Trackers still had little recognition and less understanding, but the feeling of wanting to find their own became stronger. Unbeknownst to the Trackers, however, was the fact that other people were indeed interested in what had been the outcome of the Combat Tracker Team program in the United States Army. There had been articles written about the teams during the war in various magazines and newspapers. There were also some studies going on evaluating and recommending the integration of CTT into the current peacetime Army of the 1990s.

The Trackers were also unaware that in General Westmoreland's "Report on Operations in South Vietnam," the specialty was adjudged as having accomplished "commendable achievements."[19] Major William Kelch, entitled, created another retrospective analysis "Canine Soldiers" which was published in *Military Review,* Volume LXII, Number 10-October 1982. Major Kelch's summary of Combat Tracker was, "Combat Tracker Teams were generally very effective in Vietnam. They could follow a retreating enemy and reestablish contact, follow local enemy to villages or homes, follow and recover US personnel captured by the enemy, follow and recover Army patrols or individuals who were lost or separated from their units, and backtrack captured enemy personnel. The dogs were also used for security and night defense positions."[20]

In 1998, Lt. Commander Mary K. Murray did her Master's thesis for the War College on the Vietnam Canine Experience. In her paper, entitled "The Contributions of the American Working Dog in the Vietnam War," Lt. Cdr. Murray stated, "The combat tracker program is one of the least known programs in the history of the American involvement in Vietnam. Despite the problems associated with acquisition, training and employment, the trackers and their dogs distinguished themselves in the field and provided a valuable contribution to the war effort. The lessons learned from this now deactivated program bear recording to avoid similar problems and optimize its effectiveness should the combat tracker program be required in future military operations.

"The importance of employment doctrine to a new combat program seems fundamental but was virtually ignored with the combat trackers in Vietnam. The lessons learned from the evaluation of the first provisional trackers were never incorporated in doctrine for either the tracking teams or the infantry and fire support that utilized the CTTs.

"While it would be impossible to calculate how many lives would have been saved had the tracker dogs been employed cor-

---

[19] 'REPORT ON THE WAR IN VIETNAM"-General William C. Westmoreland, COMUSMACV Monographs, June 30, 1968

[20] Military Review October 1982-Major William Kelch, US Army, "Canine Soldiers"

rectly, there is little doubt that official coordination would have resulted in a superior combat tracker program."[21]

The overwhelming reaction of the studies undertaken regarding the Combat Tracker Team program was positive. The researchers were unanimous in their belief that the program should be on going and a part of Army Specialty training because of its' favorable results. The Trackers who had created the statistics and accomplished these achievements still did not know how successful they had been. However, that would change sooner than they could imagine.

---

[21] THE CONTRIBUTIONS OF THE AMERICAN MILITARY WORKING DOG IN VIETNAM, by Lt. Cmdr. Mary K. Murray, published by the Combined Arms Research Library. June 1998

CHAPTER FIVE

In the Dogs' House

Meanwhile, "that dog" was teaching his master a new trick—how to track. While many parts of the tracker training were the same in application, the handler and dog moved out at a much faster pace. The Lab would catch the scent of his quarry and be gone—so the handler had to be ready to go with him. At a minimum, the handler also had to be able to take physical care of the Lab; to know how to interpret accurately the dog's every action; how to give medical assistance if it became necessary. Huia Woods had said that the canine brought two special assets to the team—speed and scent ability to follow the track. The importance of "that dog" became quite clear when the Teams were deployed to the War. The canines always had the best accommodations! The Department of Army reckoned that a well-trained Tracker Labrador retriever was more important, not to mention much more expensive, than an easily replaced handler was.

The #2 WDTU had a very different approach to training than their hard-core brothers on the other side of the school. On the first day of one cycle, the RAVC Instructor Corporal Loganathan "Samy" Pakrisamy took his new students Frank Merritt, John E. Dotson, Tom Presley, Gene Kuffel and Reg Maxham out of their camp, across the road, and to a ridge. As they all stood together, still in civilian clothes, their new "Guru" stood in front of them and pointed at the Visual trainees running below obviously being pushed to their limits by their Kiwi instructors. Corporal Samy waved his hand in a dismissive way as toward the Visual group along with their trainers. Then, he thoroughly

Susan Merritt

stupefied his new charges by saying, "We do not train that way. Today, we will walk a distance, tomorrow a bit more, and so on. You must think of it as 'steps within steps' and 'goals within goals.'"[1] He was instilling into his trainees that they would be undefeatable when they finished their time with the #2 WDTU. This instructor had been a Combat Tracker Team handler of great reputation in his own right. It pleased him to create a bit of competition between the physical prowess of his students and those in the "tender care" of the Kiwis. To add fuel to the fire, Cpl. Packrisamy's parting comment aimed at the sweating and physically exhausted Visual trainees and their NZSAS hard-line instructors, "THEY are nothing!" and proceeded to lead his lambs back to their new home.

The entire atmosphere at the training area overseen by the #2 WDTU was in stark contrast to the controlled mania of the "other" side of Team training. For one thing, these RAVC members did not belong to the regular BJWS cadre. They were in their own bailiwick and had their own way of doing things. It was an outpost of the British Army, albeit a small one that was highly specialized. It was so much more a regular disciplined arm of the British military that until thirty some years later the parent regiment members of the Royal Army Veterinary Corps as a whole, were completely unaware that this group had trained American troops during the Vietnam War. This entire unit and its "business" were secret—and the British did not allow "leaks." These men had been deployed as Combat Tracker Teams throughout the world where needed to defend Queen and country. As young men themselves, they had earned their stripes in Africa during the various uprisings. They had served in Oman, Cyprus, Malaya and Borneo and always with indigenous team members and their own intrepid Labs. They were capable of living "off the land" in almost any terrain and their ethos was that, "Every track has a conclusion." They were the ones who had experimented with the tactical variations and tried the various potential tracking breeds during their years in the field.

Bloodhounds, Fox Hounds and Alsatians, to name a few, had been tried for tracking but none answered the requirements as well as the Labrador retriever. The Labs were trackers by nature and benign—although some of the Trackers would beg to differ with that. The friendly black or yellow Labs would allow changes in handlers as time passed without disabling trauma. In addition, they were so adaptable to the weather that they could be used in the jungle, desert or colder climates with proper care. They were so happy to go to work—they loved the mission to find the quarry once they knew what was expected of them. They learned to avoid booby traps, punji pits, trip wires and the things that could end lives for them and their teams. The breed had a good sense of self-preservation. Their sense of smell was unparalleled and their general behavior pattern fit the purpose to a "tee." Of course, each Lab was an individual and had different "signals" (physical motions or actions), his way of telling his handler what he was sensing. The #2WDTU knew from their personal wells of experience that they would not be instructing the dogs as much as they would be instructing the students to learn from their dogs. Combat Tracker Labs were not going to perform at their peak if they were trained to strict "Schutzhund" type of obedience, or trained to receive toys as a reward. That type of training would inevitably end with fatalities of canines, handlers and the rest of the Team. The Lab had the innate ability to find quarry, the dog's trainers reinforced this natural instinct in order to help him learn to pursue a specific quarry. This did not override the dog's native abilities, but worked with them to achieve optimal results. The handler trainees were taught to observe the dog's body language and to praise enthusiastically the Lab's successful work outcomes. Of course, there were other rewards for the Labs, too. One in particular, Sambo (5A15), would later develop a taste for eating brains and eyeballs. He would be so "into his work" that he simply wanted to "share in the spoils."

Canine tracking was of such interest to the British dog-men that many other variations were explored. They had abseiled with the dogs—the British version of rappelling -; they had them on boats; and many other combinations. The American Tracker teams were inserted by choppers, so there was a jump involved from some distance—none of the Labs was terribly fond of that. But, unlike their human companions, none were reported to have broken their ankles or legs while being inserted.

Another thought that passed through the British think tanks was to try "bite dogs" for tracker teams. One particular test case involved a Doberman pinscher who was trained with his team for a prolonged period, as he was to be encouraged to be aggressive as well as to be schooled in Tracker tactics. Everyone was quite pleased with the Dobie's progress after almost a year had passed and the powers-that-be decided to put the Team into the field. The Team was tasked with a mission in a foreign country. Everything was going along well, the dog was racing along and the Team was in proper formation when the quarry entered a cave. After some discussion, the Team Leader decided that since their Tracker Dog was "bite trained," they would allow him to go "off lead" into the cave to "get the quarry." It seemed the best way to deal with this precarious situation. They loosed this particular dog of war, which was salivating at this point. The dog flew into the cave and the Team waited outside assured that their great Dobie would finish the track successfully. Unfortunately, there was more than one exit from this particular cave—and the Dobie only knew of one egress. After being very frustrated by finding nothing in the cave, he emerged out of the original opening with his eyes rolling, drool and spittle flying, and immediately charged and attacked his team! It was at this point that the Brits decided that Tracker Teams did *not* need to have a "bite dog" as part of their "kit."[22]

There were also other places to be filled in the #2 WDTU's rosters by the young Americans. For every Handler student, there needed to be Track Layers who would be creating the exercise path for the day for the Lab and his new student. These Track Layers, like "Inky" Inklaar would set up the exercise trails for the trainees and then have the rest of the day to do the rest of their work. They were also becoming proficient canine trainers. There were two types of Labs that would be available to the

---

[22] Ray "Jock" Hardie, R. A. V. C, #2W. D. T. U., & "Black Watch"—(May he rest in peace)

US Army in this new program: the first were veteran Labs who had actually been used in the field and some had experienced combat; and the "Green Dogs" who were young dogs, virtually untrained and would need six to nine months for their complete training. The Track Layers were also tasked with working with the two programs and given the choice of veteran versus the young dogs as their preference. Most of the young American kids were straightforward in their desire to work with the dogs and wanted to do it for that alone. Some were thinking that it was a great way to do the one-year commitment and then get the hell home. Quite a few started as Track Layers and had their tour extended at JWS to take either the Visual or Handler Course or go directly in as a replacement for a Tracker team. No matter what the personal choice, life with the RAVC veterans was a far different world than they ever expected when they had come into "this man's Army." One of the Green Dog trainer veterans, Dave Layne[23], said years later that he could not believe how many times he had gone up and down the hills. He felt like the Greek King Sisyphus, blind and condemned to roll the rock up the hill every day and have it roll back just before it reached the top!

The Handler trainees were unaware of the diabolical plans that their Instructors were cooking up for them along with the Track Layers. There were Track Layers assigned to certain Handler trainees and when the Instructor caught sight of certain areas of weakness, the training team would work on specific tracks and exercises to "fix" the problems. The trainees were not aware of these behind the scenes plans. Frank Merritt never knew about this until thirty-four years later at the Reunions when he learned that Dave "Inky" Inklaar had been Corporal Samy's right hand in setting up exercises to see if they could push the handler trainee's buttons to the point of explosion. When Inky did make this known, it was not as a stranger, but as a brother who had just been adopted by a different family. That was an underlying secret of the success of the specialty—the

---

[23] Dave Layne, BJWS—CTT #2—Current Combat Tracker Team Trainer

amazing attachment that united every participant of this unique "experiment." Any man who took part in this program to train these young Americans and their dangerous quest felt the intensity of what they were all going to accomplish together. Moreover, because of this, everyone grew very caring of his "lads." This was very true on the #2WDTU side of things.

The instructors and military assigned to the students at "Thornhill Lines" (one of the names for the area that the #2WDTU commanded) did not rotate out as the Visual Instructors at BJWS did. These veteran Trackers were here on station, some with their wives and families. It created a much more stable environment to say the very least. This was also a British Army outpost—that is to say, it was more "proper" in atmosphere. For instance, there was no "Kiwi shithouse" to be used as a punishment for failure at P. T. Gitti Rossell[24] would have had a fit had she heard that! However, even having said that, there was the "Monday Morning Line-Up." This ritual had been started because of a new problem that had cropped up across the Causeway in Singapore, where women were women and some men were women—especially on Boogis Street. At any rate, since most of the young men were convinced that they were "going home in a box," they tended to overindulge when in the degenerate areas of S'pore. Somehow, there were difficulties incurred with the taxi and taxi drivers who were foolish enough to agree to transport the miscreants. Truthfully speaking, more often than not, the taxi drivers thought that they had inebriated kids in their vehicles and therefore, easy prey. That was a very serious mistake. Inevitably, the taxi and/or the driver would undergo drastic alterations to their bodies. This always happened on Sunday nights—or in the wee hours of Monday mornings. Of course, there had to be a "line up" for the irate cabbie to identify the scoundrels who had accosted his vehicle or his person or both. In order to maintain his anonymity, the authorities placed a paper bag over his head with cutouts for his eyes. He would march up and down as the

---

[24] Sergeant Tony Rossell's wife who accompanied him to Malaysia and was a mainstay for many in the #2 WDTU and the trainees.

hung-over dog-men were trying to: (a) stand up; and (b) keep straight faces. It always ended the same way, the poor victims had the matching statements, "I can't tell—they all look alike to me."[25]

In addition, the Yank students received their regular pay plus a COLA (Cost of Living Allowance). The pay and mail arrived via the diplomatic pouch to the US Embassy in Singapore and was then driven to the school for disbursement. Receiving word from the "Land of the Round Eyes" was always welcome, as was the pay, which was issued in Malaysian currency. By both local and Brit standards, the students were over-compensated. The same was said of the boys as was said by the Brits of the Yanks in WWII in England, "Over here, over paid and over sexed." The only problem was getting rid of the money that was burning a hole in the students' pockets. Practical methods included hiring "Johnny Gurkha" to clean the barracks, do laundry, make up the bunks and in general keep things up to the proper military standards. The boys were always prepared for an Inspector General (IG) inspection and did not have to lift a finger. The students would "queue up" to draw weapons before going into the field. They would get their Self-Loading Rifles (SLRs) and Sten guns that were issued to them and when they returned were guaranteed to thoroughly mucked up. For a mere pittance, the Armorer would clean and secure the weapons.

As to the training itself, the handlers were not being pushed to their limits in p.t. (physical training) exercises. That is not to say that the new handlers were having a "free pass." Far from it. The first thing that they had to do was to establish a relationship with their canine partner. They did not have to like him, but they had to develop mutual respect. The dog had to obey the handler and the handler had to instill confidence and trust in the dog. If they did not have the right relationship, nothing further could be accomplished. Merritt had been given Skipper, a yellow Lab, for a partner. Initially, this seemed to be a good match. When they went out on field exercises, the dog seemed somewhat overly

---

[25] Dave Layne—BJWS—CTT #2—Current Combat Tracker Team Trainer

fond of his human partner. At first, the handler was merely suspicious, but during one exercise when both were doing a "low crawl," the Lab tried to mount his master—and that was not "appropriate." Merritt went to his instructor and asked for a replacement as "close fraternization" of this sort clearly was not going to work. Corporal "Samy" replied that he would prefer that one more trial be given. The student acquiesced but not without some serious doubts. Later that week, the students and their dogs were in swampy grounds and getting ready to spend the night on a field exercise. They had just bashaed up and the unhappy handler realized that he was almost out of water. He would have to refill his canteens and he realized that he would have to use his "water purification tabs" to make the nearby swamp water potable. That was the only water source available. Skipper, the friendly yellow Lab was with him as he went down to the edge of the swamp and as he found a large log that had fallen in to the murky water. He had to go out on the log to get to water that was not totally fouled. He carefully made his way on the slimy log, tentatively sliding the back foot after the front so as not to slip into the stinking muck. He got out far enough and carefully bent over in a curve in order to use his hand to clear the surface mess and get to the clearer water. Just as he was about to dip the canteens in, he was pushed from behind. The fucking dog had struck again. Now he was under the surface of this filthy quagmire that turned out to be much deeper than he had thought. It was over his head and he could not begin to imagine what was within the contaminated waters or what might be coming to eat him. When he flew out of the water and returned to "Mother Earth," there was no way he was going to continue with Skipper, his infatuated canine. Fortunately, there was another mésalliance in progress at the time. Mike Sheer, a Californian, a real Californian, had been given a very aggressive, veteran warrior, black Lab by the name of Sambo. They were not enjoying a good relationship as Sambo was scaring the living hell out of his young trainee. Corporal Samy felt that this might be a sign that a more efficacious outcome could be had by changing the Labs. And so it was that Skipper went on to become a great Tracker

Seek On!

for his teams and Sambo went forth to eat brains and eyeballs and become beloved by all at the 1/9th Cav.[26]

This process was not for a contest or a dog show; it was to save both of their lives, the teams' and ultimately, many American soldiers. These first steps would become the foundation for all the future work the Tracker dog would do. It was all a part of fitting the right man with the right dog. It was also a matter of acquainting each of the students to each of their dog's individual mannerisms and alerts. One of the primary commands that the Handler would learn was, "Seek!" that was the command he would use to task his dog to start tracking the quarry. Before long, the hills and dales were filled with young Americans in various stages of becoming Tracker handlers. Some of the dogs may have had more combat time than many of their new handlers. They also were not above setting "the kids" up.

On one occasion, it was a typical day in Malaysia where it seemed like the terrain wanted to ingest every living thing on its' surface. The Lab was tired and cranky and the young trainee was doing everything wrong. This continued until the poor dog had endured enough and simply sat down and refused to go another step. The apprentice handler tried absolutely everything in the arsenal that had been given to him. He became totally defeated and completely distraught. He finally went to his Instructor, Sergeant George Yeandle, (who had been awarded the Order of the British Empire {OBE}), for help. Sgt. Yeandle looked at the young man with contempt, got down on all fours in front of the recalcitrant Lab, looked him in the eyes and said, "You do want to track, don't you?" He then got up. The Lab got up, and promptly got on the track and sped off again. Lesson "learnt."

There were times when the young men got thoroughly frustrated with their four-legged partner and displayed their tempers. The instructors had a fit antidote for that—when a trainee or Track Layer had been less than respectful to his canine companion, he would then be reminded of the importance of

---

[26] Frank Merritt—BJWS—CTT #7—1/9th Cav 1967, Current Combat Tracker Team Trainer

his friend—by carrying him around in his arms for hours and hours, miles and miles, and in some extreme cases, days and days. Even for those students who only observed this "learning experience," it was an exceptionally effective way to teach the virtues of curbing one's temper.

The handler designees went through three months of increasingly difficult training if they had a veteran dog and up to six months if they had a "green dog," just the same as the Track Layers' period for the other dogs being readied for the next cycles of the program. Moreover, just as the Kiwis were very concerned about what would be waiting for these "young Yanks" when they were sent back to Vietnam and the war, everyone at the K9 wing was as apprehensive. For years, the outcome of "those kids" remained a subject of conversation whenever they were together—be it at a duty station or later after retirement. However, they were forbidden to make inquiries or to pursue anything outside of mere speculation. It was a strict prohibition from the Ministry of Defence. Only after more than thirty years had passed was there a lessening of that stricture and when there was an allowance of contact, time and distance had not lessened the strength of the bonds that had begun in South East Asia in the late 1960s. They are now stronger than ever.

Seek On!

FOR OFFICIAL USE ONLY

HEADQUARTERS SPECIAL TROOPS
UNITED STATES ARMY VIETNAM
APO San Francisco 96307

AVIA-P
LETTER ORDERS NUMBER 2-37

13 February 1967

SUBJECT: TDY

TO: Individual Concerned.

TC 200. Indiv this sta placed on TDY as indic. EPSCTDY. TDN.

MAXHAM, REGINALD T RA22883303 SGT E5 Scty Gd Co, Sp Trps USARV APO 96307
DOTSON, JOHN E JR RA19869628 PFC E3 Scty Gd Co, Sp Trps USARV APO 96307
MERRITT, FRANCIS B III RA12732968 PFC E3 Scty Gd Co, Sp Trps USARV APO 96307
KUFFEL, EUGENE F US54805623 PFC E3 Scty Gd Co, Sp Trps USARV APO 96307
COON, GARY L US54805617 PFC E3 Scty Gd Co, Sp Trps USARV APO 96307

TDY to: British Jungle Warfare School Singapore, Malaysia
Pd: 95 days
WP: o/a 18 Feb 67
Purpose: See USARV G3
Auth: VOCG
Tvl data: TBMAA on space required basis. Tvl by coml or mil air auth to include foreign flag.
Acct clas: 2172020 80-5006 P2000-21 22 S83031 (2020.3500) MK O/A 67-A-137 (10-160) $11,075.00
Sp instr: Report to USDAO Singapore upon arrival. Futher transportation will be arranged, to the Jungle Warfare School. Civ clothing will be worn for all travel and duty outside JWS. Work uniform w/o shoulder patches will be worn at JWS. Personal baggage 100 lbs. Immun cert (DD Form 737) WB in your possession at all times. Indiv is req to possess passport and visas as approp. Civ clothing allowance authorized not to exceed $100.00.

FOR THE COMMANDER:

T. A. BROWN
WO1, USA
Asst Adjutant

DISTRIBUTION:
30-EM conc
5-OO, ea unit indic
5-FDRF
5-EM 201
3-AVIA-PN
3-AVIA-MR
1-Rec set
1-Rmf set

FOR OFFICIAL USE ONLY

PHOTO 1 Orders for Training of Dog Handlers with #2 Working Dog Training Unit at British Jungle Warfare School, Johore Bahru, Malaysia. Note – no US military clothing or insignia to be worn and civilian clothing allowance given.

Susan Merritt

For OFFICIAL USE Only ORIG. TO BJWS

HEADQUARTERS SPECIAL TROOPS
UNITED STATES ARMY VIETNAM
APO San Francisco 96307

AVIA-P 9 January 1967
LETTER ORDERS NUMBER 1-10

SUBJECT: TDY

TO: Individual Concerned

TC 200. Indiv this sta placed on TDY as indic. RPSCTDY. TDN.

HOOD, JOHN W JR RA52290659 SSG E6 Scty Gd Co, Sp Trps, USARV APO 96307
WILDE, JON C RA19370670 SP4 E4 Scty Gd Co, Sp Trps, USARV APO 96307
DUNCAN, TOMMY C RA10734475 SP4 E4 Scty Gd Co, Sp Trps, USARV APO 96307
SCOTT, MITCHELL D JR RA25847760 SP4 E4 Scty Gd Co, Sp Trps, USARV APO 96307
DONGIORNO, MARTIN J RA12720066 SP4 E4 Scty Gd Co, Sp Trps, USARV APO 96307
KARNOSKI, FRANCIS A JR RA15617064 PFC E3 Scty Gd Co, Sp Trps, USARV APO 96307
KNIGHT, HENRY A US53420657 PFC E3 Scty Gd Co, Sp Trps, USARV APO 96307
FARMER, JOSEPH A JR US53433960 PVT E2 Scty Gd Co, Sp Trps, USARV APO 96307
ASINO, RODNEY T RA60014210 PVT E2 Scty Gd Co, Sp Trps, USARV APO 96307
ALBEND, ROBERT D US53422490 PVT E2 Scty Gd Co, Sp Trps, USARV APO 96307
LAYNE, DAVID O RA15003505 PVT E2 Scty Gd Co, Sp Trps, USARV APO 96307
BARTLETT, DALE W RA16000540 PVT E2 Scty Gd Co, Sp Trps, USARV APO 96307
LIBBY, ALFRED R RA10035405 PVT E2 Scty Gd Co, Sp Trps, USARV APO 96307
O'BRYAN, TERRY L RA19055055 PVT E2 Scty Gd Co, Sp Trps, USARV APO 96307
GILL, LARRY A RA16051225 PFC E3 Scty Gd Co, Sp Trps, USARV APO 96307
HEAL, KENT E US54377439 PVT E2 Scty Gd Co, Sp Trps, USARV APO 96307
HOWARD, WILLIE H US56367051 PVT E2 Scty Gd Co, Sp Trps, USARV APO 96307
DEJEWSKI, JEFFERY T US56452069 PVT E2 Scty Gd Co, Sp Trps, USARV APO 96307

TDY to: British Jungle Warfare School Singapore, Malaysia
Pd: 170 days
WP: o/a 14 Jan 67
Purpose: See USARV G-3
Auth: VOCG
Acct clas: 2172020 60-5000 P2000-21 S03031 (2020.3500) 0417-B-113
CIC: 2072020 000 03031.
Tvl data: TDWAA on space RQN basis. Tvl by coml or mil auth to incl foreign flag.
Sp instr: Report to HQ No Singapore upon arrival. Fur trans WB arranged to HQ-2 War Dog Training Unit. Civ clothing WB worn for all tvl and dy outside JWS. Work unif w/o shoulder patches WB worn at JWS. Personnel bag 100lbs. Immun cert (DD Form 737) WB in your poss at all times. Indiv is req to posses passport and visas as approp. Civ clothing allow auth not to exceed $100.00.

For OFFICIAL USE Only

PHOTO 2 Orders for Training of Tracker Teams at British Jungle Warfare School, Johore Bahru, Malaysia. Note – no US military clothing or insignia to be worn and civilian clothing allowance given. Immediately prior to transportation to Malaysia, the US State Department issued "Maroon" Passports – (Official State Department Passports) – for the prospective trainees and spirited the young men out of Saigon via commercial air transport. The return trip was quite different.

Seek On!

PHOTO 3   1/3 Graduating Class of May 1967 Visual Trackers JWS

PHOTO 4   Center third of May '67 Class with Huia Woods in Center

PHOTO 5   Final third of May '67 Class

PHOTO 6 "Abandon all hope, all ye who enter these portals"

PHOTO 7 School days included many "interesting things!"

PHOTO 8 The Outpost of Civility – The Home of #2WDTU

Seek On!

PHOTO 9   The Staff of #2WDTU

PHOTO 10   A graduating Class of Dog Handlers & K9s

PHOTO 11   Staff, Graduates and Labs

PHOTO 12 Goodwill Ambassadors to Singapore

PHOTO 13 The Officer Corps of the Future

CHAPTER SIX

Till Death Us Do Part

The time had come for the unnatural wedding of the visual team and the handler and Lab. This was expected by some classes and was an utter shock to others. This was a critical time on many levels. There were internal conflicts that had to be smoothed out when the visual tracker (VT) and/or Team felt that they did not need "no damned dog," and would then be forced to add a handler and Lab. There was a finite period to hammer five man/one Lab teams out of the pool of trainees and there was no allowance for hubris. This "marry-up" period was instructed by the NZSAS and BJWS cadre trainers. In fact, some in the #2WTDU group in their enclave were unaware that their graduates had gone for this "master's degree" program. It was not until the late 1990s that they learned of the rest of the story.

    The visual team had all become cross-trained to the point that virtually any one of the men could take position as visual tracker (VT), team leader (TL), coverman, or radiotelephone operator (RTO)—and this was the way that the teams would work in the field. Having stated that, each individual excelled at one of the positions just a bit more than another did. To make each team optimal, they were given a primary assignment in that given position, although it was not rigid. As the team went further into the field and first encountered the quarry, whoever saw the threat first "called the shots." This was a single war fighting entity made up of sharply trained individuals who functioned in as synchronized a manner as a finely crafted Swiss watch with many different abilities. With the addition of the Lab and handler, the team unit was complete and the crafty instructors and their assistants worked on tracks that were complex. They would first have the VT on point and then the point position was set for the K9 and his "interpreter." They started with "easy" routes and very quickly raised the levels to highly dangerous situations. It became clear to the visuals that the Lab brought speed and an amazing "nose" to the chase—once they could put their confidence in "that dog" and his handler. More importantly, from the handler's perspective, he was looking for a coverman that he literally could trust with his life.

This "Finishing School" was as difficult as the earlier training had been. There was one occasion when a five-man team was sent on a navigational exercise by "Snooks"—one of the veteran NZSAS Instructors. The team consisted of a certain Lieutenant who had come into the program with the attitude that, "These Brits ain't shit. They can't teach me nothing that I haven't gotten from Ranger School." This particular Officer had been an NCO who had achieved Officer's rank through Officers' Candidate School. James P. Moore, a six foot-six inch Afro-American Sergeant, and three others; Frenchy La Farlette, John E. Dotson, and Frank Merritt, filled in the other slots on the regular team. On this extremely hot day in Malaysia, the task was to navigate the team from one place on land through a swampy area to another point on land. There was an outcropping of rocks to one side of the swamp—and the swamp itself was quite wide, although it did have a shallower "shoreline" area. The swamp was filled with "Elephant grass" or as the Brits would say, "Belucca," that was eight feet tall and leech-infested water. The Officer was to shoot a heading with his compass or by any means at his disposal to get from point A to point B. The Lieutenant puffed his chest and informed all and sundry that this was an easy thing, "a piece of cake!" The team put on all of their gear, including their SLRs (British equivalent to the M-14) and followed their "Fearless Leader." The first sign perceived by some of the little troop that something was definitely wrong was when they realized that they were not in the shallows or shoreline of the swamp. In fact, the filthy water was well over their knees. The second clue that all was not well was when they could not cut a path through the elephant grass with their parangs (the sharp machete-like knives that the Malay natives used that had a "hook"-like curve at the point end). This forced a novel approach to creating a path through the swamp. One member of the unit at a time would take the point and literally fall forward with his weapon held at arms' length into the foliage and muck beating down the belucca. This would continue for fifteen minutes before the soldier was completely exhausted and another came up to take his place. Meanwhile, the erstwhile Ranger Lieutenant was trying to find his way out of the sucking mess. Sergeant Moore, the NCO, whispered to the others of the "Lost Squad," "I've been watching the shadows and checking my watch. We've been going in fuckin' circles for hours!" The entire track should have taken an hour at the most and at least four hours had elapsed under the scorching mid-day Malaysian sun. Shortly after this observation, Moore and Merritt caught sight of something on the outcropping of the rocks. It was "Snooks" and he was doubled over miming laughter. He was in tears! He motioned to keep silent and waited for the "master soldier" to notice him at which time he pointed to "Point B." It was only one hundred and fifty yards ahead.

Of course, the team was totally depleted from their marathon. At least Sambo, their team's prospective Lab, was spared this indignity. However, the Lieutenant's day was not quite over. A leech had invaded his private parts during the "March through the Swamp from Hell," and the repercussions from the disastrous day were going to remain with him for some time. Fortunately, that particular Officer and his supercilious attitude were the exception and not the rule for the fledgling teams.

The young men were very pleased that their "hosts" and their American NCOs were treating them to some relaxing evenings after the grueling days. They were quite surprised that this partying was encouraged, but, hey, they sure were not going to argue. What they did not realize was that this was the way that the Kiwis and their own NCOs were deciding who would work best together as a team. It was a great indicator to see these trainees with their guards down in a stress-free mode.

Those who had natural affinities and those who had conflicts were easy to spot after a couple of rounds under the encouraging eyes of their "minders." For what the men in charge knew without question was that once the team had been selected and worked together and blooded together in the field—nothing save death or severe wounds would separate them. The choices that were made for this mixture were therefore critical. Though there was great ebullience, the purpose for it was incredibly serious business.

Playing hard was an antidote for daily rigors of training and a great way to rid their pockets of the extra Malaysian "funny money." There were visits to the dens of iniquity in Johore Bahru and "S'pore." One of the favorites was "the Library" where they did not go to read. It was, euphemistically, a house of ill repute in Johore Bahru. Sergeant Moore was a featured player in the boys' fun. As described before, Moore was a six-foot six-inch Afro-American who was as well endowed, as the old wives' tales would have one believe. He would frequent the establishment and after picking his companion, they would retire to her room. Shortly thereafter, she would be seen exiting the room at top speed, screaming, "NO, NO, not wit' dat' t'ing!" This was a case of an asset turned into a liability. The Kiwis enjoyed this spectacle beyond words and paid for Moore's time and refreshments at the house just to observe and be entertained!

There was also the NAAFI for excessive imbibing which allowed the Kiwis and American non-coms to observe further the possible combinations for the future team assignments and to have time together, too. There was not a great deal of formality among the enlisted men of different ranks and this continued into deployment and beyond.

In S'pore, a foray almost cost the end of Merritt's career as a Tracker. Dotson had bought a motor scooter and after an evening of liquid overindulgence, Merritt was the designated driver—which was a serious mistake. Unfortunately, an obstacle threw itself in the path of the flying scooter and the guys took a serious spill. Merritt had a severe facial laceration and a local Good Samaritan took pity on the miscreants and put the bike

Seek On!

with a bent front wheel into the trunk of his vehicle, and drove the guys and bike to the British Military Hospital. Subsequently, the doctor did his stitching while John E. counted each one, then laughing like mad, left the ER. He straightened the front wheel out by hand, jumped aboard and returned to the School to report the accident.

In some respects, it was an inspirational incident for Merritt as this hospital had been erected during the British colonial period. There was no central air-conditioning, it was multi-floored and it had high ceilings with fans to provide air circulation and cooling. The wards were open affairs separated by large Roman arches. On the wall next to each ward entrance were brass plaques inscribed with names. The American patient asked an attendant for an explanation. He was told that during WWII, the Japanese Imperial Army had invaded Singapore and had defeated the British defenders. When the Nipponese soldiers entered the hospital, they went to ward after ward and bayoneted every patient to death. "Just what do you think *they* will do if they get a hold of you?" Now that utterance from his DI, back at Basic Training made abundant sense. After a brief recovery period, it was time to "get back on the horse" and return to training.

Back at school, the students were testing their skills. When they had first arrived at JWS, they had been told that certain areas were "off limits." That was just too much temptation for these highly charged guys and it was only a matter of time before those areas would have to be explored. After all, Trackers when in combat would be working in enemy territory that would be considered "off limits," right? One day at dusk, three of the usual suspects were making their way down a trail in a restricted area. They were going along smoothly when directly in front of them was a swaying King Cobra. The snake's hood was extended and his head was weaving left to right in a threatening dance. The head was at least three feet off the ground and that represented only a small portion of its total length that can be up to eighteen feet long. Not only was this serpent living up to his name but also he had another asset—he possessed venom containing a virulent neurotoxin. If this type of snake bit a person, the victim's nervous system would shut down stopping the heart and respiratory functions ensuring a quick death. The boys surrendered the field to the Cobra and beat a hasty retreat back to the NAAFI. They asked one of the Brits who was a dead ringer for English comedian Terry Thomas and a long-time resident there, "What do you do when confronted by a deadly Cobra?" He presented his "famous" grin and said, "The snake represents no threat." The Yanks were very nonplussed and asked, "How so?" The Brit put his arm forward as if in front of a snake as had been described. "You simply present your arm to the snake. His fangs are so long that they will pass through the fleshy part of the limb and the venom will harmlessly squirt out the other side!" The boys looked at one another in astonishment and went further, "But, what if the snake's fangs hit bone or if it refuses the offered arm and bites you in the leg or thorax?" The expert replied in what we consider typical British fashion, "No problem—you're dead!" So much for "The jungle is your friend."

Although they had already gone through months of incredibly difficult training, there was the "final" exam to pass before the teams could graduate. Every day, they polished the skills that they had learned by going up against the "enemy" who had disappeared in the jungle. They knew how to keep on that track until they found and fixed the quarry. They were able to tell from an area where others had been how many had been in the group, what state they had been in, what they carried for weapons and where they had gone. They were able to "feel" every nuance of the environment around them. The "enemy" could not fool them anymore. They could also assess an area for possible earlier activities. Another lesson learned was how to use their knowledge to rescue friendly personnel who had become lost or captured. They would fulfill their missions. They were ready to go. They wanted to use their skills to make a difference in a war that they could now understand. The average soldier, no matter how good his training, would have no comprehension of what the Tracker Teams capabilities were. Unfortunately, many of the line officers were suffering from the same ignorance.

Seek On!

The newly connected teams had committed to one another and they were ready for the ultimate challenge of the last test to be given them by their trainers. The track was filled with everything that the Brits, Kiwis, Gurkha, Iban and Sarawak could devise to trip up the latest members of the Combat Tracker community. It was a fifty-mile trek in less than a week and there was a night track included. In fact, one of the members of that team remembered that part of their "death march" very distinctly! It seems that the "happy little psychopaths," as Ray "Jock" Hardie of the RAVC, #2WDTU fondly called the Gurkhas, whom he thought the world of, decided that they would design that night track over an open well. Merritt was the handler of that team and remembered it because he felt the lead go upward at a sharp angle—definitely signaling that his dog Sambo had jumped. He was just able to follow suit—and realized what a terrible thing he had been spared when he heard the giggling of said Gurkha! They did love their young Yanks! For those who did not pass the final, there was no second chance and no graduation. This event took place only days after the "Flying Kiwi" had struck again. Just as Sambo had flown down the track, the ground blew up in front of Merritt temporarily blinding him with dirt and debris. Another lesson accompanied by laughter, "Mate, you've got to be aware of everything! Hahaha!"

The Teams were ready to go forward. The young men had been honed and fashioned by the best instructors in jungle war craft bar none. The handler and dog were matched to complement one another at work—and work was the only factor that really mattered. The visual team and the handler and dog were seamlessly crafted into a working unit that had no equal. There were no individuals when they were on a trail—they were a fist made up of five men and a Labrador retriever. For those who could excel at the training, they became a special breed altogether.

There was no ceremony with the families of these men when they graduated, no articles in the papers about the excellence of their achievements. However, the men were well aware of what it took to become a Combat Tracker Team member—and it enabled them not only to survive but also to protect the troops behind them, to reestablish contact with the enemy, and to find their fellow soldiers who had been captured by the NVA or VC Regulars or the VC Terrorist cell groups. These young men were perfectly aware of the skills they now possessed. Moreover, in a time when the United States Army needed the benefit of their training, they were superbly ready to serve.

The young men were sent out of BJWS in complete Teams at this time. The Trackers were anticipating using their new skills to the advantage of their fellow soldiers. They knew what the newbies of the infantry could not because the terrain of South Vietnam was home to them now. There was no intimidation about being in an alien land. For them, it was no longer strange and it did not matter if they were in triple canopy jungle or going up the rivers or sitting on the tunnels of Cu Chi. In that sense, the Trackers were much more comfortable than their peers were. Still, there was an excitement or an edge to what they were feeling. It was due to thinking of being in actual combat with these honed skills from the School.

There was also sadness about leaving Malaysia. They had become close to their instructors, the Gurkhas and other indigenous members of the cadre. They felt as if they were all family and they were leaving home again. It was because of the intensity of what they had endured, true, but it was also because of the real reciprocal feelings among a group of men that have standards second to none. There had been a tragic accident during the training of the very first classes that had started in October of 1966. In an exercise that involved river crossing, three of the original Tracker candidates had drowned. Lieutenant Freddie Lee Johnson, Private First Class Jose Munoz and Private First Class Harry Walter Murray had been on a field exercise when they met their deaths. The bodies were flown to Saigon so that the secret of the British School training American soldiers would not be compromised. Although there were "leaks" and both Reuters and U. P. I. published articles with a surprising accuracy, even on the Viet Nam Wall there is no mention of them dying at JWS in Malaysia. Having this happen so early in the new contract created a lot of misgivings and confusion in the ranks of the students. There were quite a few of the original trainees who no longer wanted to be a part of the program. There were also resentments against the Commandant of the program for what was perceived as inadequate safety measures. To be fair, part of the nature of this training was to have as close a simulation of actual combat as humanly possible for the students and this was the same intensity that the British or ANZAC special ops selectees would experience. In addition, this was done because every instructor knew what was waiting for these students in the guerilla warfare of Vietnam. They knew that the only thing that would guarantee the survival of these young "Yanks" was a complete immersion in what they would be facing "in-country."

Even this sobering thought of the training deaths could not dampen spirits of the newly minted Trackers. They were going back to their War. They felt very confident that they could really be an asset to the Army now. For those who had already served in Vietnam, there was an even stronger feeling of eagerness to help. They were well aware of how deadly the NVA and VC had played with the U. S. forces. Now, they could make a real contribution to the war effort. That British Officer who had given the "Welcome address" had been right. Now the graduates knew what that Officer knew just as he had told them what seemed like eons ago.

Meanwhile, at the end of June 1967, the first NZ SAS training squad was leaving BJWS to return home to be reassigned to regular duties. Major Huia Woods was also leaving the post at BJWS having established the program for the US Army Combat Tracker Teams. General Westmoreland personally observed every result from the Provisional Trackers as they began to work in the war in Viet Nam. He was impressed with the Teams. He did not want to lose the participation of Major Woods and the program and wanted to start a school at Fort Gordon, Georgia under Major Woods' oversight. This would involve high-level secret negotiations with the UK because of the Geneva Conference of 1954. This was when France had lost Viet-Nam and the

Susan Merritt

country had been formally split into two countries—North and South Viet Nam. The signatories were the State of Viet Nam, the Democratic Republic of Viet Nam, France, the United Kingdom, the Soviet Union, the Peoples' Republic of China, Cambodia and Laos. The United States was there as a witness but did not sign the documents. This was why the British government had to be extremely careful not to be seen as actively participating in the conflict in any manner. The consequences with the other major signatories could be catastrophic. Meanwhile, the General was so convinced of the potential of the specialty that he was not above breaking a few laws to get what he wanted. He even proposed "stealing" Major Woods if there was no other way to do things!

CHAPTER SEVEN

Deployment Vietnam—1967

The newly formed Teams had arrived "in-country." There were as many reactions to the next steps as there were Team members. They had been surprised when leaving Malaysia because they had not flown with a regular air carrier. They had been driven to an awaiting military cargo plane (C-130) with their Labs, and taken directly onboard. There were no customs, nothing to indicate that they were leaving Malaysia and nothing to show that they had ever been there. They did not want to seem too unworldly, so no one remarked on it except to one of the other Team members. Those unusual maroon passports had them arriving in Malaysia in 1966 or 1967 but never attested as having left the country. The young men were sent out of BJWS in fourteen complete Teams at this time, from February to October 1967. The Trackers were anticipating using their new skills to the advantage of their fellow soldiers. They knew what the regular infantry could not; the terrain of South Vietnam was home to them now. There was no intimidation about being in an alien land. For them, it was no longer strange and it did not matter if they were in triple canopy jungle or going up the rivers or sitting on the tunnels of Cu Chi. In that sense, the Trackers were much more comfortable than their peers were. Still, there was ambivalence or an edge to the positive feelings they had. It was due to thinking of being in actual combat with these honed skills from the School. They knew that they had been given the "keys" to do their job; to reconnect with the enemy, to be able to move through the jungle like a native—but Viet Nam was not

Susan Merritt

Malaysia and it was their turn in the barrel. What would the next weeks bring? They had a vast knowledge that was unimaginable only months before now.

There were a number of great stories to tell about Malaysia. They had taken part in a different experience that most of the guys here would never have. One of the favorites was to tell the gullible regular troops back in 'Nam was how they finally got their revenge on "Johnny Gurkha" as the British called them. They would roll out the tale by starting how one of the students would go over to the unsuspecting Gurkha and ask to see his kukri (the slightly curved, viciously sharp knife carried by the Gurkhas). "Now, according to the Gurkha tradition," said the captivating Tracker, "these feisty little soldiers could not allow their knives to be brought out from the scabbards without shedding blood!" The Tracker would spin this out and his team members thought this was great. "Why, we would line up and ask to see the Gurkha's kukris. Of course, the poor man would then cut his own arm—so as not to dishonor the tradition. The Gurkha forever after wore some unusual scars on their forearms—and could be seen to growl at those 'wicked Yanks.'" And many an infantryman in Vietnam believed this story as gospel and it still gets retold in places like Minnesota and Iowa, or Arkansas and Alaska from time to time when former fighting men get together to tell about the oddities of war.

As the teams were deployed in that first year, they were placed in many different situations. The specialty was not yet an official part of the U. S. Army. These first Teams were authorized as "provisional" to their assigned Division or Brigade and the operational control was G3 or G2 (Intelligence). They were round pegs being assigned to a myriad of square holes at this point. Fortunately, the need for their work smoothed out many of the potential problems.

It was at the very beginning of tracker deployment that the depth of their training really became evident. When they had been in school, the instructors had successfully introduced them to all types of environmental and geographical areas. Every week, the Instructors had included terrain exercises with single, double and triple canopy to acclimate the students to the total topographical possibilities that prevailed in Vietnam. It would not matter where they were sent; they were already familiar with working within the variety of terrains.

The teams had a parent organization within USARV (United States Army Republic of Vietnam)—called Special Troops. This was an umbrella HQ for many different elements including War Dog Detachment and Women in the Armed Forces in Vietnam. The teams and individual replacements would be temporarily assigned to Special Troops Detachment, HQ USARV at Tent City B at Tan Son Nhut. This was to get the administrative details in order before processing them to their assigned Divisions or Brigades. This would take a week or less usually, and the Trackers would be on their way. They would be sent throughout the Republic of Vietnam—from I Corps in the north by the DMZ to the Delta regions of III Corps. The first few weeks that the Teams were in Vietnam, their orders had been "cut," but they were in the normal cycle of "Hurry up and wait," for which the Army was famous. They were still under the "umbrella" Command of the Special Troops USARV. While they knew where they were going, the higher ups were telling the Divisions and Brigades that they were trained and ready to be deployed.

While languishing at Tent City B outside of Tan Son Nhut Airbase, the boys decided to outfit themselves. There was not a General Order pertaining to their status within the Army yet, and so they were to be "provisionally attached" to their Command groups until February of 1968. Because of this, there were no authorized uniforms, equipment, housing or any of the other "creature comforts" offered by the Army. They went to the PX Annex and set about creating "Combat Tracker Team" uniforms. Since there was no absolute in the regulations, a variety of fatigues and equipment were tried out. They chose the locally made Aussie-style "camo" (camouflage) jungle hat and attached a shoulder tab with "Combat Tracker Team" on the side, which was pinned up. Some of the guys got a little carried away and thought that the "Tiger Fatigues" were made to order for them, although not to be worn "on the job."

They also had enough time in this "holding pattern" to enjoy the hospitality of several Enlisted Men's' Clubs and Officers' Clubs. On one memorable occasion, some of the intrepid Trackers had been imbibing a bit too freely. They were combat Vets and had served with the Military Police (MP) in Sentry work before becoming Trackers. On the way back to their sleeping quarters, they had the misfortune of having to pass the MPs "home away from home." This was a G. P. (General Purpose) tent with vertical poles to hold it in shape. It was too much of a temptation for one of the guys, and he entered the tent loudly declaring that the "M. P.s were all chicken shit!" Of course, this was unendurable for the sleeping MPs and they came awake in "attack mode." The other Trackers were laughing hysterically, and had no choice but to defend their somewhat berserk Teammate and they proceeded to do so. The result of their foray was that the center poles collapsed, and MPs and Trackers became entangled in the canvas wad that had once been a tent. The MPs' Officer of the Day (O. D.) heard the commotion and came rushing over to find out what had happened. The Trackers and MPs stood at attention as the Officer screamed, "What the hell is this all about?" Several of the MPs muttered that their honor had been sullied. When the Officer looked in the direction of the Trackers, the miscreant who had started the ruckus still maintained, "MPs are ALL chicken shit, Sir!" The other Trackers explained calmly that they were about to go to their assigned Division on the next day, that they were Trackers, and that they were "Sorry, Sir!" The Officer thought about it all for a minute and recognized the line of work that the Trackers had in front of them—and dismissed them. He strongly directed them never to come near the MPs area again.

When the Trackers arrived at their respective Divisions and Brigades, nothing was ready for them or for the Labs. The first task for the Trackers was to create their new Team Headquarters. That meant that the protection of the Labs was the first consideration—before worrying about the basic comfort of the team. As a result, the Labs had better accommodations that were built by sweating and cursing Trackers who were uncomfortable in general purpose tents and command tents until the kennels were finished. In many cases, one member of the Team would be a "scrounger" or a "dog robber." The expressions were used in the military to describe someone who could do anything, procure anything, skirt red tape and in general, obtain the necessities of life for their respective units and "dog robber" had been used for a general's aide in particular. The "dog robber" did not have to be a good Tracker, because the rest of the Trackers would protect him with their lives. This was the guy who could find wood for the tent floor or a generator that worked.

The Trackers were more than ready to go to work as they completed their building projects. They spoke among themselves about what lay ahead. They would alternate between bravado and some serious cases of introspection about their upcoming "debuts." They knew that they had the best information and skills that they could have been given but would it really work? They practiced their formations and went over their hard-won knowledge, but they were not going to lose the feelings of unease until they had time in combat.

They were dispersed throughout the war zones. Each Team was met with different challenges in their new assignments. Many of the line Commanders of the units to which the teams were attached had the idea that the Trackers were to be used as permanent "point men." This was a very erroneous concept. The Teams' Mission Statement as authorized by the Army was to first—re-establish contact with the enemy; second—explore an area to determine if there had been enemy activity; and third—to rescue captured friendly personnel. The line Officers had difficulty in understanding the difference between re-establishment of contact and acting as "point." In fact, it was completely different. The Trackers were able to work completely on their own in accomplishing their missions. They were not an infantry support unit—rather, in the American Army application of Tracker, the Trackers had platoon or company sized infantry units supporting them.

The Trackers had the ability to act as a "Hunter/Killer" team as the British had used them. In the American application, there were enough infantry assets so that the Trackers could be used primarily in a pure tracking function. The BJWS graduates had no trouble adapting to different methods for doing their work. In fact, as they began to go into the field, they had the "luxury" of training some of their infantry support elements to become almost an extension of the Unit. The School's axiom, "Train hard, fight easy," was proving out. Some of the assigned Divisions had their own "chopper" assets and when this was available, the Teams would go on several missions a day to triangulate the enemy's positions. As the Teams got into their work, they learned what parts of their lessons could be used in this war and what would be left out. They began to start with small variations on the major themes of their JWS education and carefully experimented with their own changes to suit the missions they were given.

In addition, deployment was not always so accommodating. Some of the early Teams spent days in the field performing non-Tracker missions, because there was no transportation available to get them back to their HQ. Other teams worked in river and lowland areas and spent the same amount of time in the field as their attached infantry element. The proof of the excellence of the training was that there was no place that the teams could not adapt themselves. No Area of Operation (AO) was a mystery to them, or was able to present insurmountable problems in the performance of their work. If the protocols were observed to insure that it was an appropriate tracker mission, the Trackers were able to achieve their goals.

Sometimes, the CTTs would be left in the field because the support unit that had called them in had no air assets of their own. This meant that the team could literally be stuck for a period. Chances were that there would be no Officer in Command (OIC) with the team and there would be a Sr. NCOIC, instead. If the non-com were good, he would be able to stand up for the team in how they were to be deployed, whether a mission was proper for them or not. He would know when to stop on a track because the dog had alerted or because he had enough tracking knowledge to realize that the enemy was ahead and it was time for the support unit to come in and "take care of business." However, too often, the teams were not led properly or intelligently. They were thrust into situations where they had no business being or they were forced to "walk it in," when it was obvious that the quarry had been identified. The casualties taken by these teams were due to these errors rather than actual working faults of the teams. Indeed, "shit happens," and in war that is a given. Nevertheless, the abilities of the CTTs were of such high caliber that there was little rate of failure on their actual work. The most aggressive teams would, "blow through" from time to time, into actual enemy areas. Their analysis was that when the enemy was in control and on the assertive path, they were sure and positive. When they were attacked *in their home turf*, it threw them into a frenzy of disarray. They simply could not accept that their area had been breached by a team of enemy men and add to that a "devil dog," and they would literally throw their weapons down and run.

The enemy was not just terrorized by the team, but by the overwhelming firepower that could be brought upon them by the follow-up that would surely come. The arrival of a CTT was like an announcement of imminent death.

This chart shows the Divisions and Brigades to which the Combat Trackers were attached. Note that the original Teams were officially designated as Combat Tracker Teams. As of General Orders 105 issued in February of 1968, the Trackers were to be Organized and Equipped as IPCT—Infantry Platoon Combat Tracker assigned to a Division, or IDCT—Infantry Detachment Combat Tracker and assigned to a Brigade. The IPCT or IDCT was then broken down into separate teams.

Susan Merritt

THE PROVISIONAL COMBAT TRACKER TEAMS OF THE VIET NAM WAR

With their Division/Brigade attachment and their subsequent designation as IPCT/IDCT[27]

CTT # 1	66th I. P. C. T.	25th Infantry Division
CTT # 2	66th I. P. C. T.	25th Infantry Division
CTT # 3	64th I. P. C. T.	4th Infantry Division
CTT # 4	64th I. P. C. T.	4th Infantry Division
CTT # 5	61st I. P. C. T.	1st Infantry Division
CTT # 6	65th I. P. C. T.	9th Infantry Division
CTT # 7	62nd I. P. C. T.	1st Cavalry Division (AM)
CTT # 8	62nd I. P. C. T.	1st Cavalry Division (AM)
CTT # 9	557th I. P. C. T.	101st Airborne Division
CTT # 10	64th I. P. C. T.	196th Light Infantry Bde. & 4th Infantry Division
CTT # 11	76th I. D. C. T.	199th Light Infantry Bde
CTT # 12	66th I. P. C. T.	25th Infantry Division
CTT # 13	61st I. P. C. T.	1st Infantry Division
CTT # 14	65th I. P. C. T.	9th Infantry Division

The other problem that the teams encountered during the Provisional time was that the young Trackers had the knowledge and ability that outranked the more senior soldiers who had called them in, but not the chronological seniority. They were too young to be able to stand up for themselves when ordered to do something that was contrary to the Mission Statement that they carried with them:

---

[27] Courtesy of the CTT Website: *http://www.combattrackerteam.org*. Chart created from historic research by Veteran Trackers and Author.

Seek On!

THE USARV COMBAT TRACKER TEAM

I. MISSION:

The mission of the combat tracker team (CTT) is to track the enemy in order to re-establish contact. Typical missions include tracking:
A. Enemy personnel who survive friendly ambushes.
B. Enemy ambush parties after ambush of friendly units.
C. Enemy mortar or rocket crews after attack on friendly units or installations.
D. Enemy terrorists or mine-laying parties.
E. Small enemy elements, which have been observed by, ground forces or air observers.
F. Lost or missing friendly patrols or personnel.
G. To gain intelligence information such as age of track, direction of travel, and composition of party. This information can be used to attempt to block or intercept the enemy using ground forces or air power.

II. ORGANIZATION:

The CTT is composed of a team leader, a visual tracker, a tracker dog and handler, and two covermen. All team members except the handler receive visual tracker training. Although not organic to the team, a scout dog team often is attached. Each division is authorized a combat tracker platoon with four CTT and each separate brigade is authorized a detachment of two CTT.

III. EMPLOYMENT:

A. General Principles.
   1. CTT is trained to operate primarily in heavily vegetated areas. As population density increases, tracking efficiency normally decreases.
   2. CTT must have a good starting point for tracking. The visual tracker must confirm the enemy track since the tracker dog will track any scent, friendly or enemy. Friendly destruction of enemy signs or tracks prior to the arrival of CTT often makes tracking impossible.
   3. Rapid deployment of CTT is essential. Excessive time lapse between enemy activity and arrival of CTT allows signs and scent to decay and increases the probability of friendly troops or local nationals covering the track. Since many incidents occur at night, CTT are often best employed at first light.
   4. To achieve economy of force, CTT must be held in reserve until a mission develops.
   5. Team integrity should be maintained. Although visual trackers may achieve some success independently, difficult tracks require the skills of all elements of the team.
   6. CTT locate the enemy but do not normally engage him; teams should be accompanied by at least a dismounted platoon and have fire support available.

B. **LIMITATIONS**
   1. CTT cannot track tactically at night.
   2. Although humid conditions tend to aid tracking, a heavy tropical storm may make tracking impossible.
   3. A track in primary jungle is difficult to follow if it is over 24 hours old. Even less time is available in areas without canopy.
C. **SEQUENCE OF EVENTS.**
   1. The standby team is alerted. The team leader is briefed on the situation, his mission, transportation, and contact on arrival. The team leader briefs his team and moves it to the contact point.
   2. At the contact point, the local commander briefs the team leader on the current situation, all known enemy information, the limit of friendly advance and the supporting force. The team leader then briefs his team and coordinates with the supporting force.
   3. The visual tracker establishes the track and follows it until the team leader decides to employ the tracker dog. CTT formations while tracking will vary from a file to an open diamond depending on the terrain. Since the element of surprise is essential, noise discipline must be strictly enforced and visual signals used to the maximum.
   4. Under ideal conditions, CTT will track until the dog indicates the enemy is near or the visual tracker determines this fact. When this occurs, the supporting force normally passes through the team and closes with the enemy. If contact occurs unexpectedly, the team will break contact using a contact drill and the supporting force engages the enemy.[28]

This Statement was carried in a pocket size card by all members of Combat Tracker Teams. It was to be used by the teams to help them establish what missions they would accept and the "ground rules" by which they operated. Unfortunately, too often there were well-trained, twenty year old men who had been in the Army for a relatively short period of time trying to gainsay an Officer with eight years of military service who wasn't about to listen to him. Some of the results of these conversations are names listed on "The Wall."[29]

---

[28] GTA 21-4, June 1968. Mission statement card issued by the U. S. Army for all members of the Combat Tracker Teams.
[29] All CTT KIAs are listed on *http://www.combattrackerteam.org/memorial* with the designated position on "the Wall"

CHAPTER EIGHT

Workin' It Out—Deployment 1967

The Tracker Teams' history of assigned Divisions and Brigades in the Vietnam War is defined. What is confusing to objective assessment is explaining the geographical locations within their assignments. Division elements were often moved all over the length and breadth of South Vietnam, and naturally, the Trackers accompanied their Divisions or Brigades. Even the Team members themselves have difficulty relating to the areas of an earlier or later Team within their same Division or Brigade because of the position of the AO (Area of Operation) where they were utilized and in what capacity they were used. The Army also would employ "pieces and parts" of various Divisions and Brigades for specific operations.

Some of the Teams were placed with the famous First Infantry Division—"the Big Red One." It was and is an old and proud division. As before in its various commitments, the 1st ID was in force in Vietnam. The First Infantry was home to the CTT #5, CTT #13, and finally after the Activation and Organization Order of 6 February 1968, the 61st IPCT. The group had a diverse area of operations. Their initial home HQ was in Di An—which was a swamp. The Labs that these Teams brought over from Malaysia worked throughout the war. Lieutenant Ron Reed was the first CO and Chris Hodge and Roger Cool were two of his NCOs. Charles Cherry, John Reed, Dave Biancardi, Gilbert Carpenter, Roger Breeden, Tim Gress, Al Horner, Franklin Johns, John Robinson, James Stone, James Williams, Michael Vanover and race driver Jackie O'Bannon were some also on the early CTT #5. On Friday 13 October 1967, Lt. Don Hendricks with Sr. NCOIC Ted

Kirmse came in with CTT #13 from BJWS including George Battles, Roy Burchfield, Dick, Willie Cox, Tom Dodd, Al Haynes, Norm Shaw, Steve Tesdall, Dick Timmins, Ed Wheeler Jon Wilde and a few months later, Chuck Steward, Jerry Pritchett, Jerry Bates, Bill Grady and Lenny Giguere.

The Teams worked along with support groups from the 1st Infantry Division. They were awarded a Meritorious Unit Citation for their work from April 1967 through November 1, 1968. This meant that CTT #5, CTT #13 (both Provisional Teams) and the 61st IPCT were all cited in the single unit citation. This was in addition to 52 individual medals awarded to the Team members in this period alone.

CTTs #1 and #2 were the two original Teams sent to the 25th Infantry Division (Tropic Lightening). This was followed by CTT #14 in October 1967, and reorganized and activated as 66th IPCT in Feb. 1968. Their AO was from the Cambodian border to just outside of Long Bien (which was shared with the 9th Inf. Division).

They were billeted in Cu Chi, and with the Division who was very unaware that they were on top of one of the largest underground complexes and tunnels that went all the way to the "Iron Triangle." It was later learned that the VC regular elements staged the attack on Tet from this subterranean refuge. The applications of the Teams affiliated with the 25th Infantry Division were not just for that Division alone. They were "loaned out" to elements of 1st Infantry at Tay Ninh, as well as the "nonexistent, impossible" operations in Cambodia. There were times when they operated with the 4th Infantry Division near the Cambodian border, as well as with units of the 9th Infantry Division and the 101st Airborne.

They had an interesting diplomatic and political dilemma in the area close to the Cambodian border. There was a rubber plantation under French ownership. CTT #2 had been following a large body of VC and what they thought was NVA for a couple of days. They were taking their time and proceeding slowly because of snipers and other "surprises" set up for them by the fleeing enemy. They ascertained that they were following

Seek On!

at least a battalion, if not a regiment. They were able to surround the large group within the confines of the plantation. The CO of the 1/27th Infantry Regiment and 2/27th Infantry Regiment, who was the Team's Infantry support, called in for air strikes. They knew that the enemy was found and fixed and able to be exterminated.

Imagine that CO's frustration when the air strike was called off because the French ownership had demanded that these plantations had to be preserved at any cost! Further, any time an action by the U. S. and her Allies took place in a plantation area, two hours later a chopper would arrive with a French national who carefully noted any damage to the rubber trees or other parts of the plantation. It seems that the U. S. government had to recompense the French for any loss of trees *and* their calculated life span output of a rubber tree!

The 25th Infantry Division had the largest number of Teams, and that was a "double edged" proposition. It left young junior NCOs on their own, because there were not yet enough Tracker Staff Sr. NCOs and OICs to go around. The School at BJWS was turning out Trackers as fast as possible, but they would not disregard thoroughness for speed in doing so. When the first Teams (CTT #1 and #2) went to the 25th, they were very fortunate to have Lt. Don Best as their CO. There should have been a second Officer, but the other Lieutenant (Lt Freddie Lee Johnson) had drowned in Malaysia along with two students, PFC Jose Munoz and PFC Harry Murray. Some of the earliest BJWS graduates came in with Lt. Best and his Sr. NCOIC Don Eveland. Jerry Anglin, Daniel Audet, Bob Barrett, Roger Butler, Carroll Cummings, Bill Eaton, Richard Fostervold, Larry Hadzima, Peter Katzfey, Ashley Harler, Bill Hartwell, George Leon, M. "Hank" Letts, Mike Sisco, John Patrick and Denny Witt were with him, to name a few. Later, Lt. Ron Hudson, who had started with CTT #8 but had been ordered to return to JWS for more "train the trainer" time, came in to the 25th ID group with a second group of graduates. This group arrived in September 1967 led by Lt. Hudson, Robert Brede, James Roger Boyer, Mark T. Howard, Sr., Arnold Johnson, George Koon, David

Layne, Paul Monarko and Jerry Quinn. The Tropic Lightening teams were further augmented by another wave of trackers in early October with Bobby Baldwin, Ron Grove, Willie Howard, Frank Karwoski, Joe Mocki, Al Provost, Dewitt Roberts and Glen Schlecter. There was not enough leadership for the size of the unit and the teams paid the price.

The 4th Infantry Division ("Ivy") had three major sectors of Area of Operations. The First of the Fourth Infantry Regiment was sent to the area by the South China Sea; the Second of the Fourth Infantry Regiment had an area of responsibility in the Central Highlands; and the Third of the Fourth Infantry Regiment was working the Mekong Delta. The headquarters for the Fourth Infantry were located in Pleiku from '66 through '68, then Dak To, Pleiku, and An Khe at the time the Division was "stood down" from their deployment in the Vietnam War. The first CTTs to be sent to the 4th Inf. Division were CTT #3 and CTT #4. The initial Officer was Lt. Jim Myrick who would go on to play an important part in establishing the program for the American School for CTT. His Sr. NCOIC was Dan Tharp—the "senior sarge" who had "put his ear to the ground" for handlers Frank Merritt and John Dotson when he was a Sr. NCOIC at the 1st Cav during the time that the guys were doing what they considered K9 "REMF" duty. J. "Preacher" McIntosh, Jerry Seevers, Mike Sheer (along with Skipper), John Carroll, William Lumsden, Ben Johnson, Wayne Reed, Walter Simpson, James Hillard, Larry Snitgen (who went on to multi-tours as a Tracker) and Bill Vugrin went with Myrick and Tharp as a part of CTT #3. CTT #4 had Lt. Brown Payne, Sam Blibel, Marty Bongiorno, "Inky" Inklaar, Tom McCart, Marty Olhiser, George Thomas, "Dutch" Wierenga and Julian Van Dyke. In 1968, after the Activation and Organization, the Teams affiliated with the Fourth became the 64th IPCT. The Fourth Inf. Div. had come into Vietnam in 1966 and set up their first HQ later named Camp Enari near Pleiku. The Third Brigade of the 4th Infantry continued to work with the 25th Infantry Division. There were many times when Tracker Teams worked for both of these Divisions simultaneously.

The 9th Infantry Division was working the Delta area at the beginning of Tracker placement. The first Team to go with them was CTT #6, which was in place when CTT #14 was added. The second Team brought the full complement to strength status. Lt. Paul Richeson was the first Lt. of this affiliated group and was accompanied by Gary Ward as Sr. NCOIC. They brought with them Perry Calloway, Gary Coon, Steve Gadarik, Al Horner, Gene Kuffel, Mike Landers and George McDonald. Don Ferraro was brought in and trained on the job (OJT). In September, CTT #14, the last of the Provisional Teams, came in with James Friis, Gary Gattinger, Larry Gell, Stephen Hawkins, Bill Hughes, Ed Manley, BartolomeoManzanares, Larry Richards, Al Sedillo, John Simpson, Don Smith, Kenneth Thibault, Billy Upton, Porfiro Vazquez and Joe Watson. General Westmoreland and Admiral Sharp remarked on the fact that the Tracker Labs were able to hear sampans and alert the Teams to enemy presence at night. The authorization orders reorganized these provisional teams to the 65th IPCT.

CTT #7 and #8 were attached to the First Cavalry Division (Air Mobile) in 1967. They were originally attached to the 1st Cavalry Division, Headquarters and Headquarters. They were subsequently sent to the L. R. R. P.s (Long Range Reconnaissance Patrol). However, LRRPs moved with slow and deliberate movements and were a reconnaissance unit that employed stealth rather than speed. The LRRPs could also act as Hunter/Killer when necessary, but missions were "black," clandestine, making themselves a part of the environment. The Tracker Teams were different. It was their job to become "up front and personal" with the enemy. They would think nothing of going into an enemy camp—and considered it "blowing holes" through the enemy sites. They would employ concealment and noise discipline, but the goal was to find and fix the enemy on the Tracker Team's terms. The LRRPs were human "listening posts" who would spy on the enemy and just as quietly return to base with the new information. The LRRP teams were a courageous and efficient specialty and another tool needed in the warfare of Vietnam, but their association with CTT was not working. Lt. Ron Hudson, who had deployed from BJWS with CTT #8, asked Division for a more suitable attachment for the Tracker Teams They were subsequently assigned to the First of the Ninth Cavalry Squadron, the reconnaissance arm of the Division. Lt. H. Hunt and Joe "Nick" Nicholson Sr. NCOIC brought James P. Moore, Ralph Clemings, James "Frenchy" La Farlette, Frank Merritt, Juan Alvarez y Navarez, Tom Presley and Bill Reed in as CTT #7. Lt. Hudson seconded by Hugh Lamb as Sr. NCOIC brought Neil Couch, Elmer Wain Mahurin, Ken Brown, Steve Cradick, John E. Dotson, Reggie Maxham and Tom Niggermeyer in as CTT #8. After a matter of only weeks, Ron Hudson and Hugh Lamb went back to JWS for "Train the Trainer." At that point, Hunt was the Lt. for both teams and Couch became Sr. NCOIC for Team #8. There was an interesting Officer inserted for a while with the guys. A Lt. Herb Vest came in, ostensibly as an OIC for CTT #8, but he did not really fit the position and asked more questions that work with the teams. He was not there very long and left as abruptly as he had come. The Boys were unanimous in their thinking that he must have been a "spook" with uncertain affiliation. In September, John Dupla and Dennis Beuke came into CTT #7 and CTT #8 respectively along with others. The "Air Cav," with their own audacious reputation, was the perfect match for the Tracker Teams. The 62nd IPCT was the authorized attached unit after 15 February 1968. Throughout the War, the $1/9^{th}$ and the Trackers assigned with them had an excellent working relationship. The G-2 (1st Cav's Divisional Intelligence) worked with the $1/9^{th.}$ Soon they developed a close rapport with the Tracker; they grew to value the opinions of the Teams and would consult with them before sending them in on missions.

 The First Cavalry's HQ was at An Khe at this time and subsequently moved to Camp Evans in I Corps. The $1/9^{th}$ had its own helicopter assets. Because of this, the Trackers had the fast-insertion capability and were sent on more than one mission on some days. The $1/9^{th}$ also had aero-rifle "Blue Teams"—platoon sized infantry units. These Blue Teams were small enough to be integrated into the CTT adding additional firepower. The

Blues proved an asset and not a liability unlike some of the other infantry units. In this Divisional association, the Trackers were considered an important enough unit that they were very infrequently left anywhere at night. Usually, they were extracted the same day that they were inserted. If return to base was not feasible, they were at least camped in a secure area.

The 23rd Division (Americal) used the Trackers in a different aspect. They were joined with Scout Dog and Handler as well as having a Mine and Tunnel Dog and Handler under the umbrella of the 63rd IPCT. The Tracker history with the 63rd started in 1968, and was an authorized attachment from the beginning of the association. The Americal was initially headquarted in Chu Lai, and like most of the others, proceeded to work almost all of the areas. They were later camped south of Danang, after the Marines had left that area. The 63rd Tracker Teams were also at work with the 1st Division and the Trackers from the 196th IDCT. There were no Provisional teams with Americal.

The first Team CTT #10 was under the banner of the 196th Light Infantry Brigade. In the CTT #10 group, Lt. Harold Bell headed up with Sr. NCOIC Grant Golden. Bob Alberd, Kent Near, Steve Tolson, Gene Beyle, Willis Dinkins, Howard Duble, "Slug" Martin, Lavon Taylor, Mike Seniuk, Robert Phillips, Freddy Martin, Roy Matsumoto and John Wood rounded out the team. The 196th LIB had been raised at Fort Devens in 1965 and scheduled for deployment in the Dominican Republic. The War was heating up and the unit was rushed to Vietnam and put in position in the Western Portion of III Corps. They were used in major operations, Task Force Oregon and Operation Attleboro just to name two. The 63rd Tracker Teams were then augmented by the Teams who had initially been sent in to work with the 196thLIB.

CTT #9, who came from BJWS in Oct. 1967, was assigned to the 101st Airborne Brigade (Separate). The Teams were sent to the 101st Brigade (Separate) HQ & HQ in the Central Highlands. The full 101st Division was en route to the Republic of Vietnam at this time. From November through December 1967, CTT #9 "tromped up and down rugged, jungle covered mountains. The

Susan Merritt

"Para Trackers" were led by Lt. Steve Williams with Sr. NCOIC Johnny Teeters. The team consisted of Rodney Asino, Richard Boyer, Bill Cannon, Joe Farmer, David Hahn, John Harding, Ben Miller, Gene Smoot and Charlie Womack. In December 1967, the entire Brigade commenced operations in the area of Bao Loc, which was between Hue and Saigon. The February 1968 authorization placed three Tracker Teams with the First, Second, and Third Brigades of the 101st Airborne Division that had finally arrived from the States. All of the Teams worked out of HQ at Camp Eagle. These Trackers also were in the field from the Central Highlands to the DMZ (Demilitarized Zone). It is interesting to note that when the Teams first came to the 101st, they were to go through the usual routine of a week's testing and "training" by the 101st Staff. After the first morning of this "exam," the Team's Lieutenant was told that the Trackers knew more than the Airborne could teach them. The next day found the Trackers at work in the field. The reorganization name for the 101st's Tracker Teams was the 557th IPCT. The Trackers affiliated with the 101st were like the other CTTs. Although their primary attachment was to the Airborne Unit, they worked with many other elements in I Corp—5th Infantry—Mechanized in Quang Tri, the Third Marine Division in Da Nang and several ARVN (Army of the Republic of Viet Nam) groups.

There was another group sent to the 82nd Airborne. This was the 77th IDCT. They were 77th from their beginning, but many of their members were originally CTT alumni. After their time with the 82nd Airborne, the 77th was placed under the 5th Infantry—Mechanized. Again, this was after the time of the Provisional Trackers.

A little known fact from this time was General Creighton Abrams' "acquisition" of a Tracker Dog. The General would go into the area where his old tanker friends were working, the 11th ACR (Armored Cavalry Regiment) and take some time off with them. He heard that one of the Tracker Labs of the 61st IPCT attached to the 1st Infantry Division was no longer useful in the field. The General decided that no one should do anything with this dog until he got back to them. General

Abrams became the new owner of that Tracker Lab, which he renamed "Devil." It is probable that the name of the Lab was changed to "protect the guilty" in this case. At any rate, the General always had "Devil" as his companion and relied on the Lab's judgment of people. Devil became a permanent fixture wherever General Abrams established his Headquarters. If the Lab did not like someone, the General would not spend any time with that person. If Devil did like someone, the General would be a gracious host.

The 77th, unlike the other Team's control authority, were under the direct control of G-3—or Staff. In the original documents that show the new organization and activation of the Combat Trackers, two important things should be noted. The use of "TEAM" in their working description was never changed. While the groups were designated IPCT or IDCT, each was made up of two or more Combat Tracker Teams. The second unusual paragraph gave promotional, leave and award control with the Commander of the Division or Brigade to whom they were attached. However, all other control was ultimately in the jurisdiction of G-3 USARV Special Troops.

The 173rd Airborne was also in Vietnam from 1965. The Tracker Teams authorized was the 75th IDCT as of Feb. 1968. The 173rd was a major force in many of the battlefields of the War. They were initially headquartered in Tay Ninh and had the "Iron Triangle" to work, as well as general oversight of Bien Hoa and its environs. They were part of many Operations, and the 75th IDCT were part of the recon for these actions. The IDCT groups consisted of two Teams and a Sr. NCO as overall NCOIC and were headquartered at An Khe in II Corps. There was no provision for a Tracker Officer for the Infantry Detachment groups.

The 199th Light Infantry Brigade was the last of the assigned units for the Trackers. In October 1967, the CTT #11 was attached to the "Redcatcher". The AO (Area of Operations) were centered in the Northeast corner of Long Bien. Lt. Tony Witter and Moses "Pappy" Nahinu Sr. NCOIC brought their team over from BJWS. Larry Cohran, Jeff Dejewski, Bill George, Law-

Susan Merritt

rence "Chief" Iyotte, Floyd Lachney, Jim Lawson, Mitch Scott and Clive Seydell made up the Provisional team who patrolled the area of Long Bien, Saigon and Bien Hoa. The 199th was a new Brigade specifically organized for the Vietnam War. After February 1968, the authorized unit of Trackers attached to the 199th was the 76th IDCT.

While the Trackers were ready to put their education to good use, they realized that almost no one in Vietnam was ready for them! If the Visual Trainees had been surprised to know that a Labrador retriever and his Handler were going to be part of the Team, imagine the plight of an Infantry Line Officer when faced with this totally new and "different" group. The reactions would have been amusing but due to the circumstances became a total frustration for the Trackers and those who had put the whole program in motion. The addition of the teams to the Army's Infantry Divisions and Brigades had been well thought out by the highest levels of the Commanding staff, yet there existed a great chasm of ignorance between that group of General Grade Officers and the teams themselves.

It showed in large and small ways. When some of the Teams came back to the Divisional Headquarters in Vietnam, there was a great deal of "head scratching" while their superiors wondered just where to put them and what to do with them. First, most of these Line Officers only knew of the defensive canine specialties. The Scout and Sentry Dogs and Handlers had been a part of the Army since the Second World War. The "Team Concept" was equally "foreign" to the Divisional Line Officers. In addition, a Team with a dog, trained by the British special ops' standards and techniques seemed as far out as the "sniffer" machines that were being tested. They simply could not envision an autonomous Team who answered to virtually no one. On a Mission, the Team Leader had total control. This extended to having authority even over the Commanding Officer of their Infantry Support Element. The rules of the Trackers were that they would have the final word on the mission. Moreover, that was the hardest thing of all for the line officers to accept. Just who the hell were these arrogant Trackers?

CHAPTER NINE

Return of the Tracker 1998

The Vietnam vet was sitting in his office. He had recently heard from one of the guys on his Team. A former team member was talking about some veterans' association for all canine specialties that he had heard about and was joining. This was the *Vietnam Dog Handlers' Association*.[30] The veteran VT had been interested enough in the organization to send for information that he had just received. The vet had just opened a copy of "Dog Man," a newsletter that the association sent out. The issue had a lot of photos…and amazingly, an article about the Combat Tracker Teams.

As he looked through the paper, he started thinking about his time "in-country" as a Combat Tracker. He was a graduate of the British Jungle Warfare School. He wondered about what might have happened to his fellow graduates over the past thirty-some (could it *really* have been *thirty*?) years. To this day, he could remember every Lab's name that was with his Team. He could recall adventurous times in Singapore and Johore Bahru. All that hard work to learn a highly demanding skill and he understood that the Army had just dropped it. Imagine, they had even established a Tracker School at Fort Gordon, in Georgia—and then just shit-canned it all!

He found out that a close friend of his had died several weeks before. He began thinking about his Vietnam War days and could not understand himself in letting so much time pass

---

[30] *http://vdha.us*—An organization dedicated to the K9 warriors of the Viet Nam War and their handlers and supporters

without reaching out to the other guys on his Team. They were closer to his heart than any of his other friends, social and business acquaintances, or school alumni. The intense bonds of brotherhood, trust and respect were forged through the rigors of school days in Malaysia. They had been honed in combat between the members of a Tracker team. It was inconceivable that they were repressed for all these years. The desire to find and communicate with the other members of his team was overwhelming. His emotions were roiling up inside him. He had mixed feelings—should he bury this feeling, or act on it? There was a hole in his heart where all of this had been—and nothing had come close to filling it over all of the years. Maybe...

He went back to reading the article about the Trackers. In that edition were names of Trackers who had joined the Association. He stared at one in particular. The man whose name he was reading was an old drinking companion from BJWS. The e-mail address was listed. With that information, he went to his computer and called up a search engine with reverse listing. He put the e-mail address in the search query and in a few seconds, there was his friend's name, "snail mail" and telephone number. His heart was thumping harder for some reason. He kept staring at the information as if it could give him an answer as to what he should do. His eye caught an announcement of a VDHA Reunion that was coming up in a few weeks' time. The more he tried to ignore it, the more he came back to it. He astonished himself as he went through an emotional seesaw about all of this. He had to laugh at himself, though, because he was very sure that no one who knew him now would ever believe this reaction. He was very successful in business, and truthfully, regarded as being a very "cool" guy—one who seemed to be impervious to everything in his world. How amazed they would be at this reaction—he was really surprised at himself.

Those days had been dead serious and tougher than anything he had been able to relate to anyone. The things that he had seen in his time at war, especially with the Trackers, were visions from hell. The thing about it was developing a sense of "gallows" humor that was all they had to counter the horrors that they witnessed. He remembered the almost hysterical laughter on more than one occasion, but one in particular came to mind. They were on a mission in an area that had been a base for the NVA. They were working as a visual team only as the Lab was on "R & R" (Rest and Recreation) at the Tracker HQ. They entered an area that could only be described as "hairy." They could almost feel the presence of the enemy here. They moved in with careful, measured steps in a diamond formation so that the point man was covered by the two men on the side flanks and the "tail-gun Charlie" was covering the back of the team. Suddenly, there was ear-splitting thunder and a blast in front of them as the earth was torn apart! The point man who was remembering this had literally been picked up by the force of the explosion and thrown in the air, landing on his back. He watched as blurry leaves and tree limbs and dust slowly fell to the ground. He could not feel anything and was sure that he was paralyzed. His limbs began to tingle and he started to check his legs. He harkened back how he had cautiously reached for his knees, and was in total disbelief that they were still there. He was stunned by the concussive force of the detonation and was temporarily deafened. For some reason that he could not fathom he was in one piece and not bleeding anywhere. He gingerly got to his feet. The balance of the team crept forward. They were also without a scratch by the discharge of the mine's ferocious explosions. They scouted with great care and found where the claymores had been placed. One by one, they realized what had happened. It seems that the devices that were semi-circular shaped were directional land mines, and had explicit directions in raised letters on the exterior. These succinctly said, "This side toward enemy." Thank God, the enemy could not read English. The NVA personnel who had set up the ambush had placed the anti-personnel mines backward! When they checked out the area further, they spotted body parts, which were remains of the NVA soldiers who had not known what those words meant! Close call, indeed. Not only had the Team been sent to track the enemy, but in this instance, the enemy had obliged by killing themselves! When the Team returned to their HQ, they related

Susan Merritt

the incident to the other Trackers. They had all cracked up with laughter.

He also remembered how the young Trackers were fed horror stories about how the South Vietnamese were all VC just waiting to maim or kill American G. I.s. There was a barbershop at Cu Chi where all of the employees were Vietnamese. He thought that there were twelve or thirteen in all. Throughout his time "in-country," many of the barbers were known to have purposely slashed their American customers. He devised a method for dealing with any potential bloodletting desire on the part of the barber. He would settle himself in the chair, and before the barber put the razor anywhere near his skin, the American soldier put the muzzle of a .45 in an unmentionable part of the barber's anatomy. He never received as much as a scratch.

He decided to make a reservation to this reunion, but on the "q.t." He would not even tell his fellow team member who had let him know about all of this and who had sent the VDHA information to him in the first place. No, if he wanted to skip it at the last minute, it was better if he said nothing.

When he called the Hotel and gave his information to the Reservation Office, he was still ambivalent about where he would go from here on all of this. This was taking on more and more meaning for him—even as this night wore on. He shook his head as if to clear it, and looked at the newsletter again, only to see a photo of the Lab he had worked with when he was a Tracker. He had loved that crazy Lab. He often wondered whether the dog had survived the War. God, he hoped so. He had read all the stories about the war dogs of the war being left behind, he wanted to find out if anyone knew about the fate of the Tracker Labs, even if knowing would hurt.

As he sat there pondering his own reactions, he began to think of incidents and Missions, of the closeness of the Team, and the old feeling that they were like the "Three Musketeers" plus Two and a Dog. He recalled another event that evoked laughter from the Team. On a mission to an old rubber plantation, the men found all of the trees decorated with some kind of poster that they assumed the NVA had left. There searched the area thoroughly, and as there was no enemy activity and had not been for some time, removed some of these leaflets to take to G-2. When they returned to base camp late in the afternoon the group at G-2 was "closing up shop" for the day. The Team Leader, who was the Lieutenant of the Trackers, gave the paper to one of the intelligence Officers who had been standing there. The Intelligence Officer who could read Vietnamese scanned the poster quickly, and started with a snicker that ended in howling laughter. The other G-2 staff took the paper from him, and they, too, read it and just about fell down in whoops of laughter. The young Lieutenant was getting red in the face because he did not understand any of the intelligence guys' reactions. The first man who had read the poster wiped tears away from streaming eyes. He gulped and tried to explain himself. The leaflet was a "Wanted Poster" left by the NVA for the local population. It said that they would pay an enormous sum for proof of a dead Tracker Lab, half of that amount for a dead Tracker, and a small percentage of that for a Tracker Commander. It was a good thing that the Lieutenant had a splendid, if not warped, sense of humor.

He had been so innocent when he enlisted in "this man's Army." He remembered that wretched, sadistic Drill Instructor at Basic Training. Man, he could remember how the DI could bait him and push his buttons. He had done well in the training. The Army was going through draftees and newly enlisted guys like crazy. While many of the men wanted to go anywhere but Vietnam, he had volunteered for it. One night after a day of forced marches, endless sets of push-ups, and other harassment to make individuals part of the Army, he had asked the DI, "Sergeant, why are you so tough on all of us?" The veteran of many combat actions looked at him and replied, "Just what do you think THEY will do if they get a hold of you?" There was no resistance after that. The new recruit realized what his DI was trying to tell him—and from that day on, went through all the exercises as if his life depended on it. It did.

He also had arrived at Ben Hoa Airbase outside of Saigon and proceeded with all the other clean-shaven, spic and span replacements for the war effort. The surrounding land around the Airbase looked like an imagined vision of Mars. There were rolling hills all around it that had been stripped of all vegetation. It looked like there was a virtual city of wooden hooches where foliage had once been. However, perhaps the oddest thing about the terrain was the "red clay." It was everywhere. Everything would be covered with it. This was an enormous staging area. He felt as if he had been transported to one of the stateside bases in Georgia. In fact, he began to suspect that the Army had done this on purpose!

 The newly arrived men had just come from Advanced Individual Training (AIT) Schools. They were dressed in their uniforms as if they were going to be billeted at an American, European or South Korean post. The vets were in various states of tropical uniforms. They wore jungle fatigues and other strange gear for the Vietnam environment. This was certainly a different Army than he had expected to see. He was startled by the expressions on the faces of the veteran soldiers around him. They were his age—but seemed much, much older somehow. While at the Holding Area, a tough looking Sergeant First Class was addressing different groups of the recently arrived soldiers. He was asking for volunteers who wanted to be a part of a dangerous special ops program that included working with dogs. The Sergeant went on that if a man had high scores on his GT tests and had a good record from Basic and AIT he would be interviewed for this specialty. The young man who had volunteered for everything else so far held his hand up. The SFC looked him over and asked for the young soldier's paperwork. The soldiers were all carrying their abbreviated records with them as the entered Vietnam. After going through all the papers' codes and acronyms, the Sergeant motioned the young man to follow him. In a room at the holding area, there was a Captain[31] sitting behind the desk. There was a cursory interview with the young soldier who answered as best he could that he would indeed like to be a part of the new specialty group. The young

---

[31] Captain William Welch, Liaison Officer for the CTT Program

soldier said this without really knowing what he was getting into. The Captain nodded to the SFC, and it was understood that the recruit had been accepted for this new program.

Within a few weeks, he was arriving in Malaysia with a maroon passport, all civilian clothing and no Army identification. The BJWS' "lorry" (truck) came to take him to his new home for the next three and a half months. Man, it was like being initiated into a secret warrior society in another world. The men who taught them and cared for them and reshaped their lives were a breed apart. There was a sense of honor that was also a part of every lesson—it was not spoken, it was just expected. There were moral ethics that were a part of warfare. It was a time when a handful of men became closer than any of them could ever explain to an outsider. They had been hammered and honed and molded and melded. As ultimately difficult as the "lessons" had been, the play was as intense! And what a time it had been.

He was lost in these reveries, and all of a sudden, the thought came to him. He wondered if anyone had ever taken those little figurines from the crotch of that tree.

CHAPTER TEN

Indian Country 1967

The teams were now working on a more regular basis. There were those who were fortunate enough to have an available chopper to ferry them back and forth. On the other hand, that could be a mixed blessing because it meant that G-2 could put them all over the AO (Area of Operations) in a single day. Some of the other teams were stationary in an area because there were not enough available assets to enable them to do more than one mission in a day. In addition, there were instances where the teams might be forced to remain in the field for a week or longer, because they were at the mercy of the affiliated unit's transportation. They did not have to live off the land while in the field like their #2 WDTU instructors. Unlike their former #2 WDTU instructors, they did have sufficient rations while in the field and were not forced to "creative culinary experiments" with indigenous flora and fauna. These were not long-range hunter/killer assigned journeys into the deepest heart of the jungle.

Back at their in-country bases, the Landing Zone (LZ) where they were temporarily quartered, their "dog robbers/scroungers" were hard at work to create an aura of normalcy. In one instance, a savvy Sergeant somehow procured a Jeep for the Team. They painted it with ersatz bumper identification numbers—and tooled around in it proudly. Unfortunately, an Officer came to the Team's compound and questioned their Table of Organization and Equipment (T. O. & E.) specifically in reference to the team vehicle. He then checked the serial numbers of the Jeep, only to discover that the vehicle had been "totally destroyed" by a land mine two years before! The Trackers were reduced to walking once again.

One of the teams worked a track where they found distinct indications that someone had left the trail. It was an example of using the skills of the Visual Tracker and the Handler and Lab in terms of their individual assets. The Visual Tracker might well have passed the area as it was off the track. The dog was working on his long lead when he inexplicably turned his head sharply to the right just for and instant and then resumed the track. The handler had never seen this unusual reaction from his dog before and knew there must be an explanation. He signaled a halt for the rest of the team. The VT was called up and examined the area to the right of the trail. There he found indication that someone stepped off the trail and had done their utmost to leave no sign. The VT and handler followed this new track a short distance to a tree. Carved in its trunk were numbers indicating specific units and adjacent to the tree was a small sapling, which had been staked to the ground so that it pointed sharply to the left. The NVA scout or VC local guide had gone off the trail to create "markers" that would direct the NVA who would be following the trail. The NVA was very unfamiliar with the area—as much as the Americans were. Trees were used as message boards. These became obvious signs to the Team, but for the regular infantry units who would go through this area, they would have gone unnoticed. When the team was scouting ahead, they realized that these indicators were for an upcoming junction in the trail. Through these signs and symbols, the Team now knew that they were following a regiment-sized element, its numeric designation and the direction of their movement. The enemy was completely compromised. They had solid information to give to G-2 on their return.

They also noticed little handmade figures that had been placed in the crotch of the tree to ask the local gods' blessing. Some of the indigenous people in the area were pagan and had left these gifts of supplication. No one knew the ages of them. The team was fascinated by this—and was tempted to take the little idols. However, had they done so, it would have "tipped" their hand to the enemy and somehow, it would have seemed sacrilegious. The team left the little hallowed statues in place. When they were extracted, they reported all of their findings. Out of a thousand people who might see that scene—perhaps one would realize what they were really looking at. This was all a part of the teams' training—to be able to see everything around them and miss none of it.

Meanwhile on missions, the Teams were still trying to cope with Infantry line commanders who had not had the time or had not taken the time to learn about the Trackers or their missions. One of the Teams had been requested to run a track in a very "hot" area. They were inserted and the Team Leader asked the Infantry unit's Captain for a briefing of the situation. The Team Leader was specific in asking whether there were "friendlies" (indigenous Montagnard or South Vietnamese troops) in the area. The Infantry Captain responded in the negative and told the Team Leader that he was sure there was a unit of enemy troops ahead. This was an area with triple canopy with full low, medium and high strata of foliage. The Lab caught the scent and was off like "a bat out of hell." Soon, they were at least a quarter of a mile in front of the Infantry unit. The Lab was alerting before the Team came to a bend in the trail. The next thing that the Handler saw was first one, then two, and finally three men ahead in "black pajamas and camo." The Handler was a hair's breadth away from pulling the trigger to take out all three, when the last man in the file turned to his left. The "enemy" had finally heard the approaching Team, and he was about to defend his group. In turning, he revealed the identifying patch of the Army of the Republic of Vietnam (ARVN) Ranger on his sleeve. The Handler and the Team realized that they were dealing with "Friendlies" and with hand signals returned the ARVN's recognition. These were Montagnard ARVN Rangers, and they had their families with them. The ARVN Rangers would have defended them to the death. The 'Yards pulled off to the side of the trail. The Team passed them by. The Team Leader had many emotions running through his mind as they waited for the Infantry unit to catch up to them. He reasoned that he and his Team were here for a finite period, while the indigenous people who were helping the Americans and their Allies were here forever. Further, he realized that these ARVN Rangers thought they were acting as a "point" element for the infantry unit who had called for the Tracker Team. These courageous native soldiers were helping their American allies, while the Captain of the infantry element was setting them up as prey. He remembered his training that had been so well done at BJWS, how they had been prepared for split-second decisions. If they had not been, the ARVN Ranger clan would have been decimated. It also pointed out that each member of the Team was working in full synchronization with the others. The unity of these individual men was so complete that no one had followed through in the potential attack. It was not just the Team Leader's recognition of the ARVN. It was a reaction shared simultaneously by each member of the Team.

He then turned his thoughts toward that Captain who had sent them on this trail. He knew that the son of a bitch had been completely aware of the ARVN Rangers ahead. When the Infantry element finally arrived at the place where the Trackers were waiting, the Team Leader asked the C. O. why they had been sent after "friendlies." The answer was, "They're all gooks, aren't they?" The Team could not disguise their abhorrence of that reply. The Team Leader demanded that the Captain arrange an immediate extraction for his men. The Captain not only refused the request, but asked him, "Who the hell are you to give me orders?" The Leader's response was, "According to our Mission Statement, I am in control when the Team is called in. Furthermore, if you doubt that or want to know more about my orders, Sir, I suggest you call Division Headquarters now." The fuming Captain told his R. T. O. to call Division HQ at once, and walked out their hearing range to lodge complaints and charges against these impertinent bastards. A few minutes later, he came up to the Trackers barely controlling his fury. He had been dressed down by Division HQ in no uncertain terms. He spoke so quietly, that only the Team Leader could hear him, and intimated that given an opportunity he would screw them to the wall if he possibly could, but he did not have the authority to do it. The men stood in silent disgust yet their feelings were as eloquent as if they had been shouting.

Back at the Tracker Team's compound, they went through what would become SOP (standard operating procedure) after a mission. It was time for the Team to dissect the mission and the details of their own performance. It would not only correct small problems that could become a matter of life or death in combat, but it also allowed them to examine their own ethics in combat situations. They were all sickened by the attitude of the infantry Captain. One of the men brought up the hypotheticals of the incident. It became a "What if?" conversation. They took the mission apart completely to formulate different solutions to the variety of possibilities. They went over reaction responses to situations that might be encountered. These sessions enabled the Team to be prepared for the diversity of combat situations.

One critical problem that the teams incurred on almost every mission was the delicate balance of surviving the "Safety See-Saw." They all had a deep understanding of what would happen if they were inadvertently caught between the newly found enemy and their infantry support element. This was a distinct prospect, which could happen in this American application of the Tracker Team concept. Unlike the Hunter/Killer Teams that the British had developed, the Combat Tracker Teams of the U. S. Army had infantry support for their missions. There were times when they felt that there was a greater danger from their own people because the support guys were so aggressive—or perhaps not too well trained trigger happy "kids" that really didn't want to be there in the first place. In some cases, there had been teams who had been fired on from our own gun-ships because the following troops had called in Air Support! In a casualty situation that the 25th Infantry Division (ID) Teams had suffered, the NCOIC was physically between the Tracker Team and the follow-up (support) unit. When the Trackers were ambushed, the NCOIC ran back to the support group while calling out for artillery. There was only one serious problem with this—there was one survivor on the team—and he had been completely unharmed in the ambush. As a result of this and other near misses, they discussed how to best utilize their infantry support. One of the reasons that the Teams did not wear "tiger fatigues" in the field, or use AK 47s as their weapons was because of this possibility. If they were somehow caught in a "kill zone"—it was imperative that they were easily recognized as fellow American troops. As the saying went, "There is nothing 'friendly' about 'Friendly fire!'" They went over plans for reacting to this situation until it became second nature. After one particularly "hairy" day after multiple missions, one of the teams came in and had just about enough energy left to climb up on a berm that was alongside their "luxurious estate" at LZ Two-Bits. As they sat there, drooping with exhaustion, they looked at the setting sun and one of the boys remarked, "Well, God must have been with us today." That was it. On that occasion, there was nothing more to be said.

All of the classroom work and field training had paid off and now with combat time under their belts the Teams could write their own book. They now had enough time in the field to be able to create their own set of standards. They all knew that the success of a mission was determined by the effort and concentration put into it by the Team. When called in to reestablish contact with the enemy, the Visual Tracker (VT) would search the area for telltale signs of recent enemy activity. The VT and the others would look for evidence that would supply them with the age of the track, with the estimated size of the enemy element, and the direction of the enemy's movement. Every aspect of the trail was minutely investigated. When the VT had ascertained the proof he needed for defining the track, the Lab was brought up to follow the scent. At that time, the Dog Handler was the predominant member of the Team. He was the Lab's "translator"—and not reading the Lab's actions could mean death to the entire Team. The Handler had to focus entirely on the Lab's performance. He knew the dog so well that a "twitch of an ear" could be a sign. The Handler could not take his eyes off the dog for a moment. Things happened that fast in combat. The Team Leader would have the responsibility of judging the suitability of the mission. He would determine when to use the visual or canine asset. It was his call as to whether or not they would probe further, or be of no use, or decide that the mission should be pursued. He was the liaison between his Team and their support. It would be his judgment whether to have the Team fall back, to bring on the support and/or to call in for artillery and air strikes in conjunction with the support element. The Coverman was the "guardian" of the team member who was on "point." There was one for the Visual Tracker or the Handler and Lab. Sometimes the same coverman would protect whoever was on point, VT or handler. It was his responsibility to continually scan the environment for potential threat. The Team worked and thought in unison. It was a practiced reaction. It should also be said here that the Team Leader could be any member of the unit. It was a part of their cross training. If there was a loss of one of the Team for any reason, the others could act in his place. The completion of the mission was the goal.

Once the "track" was confirmed by the VT, the Team had a good estimate of the number of enemy they were following as well as the age of the track. They could tell in what direction they were heading, and in some cases, thorough inspection of signs left by the enemy, they would actually know the unit's designation.

The difficulties that had proved so frustrating in the early dealings with the line officers who had called for the Team were lessening. There was still a bit to be learned. One of the team leaders who were attached to the Cav got an unusual call from an armored brigade. The team leader did not think it that strange as they had done some missions for the armored Cav before. The team leader reported to the brigade headquarters that was a huge, dark mountain of green sand bags all piled up and surrounded by wire. He had to descend down it's depths via a long sloping tunnel of stairs that opened into a cavernous room. The staff was assembled in the center of the area. The brigade commander was sitting in a chair with his attending people behind and to the sides of him forming a semi-circle in the dim yellowish light. The whole scene reminded the team leader of some dusky mosaic of the Emperor Justinian and his imperial court. The "Emperor" spoke, "I want you to take your Team and assist my troops in finding the enemy." The team leader replied, "Well, we don't normally work with tracked vehicle units. How can we do this?" The commander replied, "My tracks will follow you!" Nonplussed, the team leader asked, "What do you mean 'follow us'? I can't be on a trail with a M113 APC (Armored Personnel Carrier) crashing along behind!" This was met with a confident response, "No problem, we'll just put your dog on the lead track." The tracker team leader could not believe what he had heard and came back with a very unmilitary, "What?" The brigade commander had it all figured out. "Yes, we'll put your dog on our lead track and he can alert us when he finds the enemy." Now the tracker was torn between absolute disbelief and hysterical laughter. "Well, sir," he was able to choke out, "you see it doesn't work that way." "Why not?" The team leader tried again to explain, "The dog doesn't alert like a scout dog, sir. He has to actually follow the scent and is trained to follow that trail." This did not impress the commander, "So, we'll follow the trail too; just have the dog tell us how to turn." The completely astonished team leader could not even imagine this latest adaptation. "Sir, what? While he's sitting in a track?" The officer benevolently added, "Yes, he can sit up front." However, the madness continued, "Excuse me, sir, but how is he going to follow the track? How will your driver know which way to turn?" The reply was quick, "The driver can watch his head." "Whose head, sir?" The commander was now frustrated with the team leader, and snapped, "The dog's head—the driver of the track can watch the dog's head turn and when the dog turns his head to follow the scent, the driver will turn that way." The tracker was way in over his limit, "Ah, well, er, Sir, the dog only works with his handler." The brigade CO still had enough patience to explain to the team leader, "OK, then, you have the dog and the handler in the front. The dog will show the handler which way to go, and the handler will tell the driver." The complex possibilities were astounding. The tracker finally said, "Sir, the dog isn't going to be able to sit on a track and…" "Are YOU refusing this mission, Trooper?" "What I am saying, Sir is that as Team Leader I am authorized to decide on the best method of employment of the team and this won't work." The Armored CO bellowed at him, "Do it! Your commander has offered the use of your Team to me!" Again, into the perilous pit, "Sir, with all due respect, my commander has nothing to do with the tactical employment of the Team. I am the final authority according to USARV Regulations and I say…" "REGULATIONS MY ASS! DON'T YOU KNOW THERE IS A WAR ON? DON'T TELL *ME* ABOUT REGULATIONS!" The emotionally drained but strong-willed team leader stated firmly, "Sir, I am not going to sit my dog on your track and try…"

The "Emperor" leaped to his feet, as the staff scattered like so many disturbed ants, and pointed to the exit, screaming, "OUT! OUT! GET OUT OF MY TOC (Tactical Operation Center)!"

This particular episode is the more interesting as two other veterans were able to add their recollection of this event. One was the team leader's CO who remembered trying to direct a Cav group. He went well in advance to set up the direction of the fleeing enemy. Having done so, he gave the armored group the way to go. His comment was, "Once the general direction was established, the tracks and tanks (TANKS!) Let us go, and they pursued in a cloud of dust, cracking jungle flora and clanking on down the trail.

The other retired Officer agreed, "The story is entirely credible. No one knew much about Trackers and their employment—especially in mechanized units. Even though most cavalry units did a good bit of scouting and patrolling, everyone looked on them as doing their scouting "mounted." Therefore, as opposed to leg infantry who went, at least part way in helicopters and the rest of the way on foot, armored Cav units had little or no need for Tracker teams—or so people thought. The 1st Cavalry Division had Trackers attached, but I never encountered them as I was with the armored element. However, had I done so, I certainly never would have turned them away or suggested that the tracker team commander was not the one to say how they might best be employed."

CHAPTER ELEVEN

Good News/Bad News

CTT #7 and #8 had been attached to the Head and Head of the 1/9th Cav and had been operating well in the Central Highland area of II Corps. They were successful at bringing in the information necessary for the Infantry to thwart the enemy's plans. As a bonus, the Teams had not only found the base camps of the NVA or VC regulars, but had been able to capture large caches of weapons, ammunition, rice, and more importantly, the enemy's documents and plans for future action. They had become very valuable to G-2 (first Cav Division Intelligence). They were permitted to have a say in what Missions they felt were going to be most productive and were now writing the "After Action" reports. These were the "hairy early days" of the Tracker Teams—still provisional and still without many Officers that were permanently in charge. Those Lieutenants that really had shown promise were being rotated back to BJWS to be trained as trainers or given more training for future team deployment. Those that had no affinity or were a liability to the program were getting as far away as possible. Some of the Officers surmised that this "crazy Tracker program" was a sure-fire way to destroy their future in the Army and they wanted to remove themselves "di-di-mau" (fast!).

The new Teams were given a lot of leeway but there was a negative side to this "success." Their attached unit had the assets to insert and extract the Teams several times in a given day. They were asked to do this to "triangulate" enemy concentrations. After a prolonged period of two and three missions per day, some of the Labs were exhausted and the Teams petitioned for a break. Finally, Merritt and Dotson, two of the handlers of the teams that made up the attached CTTs, were given a short reprieve, known as a "stand down." They took their Labs, Sambo and Shadow, to the Tracker Teams' Veterinarian for their regular checkups. The Labs, like their two-legged companions, were vulnerable to parasites and other health problems that were rife in the tropics. The climate encouraged the growth of bacteria, and it was a not an unusual event to take the dog to his medical clinic at Ton Son Nhut.

On this occasion, there was another handler at the Veterinary Clinic. They had not seen him since "School Days" at BJWS. This Tracker was working out of Cu Chi with the 25th ID in a very different set of circumstances. Since the dogs had to remain for a while in the clinic, the Trackers decided to go to a local bar and wait. The Cu Chi Team hander told the others what had been happening to them. When a line Officer of their divisional affiliation called for a Tracker Team, no one would even brief them beforehand. They would be at their camp, and be told that a chopper was coming to pick them up. There was enough disorganization at this time so that there was only one OIC (Officer in Charge) who was trying to keep up with supervising the Teams and Labs. The accident at BJWS in Malaysia had necessitated that the one Officer was in charge of two complete sets of Teams. In this time, that meant four five-man teams and four Labs. Normally, there would have been an OIC for each ten man, two team group that had been assigned to the Division. There should have been more direct intervention by the Sr. NCOICs (Senior Non-Commissioned Officer in Charge) assigned and there should have been other non-coms, at least two of them with seniority. There was supposed to be someone available with enough seniority or authority to deny missions that were not part of the Team's responsibilities. However, due to the circumstances, the groups of 18, 19 and 20 year-olds were on their own. Some of them had prior time in the Army, but very few. Moreover, even with some of the Sr. NCOICs, none of the novice teams had enough experience in the bush to be able to deal with a situation when the shit hit the fan. Without that prior knowledge, there was every possibility of a team being wiped out when an ambush was laid for them. The U. S. Army had not offered any courses to deal with this in AIT classes.

The Cu Chi Team told their old school-mates how many times a line Officer (the infantry Officer who had called for the Trackers) had not been thoroughly briefed on the Team's Mission Statement and did not know how to apply them. This was supposed to a part of the process to integrate the new Combat Tracker units into the Army, but it had not happened as planned. Because of the complexity and unusual skills that a Combat Tracker Team brought with it, proper use was critical and if not used correctly, serious problems might arise. And, they did. The men from Cu Chi said that they never spoke directly with G-2. In fact, there were many times when a line Officer had been in the field for a long time, and called up a Team to relieve some of his men from "walking point" (a scouting position—probing the area in front of a unit). The Trackers could do that easily, but it was a waste of their time and training. BJWS had prepared them so well, that functioning in any capacity in the field was a simple task for them. However, putting them to uses like that took time away from saving the lives of other troops, which is what their missions would accomplish. The dog handler from the Cu Chi group asked his fellow handler from the Central Highlands, "How does a nineteen year-old Spec 4 say 'No' to a Captain?" The other Handler who was on his second tour looked at him, and said, "Just says 'No'. If the Captain questions you for refusing the Mission—show him the Mission Statement that you got from USARV. Also, you have to get your OIC involved. There has to be a way for you to get them aware of this and you have to get them to speak up for you. In the end, if you can't get the LT or the NCOIC to do it—stick to your guns—it's your team on the line!" The nineteen year-old thought about it, knew he should do that, but still did not have the experience to be able to pull it off.

A few weeks later, the Team in the Central Highlands heard about one of the Cu Chi handlers being ambushed. It was as a result of the Handler seeing his Lab alert and then being told by one of the Sr. NCOICs to "Walk it in!" (Keep going forward!), despite that. The Sergeant had never worked with a dog, and did not believe the Handler about the alert. The young Handler went forward on the Sergeant's orders, and was killed instantly. The rest of the Team spent time being pinned down until their infantry support was able to lay down enough supporting fire for them to withdraw.

The Teams at Cu Chi had not been working more than six weeks after this, when another blow was dealt to their ranks. In this case, Lt. Hudson, who had come back freshly trained from JWS to be able to straighten out the situation at Cu Chi, led CTT #2 into the field. Bob Brede was the handler and his dog Bodie was with him on the Mission, Arnie Johnson, George Koon, and Mark Howard, who was about to become a Dad for the first time, made up the team. A Sr. NCOIC was also with them and was to work as the RTO and liaise between the Team and the support element. The Trackers arrived in their slick (chopper) and were closely followed in by the support in their birds. They looked out and saw that there was an open field that had been cleared by Roman Plows and the foliage and debris had been pushed to an end of the area creating an artificial berm. As the Trackers landed and jumped off of their ships, Bodie began to tug and alert almost immediately. Brede and Lt. Hudson noted his actions and realized that he was alerting and pointing toward the area of the berm. As the team came out behind them, they all started running toward that area as the Lab's alert became stronger. The Sr. NCOIC took shelter behind a tree to set up his position for communication between his Tracker team and the support. Within minutes, the ambush had started and Bob Brede was cut down and Bodie was fatally wounded—but still moving, yelping horribly. Mark Howard, Arnie Johnson and George Koon were slaughtered within minutes of their handler and their Lab. Lt. Ron Hudson had been wounded, but was not dead. He needed to be rescued from the killing field immediately or his life would probably be lost. The Sr. NCOIC froze and did not lay down covering fire for his LT, which would have saved Hudson from additional wounds that ended his time in Viet Nam. After what seemed like forever, ARA came in and took out the bad guys. Hudson suffered a lot more than he should have, but he did survive—although it took years to recover from the wounds of that day. The Trackers lost a good Officer and a team of good, young men and a wonderful Tracker Lab. Shit happens—but there are things that can be done to mitigate the damage.

After the word spread about that ambush, all of the Teams had a new determination to stand firm when they read the Lab's alerts. They also would refuse Missions that were not part of their specific duties. They also grew closer as people and that included being tight with their non-coms and sometimes with their Officers. The Trackers' reputation grew throughout the Army in Vietnam.

Meanwhile, at about this time, new Tracker Officers were coming in from BJWS. They brought with them the authority needed to take care of their Teams and to educate the line Officers. It was not easy for them either. Many times, a fellow Lieutenant or Captain would be out in the field for months, and plead with the Tracker Lieutenant to please leave just one of his four teams out with them. They really performed "miracles" when used on point, and the infantry troops really needed the break. The Tracker Lieutenant understood his peers, but would not put his fellow Officer in front of the well-being of his Teams. They were Trackers. This did not endear the Officer to his peers and served to alienate him even more.

The young Lieutenants had other problems, too. Besides the requests for "point men," he had seen infantry Officers put flanking units out on his Teams. He had occasions when the infantry commander would leave the Team out in the field until the dead had been counted. It was even more frustrating when the Team would move out on a track at a dead run, and their infantry support element would jog along not trying to keep up at all. At least when the support group heard rifle fire, they would think about catching up! When they finally caught up near the Tracker Team, they would open fire—hopefully not hitting the Trackers. On one Mission, Ed Wheeler and Sam, Handler and Tracker Lab for CTT #13, were both hit with shrapnel from an M79 grenade that exploded in a tree next to them. Wheeler had memorized the line from a John Wayne movie, where the "Duke" says, "As soon as I plug up this hole, I'll be with you." When the time came for the young handler to employ his memorized words, all that came out was, "Plug up the leak! Plug up the leak!"

When requested to go on a Mission, the CO of CTT #13, Don Hendricks, would radio ahead and ask what they were being called for. In his words, "If it was a waste of time, we didn't go. We waited for the next one. If you were a Spec-4 on a Team, you did not have that liberty. I took that liberty; they didn't give it to me."

Of course, things did not always go like "clockwork" with the Teams in the Central Highlands. CTT #7 had been going on two or three missions daily for weeks. It was wearing the Team down and Sambo had lost his usual good disposition—(Some would say "what good disposition?"). The dog was just plain tired. On one mission after this long period of day-in and day-out work, Merritt, Bill Reed, Poncho Alvarez y Navarez and Sgt. Joe "Nick" Nicholson were called to go with a "Blue" Team into a very hot LZ (landing zone). The Team and the Lab were loaded into the Chopper and were working to sustain the "edge" needed to do the job at hand. Now, Sambo was never happy about jumping out of a helicopter. He would do his level best to remain on the webbing of his seat to avoid "disembarking." Helicopters in the area had been taking ground fire and the pilot of the chopper did not want to waste a second getting rid of the Blues and Trackers. He was sure he was going to get shot up in the next few seconds. In addition, there was no way he was going to have his ship shot out from under him. The Crew Chief made it clear that he expected everyone to jump from the Chopper at height and that they had no intention of touching down. As the ship came in fast to the drop off point, the Crew Chief screamed at the departing troops to "Lock and Load, Full Auto" (Ready the weapons for full automatic fire). The Blue Team was ready to go, and the handler was ready to "assist" his Lab to the ground. The handler was carrying his weapon in the left hand,

and grappling with the dog's lead with his right. The pilot did his best to dump his passengers. He did not want to hang around a second more than necessary. The Blues went out and the other Tracker Team members went out. The Handler was standing on the helicopter's skids while trying to cast the Lab out—when he realized in the confusion, he had not put his hand through the loop at the end of the lead. The Lab touched down, and took off. He was hot, tired and hated chopper rides. As he ran like the devil was right behind him, the lead unwrapped from the handler's arm—and the dog was gone! Merritt was very astonished as he looked at his empty arm. Reed, his coverman, had a mirrored expression of horrified shock. Meanwhile, the Blues were securing the perimeter of the area. The pilot was "outta" there and the Labrador retriever, which had cost the Army an enormous sum of money, was nowhere to be seen.

The handler and his coverman were totally stymied as to their next move—you cannot just go out in enemy territory yelling "Sambo, COME". The Blue Team Lieutenant was unaware of the run away dog. He gathered the CTT for a briefing and when he was finished, the embarrassed handler reported the mishap. The Lieutenant had his RTO call the circling Light Observation Helicopters (LOH—pronounced "Loach"), and explain that the Tracker Lab had gone AWOL. Merritt and Reed waited anxiously for any word of the runaway. Finally, one of the Loaches spotted the Lab and called in to the Blues with the information.

The handler and coverman looked at one another when they realized that none of the Blue Team had the slightest intention of leaving the newly secured area. Poncho and Sgt. Nicholson most certainly were not going anywhere outside the perimeter—hell, they did not lose the damn dog and besides they were laughing too hard to be of any use. Off went Merritt and Reed into Indian Country through high elephant grass and into the tree line, to find the frustrated canine fugitive. The Loach who had found the dog was circling the area. He would lead the Trackers to the escapee but he would not remain stationary, as he was very aware of the sporadic firing coming from the ground area. Just maybe, the twosome would find the source of that ground fire and live to tell about it. Hopefully they could accomplish the task at hand and so they followed the sound of the helicopter that had become their "eye in the sky."

They went about a sixteenth of a mile out of the secured area, and heard the sound of running water. They saw the Loach dip overhead as a signal. There, with his tongue hanging out, lying on his back, with the cool water flowing over his private parts, was the happiest Labrador retriever in all of Viet Nam. He was obviously suffering from his own brand of post-traumatic stress disorder—or maybe he just wanted the day off. Nevertheless, for once, he had been in control. Needless to say, that was the last time that handler did not have his hand through the loop of the leash and wrapped firmly around his wrist. The story made the rounds and there is no doubt that the Lab enjoyed that as much as he had his AWOL adventure!

Sgt. James "Poor Moore" Moore had been with that team in the Central Highlands and was a true believer. He had made it through BJWS and had been put on the Team by Sgts. Nicholson and Couch to "ride herd" on the boys of CTT #7 because everyone else, quite frankly, was scared to death to go out with them. They had some sort of "Mojo" going for them and "the powers that be" had told the LT and the two Sr. NCOICs to "give them all the rope they can handle." The reason Sgt. Moore had been given the moniker "Poor Moore" is that he had become somewhat accident-prone. Of course, it could have been that as an unusually tall, slender man in a stealthy unit, it was very difficult to keep a "low profile!" He had received two wounds in action previously and was just being released from the hospital as this particular incident took place. Frank Merritt and John E. Dotson were on "their berm" making small talk. Sgt. Moore had entered the perimeter gate and was walking up the road favoring one leg from the action that had given him his third Purple Heart in as many months. He was coming in to take his assigned place with one of their teams. The boys watched him far in the distance as he neared their "home" at LZ Two-Bits. Just at that moment, there was a change in atmospheric pressure—the kind that always happened just before some major "in-coming" was about to make a serious change in someone's day. And, they say you never hear the one that will kill you. Moore was still limping along the road toward the boys. Dotson and Merritt looked at each other and hit the dirt hoping for the best. The artillery round went directly over them sounding louder that a freight train—thank God for that noise. It flew over the village and hit the CP (Command Post) at LZ English killing a trooper. The explosion, noise and damage were truly awesome and the handlers were pleased not to be directly on the receiving end. Poor Moore, on the other hand, saw this as a sign from God. He took off running toward the village that was next to the encampment and was not seen for three days. However, he was a Tracker—and nothing was said.

The Trackers were definitely a "different breed." One of the teams was sent back for an in-country "refresher course." This was not a completely thought-out concept. It seems that the first day the boys started on a practice track and one of the trainers yelled, "CONTACT!" This is what would be called out in training to simulate the team coming under enemy attack. Unfortunately, the team had been in constant combat for over nine months at the time, and they reacted accordingly. Their weapons were loaded—despite the suggestions by the trainers that they not take live ammo. Combat soldiers feel naked without live ammunition and they worked out a deal with the trainers that would enable them to have their ammo, but without having a live round chambered. When the incident occurred and the team went into their normal reaction, there were some seriously panicked trainers who had some immediate laundry changes to perform. It was a lesson to those who sit and create the schedules for such things. The Trackers were not invited to any more "refresher courses" in the future.

Susan Merritt

```
VV  VAN785
PP RUEPDD
DE RUMSVA 4468 1891527
2NY CCCCC
P 0815002 JUL 67
FM CG USARV TSN RVN
TO RUEPHD/ DA WASH DC
INFO ZEN/ USARPAC
BT
```

CM-IN: 114886 VC
CONFIDENTIAL
PRIORITY
PG 1 OF 8 PGS

RECEIVED 11 JUL 1967 USARPAC OPNS CTR

DECLASSIFIED AFTER 12 YEARS DOD DIR 5200.10

NO RECORD OF RECEIPT THIS MSG IN AG-C PRIOR TO 112245Z

C O N F I D E N T I A L AVBCC-O 47855 SECTION 1 OF 2
SUBJECT: COMBAT TRACKER TEAMS IN VIETNAM (U)

1. (C) SINCE OCTOBER 1966 USARV HAS HAD US ARMY PERSONNEL STATIONED AT THE BRITISH JUNGLE WARFARE SCHOOL (JWS), JOHORE BAHRU, MALAYSIA UNDERGOING TRAINING AS COMBAT TRACKER TEAMS.

2. (C) THE COMBAT TRACKER TEAM PROGRAM CALLED FOR THE BRITISH TO TRAIN FOURTEEN US ARMY TEAMS OF TEN MEN EACH (TWO VISUAL TRACKERS, TWO TRACKER DOG HANDLERS WITH LABRADOR RETRIEVER TRACKER DOGS, AN NCOIC, ANNCO SECOND IN COMMAND, A RADIO OPERATOR, AND THREE COVER MEN FOR SECURITY). THESE TEAMS WERE TO BE ASSIGNED TO US ARMY UNITS IN VIETNAM ON THE BASIS OF TWO TEAMS PER DIVISION, ONE PER SEPARATE BRIGADE. EIGHT OF THESE TEAMS HAVE BEEN TRAINED AND DEPLOYED. SIX TEAMS WILL BE TRAINED AND DEPLOYED BY OCTOBER 1967, REPRESENTING COMPLETION OF THE PRESENT AGREEMENT BETWEEN USARV, BRITISH FAR EAST LAND FORCES (FARELF) AND JWS.

3. (C) THE TRAINING COURSE FOR COMBAT TRACKER TEAMS IS FIVE WEEKS FOR VISUAL TRACKERS, THREE TO NINE MONTH TRAINING FOR DOGS

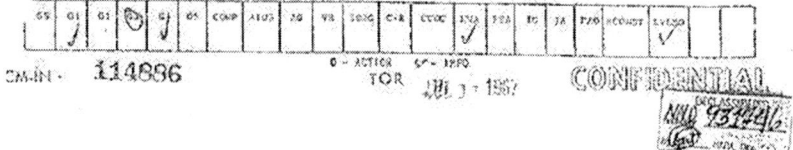

PHOTO 14 This is the first page of an eight page confidential telex written by General William Childs Westmoreland in July 1967

Seek On!

CONFIDENTIAL

DOGS AND DOG HANDLERS. THIS GROUP IS COMPOSED OF PERSONNEL FROM THE ROYAL ARMY VETERINARY CORPS, WHICH IN THE BRITISH ARMY IS RESPONSIBLE FOR ANIMAL MANAGEMENT AND TRAINING. BRITISH PERSONNEL INVOLVED ALL HAVE EXTENSIVE EXPERIENCE WITH WAR DOGS. CPT D. H. HALL-SMITH, 466455, RAVC HAS DIRECTED THIS PROGRAM. US -4.6 D-45,- NELL USED TO TRAIN THE FINAL GROUP OF EIGHTEEN DOGSHAVE GAINED SOME EXPERIENCE WITHE DOG TRAINING FOR TRACKER DOGS. THSI EXPERIENCE LEVEL WILL BE MAINTAINED AT JWS FOR BRITISH ARMY TRAINING AS WELL AS ADDITIONAL US ARMY TRAINING WHICH MIGHT BE AGREED UPON. THE COMBAT TRACKET WING AT JWS HAS BEEN COMMANDED BY CAPTAIN F. H. WOODS, AN OFFICER OF THE BRITISH ROYAL ARMY EDUCATION CORPS WHO HAS BEEN ON LOAND FROM HIS CORPS TO FARLEF- JWS FOR THE EXPRESS PURPOSE OF SETTING UP THE TRACKER COURSE FOT THE US ARMY AND ADVISING COMMANDANT, JWS ON THE CONDUCT OF THE COURSE. CAPTAIN WOODS IS A FORMER NEW ZEALAND ARMY OFFICER, WIDELY RECOGNIZED IN THE BRITISH ARMY AS THE LEADING CONTEMPORARY EXPERT ON COMBAT TRACKER OPERATIONS DUE TO HIS EXTENSIVE EXPERIENCE IN MALAYSIA AND BORNEO. TO ASSIST HIM IN COMBAT TRACKER TRAINING, CAPTAIN WOODS OBTAINED ON LOAN THE SERVICES O ONE OFFICER AND SIX ENLISTED MEN FROM THE NEW ZEALAND SPECIAL AIR SERVICES SQUADRON, ALL WITH EXTENSIBE EXPERIENCE IN COMBAT TRACKING OPERATIONS IN MALAYSIA AND BORNEO. CAPTAIN WOODS RETURNS TO DUTY WITH HIS CORPS ON +9 JUN, THE NEW ZEALANDERS RETURN TO THEIR SQUADRON ON +5 JUNE. THE LAST SIX US ARMY COMBAT TRACKER TEAMS WILL, BY AGREEMENT BETWEEN USARV AND JWS-FARELF, BE TRAINED BY US ARMY OFFICERS AND NCO'S TRAINED BY CAPTAIN WOODS AS INSTRUCTORS, OPERATING UNDER THE DIRECTION OF THE COMMANDANT, JWS. BOTH FOR BRITISH ARMY TRACKER TEAM

CM-IN 114886   **CONFIDENTIAL**   PG 5 OF 8 PGS

Susan Merritt

CONFIDENTIAL

DOGS AND DOG HANDLERS. THIS GROUP IS COMPOSED OF PERSONNEL FROM THE ROYAL ARMY VETERINARY CORPS, WHICH IN THE BRITISH ARMY IS RESPONSIBLE FOR ANIMAL MANAGEMENT AND TRAINING. BRITISH PERSONNEL INVOLVED ALL HAVE EXTENSIVE EXPERIENCE WITH WAR DOGS. CPT D. H. HALL-SMITH, 466435, RAVC HAS DIRECTED THIS PROGRAM. US -A.G DOGS,-NELL USED TO TRAIN THE FINAL GROUP OF EIGHTEEN DOGSHAVE GAINED SOME EXPERIENCE WITHE DOG TRAINING FOR TRACKER DOGS. THSI EXPERIENCE LEVEL WILL BE MAINTAINED AT JWS FOR BRITISH ARMY TRAINING AS WELL AS ADDITIONAL US ARMY TRAINING WHICH MIGHT BE AGREED UPON. THE COMBAT TRACKET WING AT JWS HAS BEEN COMMANDED BY CAPTAIN F. H. WOODS, AN OFFICER OF THE BRITISH ROYAL ARMY EDUCATION CORPS WHO HAS BEEN ON LOAND FROM HIS CORPS TO FARLEF- JWS FOR THE EXPRESS PURPOSE OF SETTING UP THE TRACKER COURSE FOT THE US ARMY AND ADVISING COMMANDANT, JWS ON THE CONDUCT OF THE COURSE. CAPTAIN WOODS IS A FORMER NEW ZEALAND ARMY OFFICER, WIDELY RECOGNIZED IN THE BRITISH ARMY AS THE LEADING CONTEMPORARY EXPERT ON COMBAT TRACKER OPERATIONS DUE TO HIS EXTENSIVE EXPERIENCE IN MALAYSIA AND BORNEO. TO ASSIST HIM IN COMBAT TRACKER TRAINING, CAPTAIN WOODS OBTAINED ON LOAN THE SERVICES O ONE OFFICER AND SIX ENLISTED MEN FROM THE NEW ZEALAND SPECIAL AIR SERVICES SQUADRON, ALL WITH EXTENSIBE EXPERIENCE IN COMBAT TRACKING OPERATIONS IN MALAYSIA AND BORNEO. CAPTAIN WOODS RETURNS TO DUTY WITH HIS CORPS ON 19 JUN, THE NEW ZEALANDERS RETURN TO THEIR SQUADRON ON 25 JUNE. THE LAST SIX US ARMY COMBAT TRACKER TEAMS WILL, BY AGREEMENT BETWEEN USARV AND JWS-FARELF, BE TRAINED BY US ARMY OFFICERS AND NCO'S TRAINED BY CAPTAIN WOODS AS INSTRUCTORS, OPERATING UNDER THE DIRECTION OF THE COMMANDANT, JWS. BOTH FOR BRITISH ARMY TRACKET TEAM

Seek On!

CONFIDENTIAL

ASSIGNED ARE REORGANIZED, EACH DIVISION WIL HAVE ONE PLATOON OF FOUR FIVE MAN TEAMS, AND EACH SEPARATE BRIGADE A PLATOON OF TWO FIVE MAN TEAMS. USARV STUDY INDICATES THE ONLY FEASIBLE WAY TO EXPAND THIS PROGRAM IN PERSONNEL AS WELL AS DOGS, IS TO LEVY THE REQUIREMENTS OF THE CONUS TRAINING BASE.

5 (C) USARV PROPOSES TO REORGANIZE COMBAT TRACKER TEAMS ALONG THE LINES INDICATED IN PARA 4 ABOVE. AT THE SAME TIME IT WILL BE NECESSARY TO RETURN SOME DOGS FROM VIETNAM TO JWS TO PROVIDE REPLACEMENT DOGS AND DOG HANDLERS FOR REPLACEMENT TEAMS. IN GENERAL THIS WILL MEAN HALVING THE NUMBER OF DOGS IN SOME PLATOONS TO PROVIDE THE REPLACEMENT BASE.

9. (C) USARV FURTHER POPOSES TO REACH AN AGREEMENT WITH FIARELF-JWS IN THE NEAR FUTURE TO CONTINUE TRAINING US ARMY COMBAT TRACKER REPLACEMENT PERSONNEL TO JWS IN EXTENSION OF THE PRESENT AGREEMENT, THAT IS BEYOND OCTOBER 1967. THIS TRAINING MUST BE THE SUBJECT OF PLOITICAL NEGOTIATIONS BETWEEN HM GOVERNMENT, THE US GOVERNMENT, AND GOVERNMENT OF MALAYSIA. US AMBASSADOR, SAIGON HAS BEEN REQUESTED TO BEGIN THESE NEGOTIATIONS. THE USARV PROPOSAL TO FARELF-JWS WILL INCLUDE A PROGRAM EXTENDING FROM OCTOBER 1967 THROUGH NOVEMBER 1968 TO TRAIN SEVEN GROUPS OF ABOUT FORTY TRAINEES EACH, IN EIGHT WEEK COURSES, TO BE REPLACEMENTS FOR THE COMBAT TRACKERUNITS NOW IN VIETNAM. THIS WIL SUFFICE TO SUPPORT THE REORGAIZATION OF THESE UNITS INDICATED IN 4 ABOVE. NEW DOG HANDLERS WILL BE TRAINED ON EXPERIENCED DOGS BY REDUING THE NUMBER OF DOGS AVAILABLE TO COMBAT TRACKER UNITS IN VIETNAM, THOSE DOGS BEING RETURNED TO JWS TO PROVIDE

CM-IN 114886   **CONFIDENTIAL**

Susan Merritt

CONFIDENTIAL

ASSIGNED ARE REORGANIZED, EACH DIVISION WIL HAVE ONE PLATOON OF FOUR FIVE MANT TEAMS, AND EACH SEPARATE BRIGADE A PLATOON OF TWO FIVE MAN TEAMS. USARV STUDY INDICATES THE ONLY FEASIBLE WAY TO EXPAND THIS PROGRAM IN PERSONNEL AS WELL AS DOGS, IS TO LEVY THE REQUIREMENTS OF THE CONUS TRAINING BASE.

6 (C) USARV PROPOSES TO REORGANIZE COMBAT TRACKER TEAMS ALONG THE LINES INDICATED IN PARA 4 ABOVE. AT THE SAME TIME IT WILL BE NECESSARY TO RETURN SOME DOGS FROM VIETNAM TO JWS TO PROVIDE REPLACEMENT DOGS AND DOG HANDLERS FOR REPLACEMENT TEAMS. IN GENERAL THIS WILL MEAN HALVING THE NUMBER OF DOGS IN SOME PLATOONS TO PROVIDE THE REPLACEMENT BASE.

9. (C) USARV FURTHER PROPOSES TO REACH AN AGREEMENT WITH FARELF-JWS IN THE NEAR FUTURE TO CONTINUE TRAINNG US ARMY COMBAT TRACKER REPLACEMENT PERSONNEL TO JWS IN EXTENSION OF THE PRESENT AGREEMENT, THAT IS BEYOND OCTOBER 1967. THIS TRAINING MUST BE THE SUBJECT OF PLOITICAL NEGOTIATIONS BETWEEN HM GOVERNMENT, THE US GOVERNMENT, AND GOVERNMENT OF MALAYSIA. US AMBASSAADOR, SAIGON HAS BEEN REQUESTED TO BEGIN THESE NEGOTIATIONS. THE USARV PROPOSAL TO FARELF-JWS WILL INCLUDE A PROGRAM EXTENDING FROM OCTOBER 1967 THROUGH NOVEMBER 1968 TO TRAIN SEVEN GROUPS OF ABOUT FORTY TRAINEES EACH, IN EIGHT WEEK COURSES, TO BE REPLACEMENTS FOR THE COMBAT TRACKERUNITS NOW IN VIETNAM. THIS WIL SUFFICE TO SUPPORT THE REORGAIZATION OF THESE UNITS INDICATED IN 6 ABOVE. NEW DOG HANDLERS WILL BE TRAINED OF EXPERIENCED DOGS BY REDUING THE NUMBER OF DOGS AVAILABLE TO COMBAT TRACKER UNITS IN VIETNAM, THOSE DOGS BEING RETURNED TOJWS TO PROVIDE

Seek On!

CONFIDENTIAL

CONFIDENTIAL AVHGC-O 47256 SECTION 28 OF II ABOUT $134,000.

10. (C) TO SUPERVISE TRAINING OF US ARMY PERSONNEL AT JWS, USARV HAS ORGANIZED UNDER USARV GO 4053, 31 MAY 1967 THE US ARMY WAR DOG TRAINING DETACHMENT (PROVISIONAL) WITH FOUR OFFICERS AND 29 ENLISTED MEN. THIS UNIT WILL PROVIDE INSTRUCTOR GROUP, DOG TRAINERS, TRACK LAYERS FOR DOG-DOG HANDLER TRAINING, AND A SMALL ADMINISTRATIVE STAFF AT JWS. WHEN THE CONUS TRAINING BASE CAN SUPPORT USARV REQUIREMENTS FOR TRAINED COMBAT TRACKER TEAMS AND REPLACEMENTS THIS UNIT WILL BE RETURNED TO VIETNAM TO CONDUCT ORIENTATION TRAINING, QUARANTINE OPERATIONS FOR DOGS, AND OTHER MATTERS INCIDENT TO THE WAR DOG PROGRAM, BOTH TRACKER AND SCOUT DOG, IN VIETNAM.

11. (C) IN ADDITION TO THE REQUIREMENT FOR TRAINING COMBAT TRACKER TEAMS, THERE APPEARS A FAR GREATER REQUIREMENT FOR VISUAL TRACKERS THAN WAS ORIGINALLY ANTICIPATED. THIS FACT MAKES IT, WHILE NOT DESIRABLE, AT LEAST FEASIBLE TO WITHDRAW PART OF THE DOGS FROM TRACKER TEAMS IN VIETNAM TO PROVIDE A REPLACEMENT BASE AT JWS. THERE ADDITIONALLY APPEARS A REQUIREMENT TO TRAIN VISUAL TRACKERS FOR DUTY WITH LONG RANGE RECONNAISSANCE PATROLS, INFANTRY RECONNAISSANCE UNITS, AND FOR DUTY IN INFANTRY RIFLE SQUADS OF MANUVER BATTALIONS IN VIETNAM, A FACT WHICH MAKES IT EVEN MORE DESIRABLE THAT THE CONUS TRAINING BASE BEGIN VISUAL TRACKER TRAINING.

12. (C) AS THE COMBAT TRACKER PROGRAM NOW STANDS IN VIETNAM, USARV BELIEVES THE FOLLOWING TO BE A VALID USARV REQUIREMENT:

CM-IN 114886   **CONFIDENTIAL**

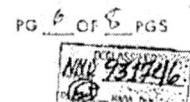

CONFIDENTIAL

A. TO FORMALIZE BY TOE THE ORGANIZATION AND EQUIPMENT OF COMBAT TRACKER PLATOONS. PROPOSED ORGANIZATION AND OTHER REQUIREMENTS WILL BE SUBMITTED BY SEPARATE MESSAGE.

B. FOR DEPARTMENT OF THE ARMY TO TASK AN APPROPRIATE AGENCY TO PROCURE AND BEGIN TRAINING, AS SOON AS POSSIBLE, LABRADOR RETRIEVERS AS TRACKER DOGS WITH A GOAL OF ABOUT EIGHTY OPERATIONAL TRACKER DOGS TO BE PROVIDED TO USARV BY END OF FY 69. USARV PERSONNEL ROTATING FROM COMBAT TRACKER TEAMS IN VIETNAM SHOULD BE USED AS A TRAINING CADRE TO ESTABLISH THIS PROGRAM.

C. DEPARTMENT OF THE ARMY TO TASK AN APPROPRIATE AGENCY TO DEVELOP AND ESTABLISH TRAINING PROGRAM FOR VISUAL TRACKER PERSONNEL, AND COMBAT TRACKER TEAMS TO BE ASSIGNED TO COMBAT TRACKER UNITS; AND VISUAL TRACKERS TO BE ASSIGNED OTHER INFANTRY UNITS OF THE US ARMY AS REQUIRED.

D. ESTABLISH A TARGET DATE OF SUPPLYING THE FIRST CONUS TRAINED COMBAT TRACKER PLATOONS TO USARV BY SEPTEMBER 1968.

E. ESTABLISHMENT OF THE CONUS BASED COMBAT TRACKER PLATOON TRAINING PROGRAM ON THE BASIS OF TRAINING AND SUPPLYING TO USARV A TOTAL OF ABOUT TWENTY TRAINED COMBAT TRACKER PLATOONS BY THE END OF FY 69, REPLACING THOSE PLATOONS AT INTERVALS OB ABOUT ELEVEN MONTHS, AND EXPANDING THE PROGRAM AS THE FORCE LEVELS IN VIETNAM INCREASE. THE TARGET BASIS OF ASSIGNMENT OF COMBAT TRACKER PLATOONS SHOULD REMAIN AT TWO PLATOONS PER DIVISION, ONE PLATOON (FULL FOUR FIVE MAN TEAMS) PER SEPARATE BRIGADE, UNTIL USARV EVALUTION OF THIS BASIS IS COMPLETE. THIS MATTER WILL BE THE SUBJECT OF SEPARATE CORRESPONDENCE.

CONFIDENTIAL

Seek On!

CONFIDENTIAL

F. DEPARTMENT OF THE ARMY TO SOLICIT OF THE BRITISH ARMY THE SERVICES OF CAPTAIN F.H. WOODS, 470541, ROYAL ARMY EDUCATION CORPS, TO SET UP A PROGRAM AND ADVISE THE US ARMY ON THE CONDUCT OF TRACKER TEAM OPERATION. FAILING IN THIS DEPARTMENT OF THE ARMY TO OFFER CAPTAIN WOODS A SUITABLE CONTRACT WITH THE US ARMY UNDER WHICH HE WOULD COME TO THE UNITED STATES, SET UP THE COMBAT TRACKER PROGRAM, AND ADVISE THE US ARMY ON COMBAT TRACKING OPERATIONS.

G. DEPARTMENT OF THE ARMY TO SOLICIT THE ASSISTANCE OF THE BRITISH ARMY FOR THE SERVICES OF AN OFFICER OF THE ROYAL ARMY VETERINARY CORPS SUGGESTING CPT D.H. HALL-SMITH, 466455, RAVC; TO ASSIST IN DOG-DOG HANDLER TRAINING OF RETRIEVERS UNTIL SUFFICIENT NUMBERS OF US ARMY PERSONNEL CAN BE TRAINED TO CARRY ON THE PROGRAM.

H. DEPARTMENT OF THE ARMY MAKE AVAILABLE TO USARV NECESSARY FUNDS TO MEET REQUIREMENTS AND THE REPLACEMENT TRAINING PROGRAM AT JUNGLE WARFARE SCHOOL, ESTIMATED TO BE ABOUT $195,000.

13. (U) IT IS THERE FORE REQUESTED THAT, AS A MATTER OF PRIORITY, DEPARTMENT OF THE ARMY TAKE NECESSARY ACTION TO ESTABLISH A PROGRAM MEETING THE REQUIREMENTS SET FORTHE IN PARA 12 ABOVE.

GP-4
BT

CONFIDENTIAL

Susan Merritt

```
                    DEPARTMENT OF THE ARMY
                    HEADQUARTERS SPECIAL TROOPS
                    UNITED STATES ARMY VIETNAM
                    APO San Francisco 96307

SPECIAL ORDERS           E X T R A C T                    30 May 1967
NUMBER    150

     7. TC 261. ATTACHMENT dir as indic this sta Scty Gd Co Sp Trps APO 96307

Personnel making up USA Combat Tracker Team No. 6
RICHESON, PAUL E 05329717 1LT Inf
WARD, GARY C RA15668792 SSG E-6
MC DONALD, GEORGE S RA19072894 SP4 E-4
CALLOWAY, PERRY W US54710407 PFC E-3
LANDERS, MIKE P RA16670413 PFC E-3
HORNER, ALFRED L US52051220 PFC E-3
GAYDARIK, STEPHEN D US52686209 PFC E-3
COON, GARY L US54805617 PFC E-3
KUFFEL, EUGENE F US54005623 PFC E-3
   Atch to:  9th Inf Div APO 96370        Rept date:  1 Jun 67
   Pd: Indef                              Auth: VOCG USARV
   Purpose: For rats, qtr and Admin. To provide tracker dog support
   Sp instr: NA

Personnel making up USA Combat Tracker Team No. 7
HUNT, HOWARD 05329669 1LT Inf
NICHOLSON, JOSEPH RA52097279 PSG E-7
MOORE, JAMES P RA14506620 SGT E-5
CLEMINS, RALPH RA25700439 SP4 E-4
NEVAREZ, JUAN RA50156662 PFC E-3
LA FARLETTE, JAMES B RA16748355 PFC E-3
PRESLEY, THOMAS G RA14750435 PFC E-3
REED, WILLIAM A US56695961 PFC E-3
MERRITT, FRANCIS B RA12732968 SP4 E-4

Personnel making up USA Combat Tracker Team No. 8
HUDSON, RONALD J 05327376 1LT Inf
LAMB, HUGH E RA17496404 PSG E-7
COUCH, NEIL P RA15440074 SSG E-6
MAXHAM, REGINALD T RA22083303 SGT E-5
WALTZ, GEORGE A RA16426494 SP4 E-4
BROWN, KENNETH US53436217 PFC E-3
CRADICK, STEVEN US55055532 PFC E-3
MAHURIN, ELMER W US55903920 PFC E-3
NIGGERMEYER, THOMAS A RA17716355 SP4 E-4
DOTSON, JOHN E RA19069620 SP4 E-4
   Atch to:  1st Air Cav Div (Airmobile) APO 96490
   Rept date: 1 Jun 67                    Pd: Indef
   Purpose: For rats, qtr and admin. To provide tracker dog support
   Auth: VOCG USARV
   Sp instr: NA
```

PHOTO 15 This order created three of the original "Provisional" Combat Tracker Teams (Numbers 6, 7, and 8). The new teams were subsequently flown out of Malaysia secretly on military transport and brought back to the operations areas with as much or more jungle warfare training than any other specialty at that time. They had had a minimum of two months of intense training at the hands of the experts.

Seek On!

HEADQUARTERS
UNITED STATES ARMY VIETNAM
APO San Francisco 96307

GENERAL ORDERS
NUMBER 2269

20 May 1967

1. TC 002. Following unit ORGANIZED

UNITED STATES ARMY COMBAT TRACKER TEAM NO 7 (PROVISIONAL)
Assigned to: United States Army Vietnam
Effective date: 20 May 1967
Authorized strength: OFF WO EM AGG
                         1   0   9   10
Equipment: Will be provided by 1st Cavalry Division (Airmobile)
Personnel: Will be provided from United States Army Vietnam resources.
           Replacements will be provided by volunteers from subordinate
           units.
Files: In accordance with Army Regulation 345-210
Morning report: Feeder morning report will be submitted to parent
           organization.
Mission: To follow retreating enemy groups by the use of tracker dogs
         and visual trackers and re-establish contact. Investigate
         areas of suspected enemy activity and follow tracks which
         are found. Train selected personnel of other units in the
         art of observation and visual tracking.
Authority: Verbal orders of Commanding General
Fund obligation: In accordance with current fiscal pocess
Special instructions: Attached to 1st Cavalry Division (Airmobile) APO 96490

FOR THE COMMANDER:

FRANK D. MILLER
Brigadier General, US Army
Chief of Staff

S. A. MacKENZIE
Colonel, AGC
Adjutant General

DISTRIBUTION:
G Plus
7-CINCUSARPAC
2-CINCUSARPAC, ATTN: Hist File
3-COMUSMACV
1-COMUSMACV, ATTN: 27th DPU
10-AVHCP
10-US Army Combat Tracker Team No 7 (Provisional)
10-1st Cavalry Division (AM) APO 96490

3-AVHAG-D
2-AVHAG-S
2-AVHGC-OT
2-AVHAG-M
3-AVHAG-A

SPECIAL DISTRIBUTION:
20-TAGO, ATTN: AGSD

PHOTO 16   Reverse of Orders for creation of Provisional Combat Tracker Teams #6, 7, and 8.

Susan Merritt

Seek On!

Susan Merritt

Seek On!

CHAPTER TWELVE

An Officer's Reflections 1999

An amazing message was on the former Tracker Lieutenant's e-mail program. He couldn't believe after all these years; he was being remembered as a Tracker Officer. It was thrilling and scary—and he didn't quite know what to do about it. The Trackers were reuniting and finding each other. His emotions were swinging wildly.

In his heart of hearts, he would always be a Tracker. He recalled the intensity of the bonds he had with his men—his Team. They had all been just "boys" then, and the Officer was only a few years older—but felt very protective of them-paternal, even. They were truly dear to him, and although it had been more than a quarter of a century since he had last seen them, it was like yesterday. Though he had gone on in life far from that place and that time—he revisited it in his mind even now.

Here on his computer screen was a message for him from the Combat Tracker Teams. He had shed private tears when "his men" had been wounded, or one of the Labs had been hurt. It had been such a bizarre time. The Army refused to let the Officers share their Quarters with the enlisted men, yet they had been trained as a unit. All of them united made one very potent entity. But, he wasn't supposed to fraternize. On the other side of things, as a Commanding Officer of a Combat Tracker Team, he hadn't been accepted by the main stream Officer Corps. It was too odd a specialty, and it almost guaranteed the Officer would never go up the chain of command to general grade. That had happened before in the Army's history when new specialties had been developed. It made a young Officer stand out in a negative way—it was too different a concept. The prejudice wasn't important to him then or now, what was important was "his men".

Now he was in turmoil. Part of him was elated at being found by his Trackers and part of him wanted nothing to do with it. It was a veritable quandary. So many memories were evoked by that simple message. He thought of the days and nights at BJWS. Some of his team were so inventive and funny that as he recalled specific incidents, he had to laugh aloud. He remembered that he had courses in basic Vietnamese expressions which were supposed to be a help in dealing with the people. He recalled his first use of the language in Vietnam. He asked an old lady, "Hum nye ba man yoy?" He was totally nonplussed when she hit him over the head with her umbrella. He was flabbergasted at the response. It wasn't until later that it was explained to him that instead of asking her "How are you, esteemed lady?" he had used the wrong inflection and endearingly said, "How are you, old cow?" That was both his first and last attempts at using conversational Vietnamese.

There were other memories—those of loss and the feeling of inadequacy in not being able to protect his people from earning "Purple Hearts"—or worse. This was becoming a roller-coaster ride of feelings. He remembered well when his team, CTT #13, left Malaysia for Vietnam. It was on a Friday, the 13th of October in 1967. They left at 1300 hours with 11 men and 2 dogs. They were being transported in a C130. In fact, the first takeoff attempt had been aborted because two pallets of dog food plus the men and dogs had been too heavy. One pallet of the food was unloaded—and the plane was within its weight limit.

They went back through Tan Son Nhut and then were driven to Bien Hoa to be housed at the new CTT HQ until their Division was ready for them. They had been issued no equipment, no arms, no housing. There were two five-man Teams at the 1st Division HQ who had been some of the very first graduates of BJWS. They were located in Di An in two tents near the HHQ Company of the 2nd Brigade.

He and his NCOIC were sent to Di An to get the area ready for the teams. He was able to commandeer an excellent NCOIC,

Ted Kirmse, who had already been on missions for the Big Red One. On his first mission out to reestablish contact with the enemy, they were supremely successful. He received his Combat Infantryman's Badge as a result of a successful track into a VC encampment.

The Standard Operating Procedure for the 1st Inf. Div. was that all new personnel would go through thirty day acclimatization before doing any work in the field. Since the Trackers had been trained in Malaysia at BJWS, they were exempted from that policy. They were battle ready—except that they had no arms! They then drew weapons and ammo from HHQ. The team chose M16s for all but the Dog Handler and himself. He chose a .45 caliber handgun and an M16. The handler stayed with a .45 as his hands were full with the dog's lead. Some other handlers opted for the CAR 15. Within the first week, the team changed their original choices to include one M79 grenade launcher per team, and the rear guard carried Remington shotguns with flechette rounds. On the first mission, the M16s jammed—rounds got stuck in the chamber even though the weapons were clean. First order of business was to get those switched for the A1 version that had chromed chambers and were more dependable that the older version. That didn't help the handlers as no CAR15 ever was made with a chromed chamber and they continued to have problems throughout their tour. The former Lieutenant refused to carry an M16 after the jamming problems persisted. He opted for an M79 with close arming WP (White Phosphorus—"Willie Peter") rounds for the first half of his year, and switched over to the Chinese-made Thompson submachine gun (.45 cal.) for the remainder. He had "liberated" the weapon from a cache that the team had found.

The Provisional Trackers were still without technical authorization and they had to find ways to talk Division out of new tents and other equipment. The men moved in with no problem when the tents were set up. He was remembering that there had been no bunks, no tables, no electricity, but there was a place for them inside the perimeter—it was located in a swamp! They learned how to trade items located on missions for important things that they needed—plywood, beer, LRRP rations, generators, wire, etc. An RPG (Rocket Propelled Grenade) launcher (just the tube) was worth two 4 X 8 sheets of plywood, while a VC flag and sandals were worth one sheet.

The men of his platoon would go on "recon" missions to find useful things for their camp. An unused gas bladder for jet fuel became their shower, trips to the Air Force Base in Saigon yielded cots and fans, plus a few five-finger discounts accounted for generators, refrigerators, etc. He was very proud of his team when they came back with a baby-blue generator that obviously was not Army issue—it got quickly re-decorated in "camo". Once they had electricity, there was cold beer and other people started visiting their "bar/tent" with great frequency.

Vehicles were another matter. There was a 3/4 ton that had been "redlined" and listed for disposal. To get another vehicle, he could not "redline" an already "redlined" vehicle—they had to dispose of it. After numerous tries to "kill" the old beast, they finally ran it driverless into a minefield where it stayed intact for the remainder of the war. Then, and only then, could he talk the Division out of a 3/4 ton truck!

They had special people who became friends of his team. There was a Veterinarian who enjoyed the ambiance of the CTT's new accommodations. Many people weren't aware that the Vet was also the meat inspector for all the meat that came into the Division. It seems that the Vet decided that there were quite a few steaks and chickens which were not fit for the Officer's mess—and these undesirable foodstuffs would be donated to the CTTs. In fact, the Officer remembered clearly the first all-team project—building the barbecue pit! The Vet was held in such high esteem by the platoon that he became their first—and frequent—guest.

He thought of the dogs that had accompanied the team to the war. Of the four, three were capable. One couldn't be taken on a mission until he had greater training. He was just too green. Another of the three had been WIA, and he and the handler were in Saigon. The incident had occurred with the first provisional team sent to the 1st Inf. Div. He rotated the dogs and his men for optimum results. He recalled watching his men operate at BJWS, and had their placements in mind before they ever went out on a mission. He also had a vivid memory about the non-fraternization rule. Officers and enlisted were not supposed to be billeted together—so a separate tent was set up for him—and that became the "bar" area. He would feign use of it whenever HHQ inspected their area.

For the first month, missions were follow ups from ambushes that the Big Red One had experienced and totally fouled and for VC activities (typically mines on the roads). After the first month, he had created a pamphlet for explaining the specialty and its uses for the line officers of the 1st Infantry Division. The missions became more frequent and diverse after that. One very successful mission that he remembered had happened during an incident for the First of the Fourth Cavalry. The Lab had alerted on an area where a Rome Plow had pushed all of the trees over. They had been huge trees, and were all broken and lying on the ground. Recon choppers had flown over the area several times and had seen nothing. The helicopters hadn't been fired on either. The dog kept alerting. An infantry squad followed the tracker team in. Under the logs was an entire platoon of NVA divided up so that they couldn't be spotted from the air. Artillery was called in, and the enemy was terminated.

His men received great recognition. In fact, Major General Keith Lincoln Ware, the Commanding Officer of the Division, came to their camp and visited and spoke with them about what a good asset the trackers were. After the Major General's visit, the teams were called in for the types of missions that they had been trained to do. Also, from that time on, the General would send his own helicopter to pick up the team if no other transportation was easily available.

The Officer remembered how he had been promoted to First Lieutenant, and had gone to Hawaii to get married. The timing was off, however, as he received word that the Tet Offensive had started and he had to return to Vietnam. Once he landed and signed in at CTT Head Quarters (HQ) with USARV Special Troops, there was no transportation to Di An and his teams.

He spent the rest of Tet at the HQ. But, since there is no such thing as coincidence, something happened at the HQ that would impact on all of the Trackers. While he was there one afternoon, he had a visit from a rather unusual person who wasn't "really there"—they had lunch together. He was able to tell all about the CTT program and how it was going and what they were doing. An extremely senior Officer wanted the details and got them. It was at this time that this General was about to authorize the adoption of the new Table of Operation and Equipment (TO&E) for all the Trackers. He wanted to discuss what was happening with them. The Officer could still remember the General's piercing blue eyes—they saw everything. The General had a lot of questions that a young Lt. wasn't very well equipped to answer, but he had done his best. The General said that after Tet, the Tracker units would prove invaluable to clean up the hot spots left behind by the VC and NVA. The young Tracker Officer was then dismissed, and the ranking officers continued their meeting with "He who really wasn't there."

As a result of the discussions, the Trackers had a TO&E, material, even tents. The former Tracker Officer realized that he had never said anything about that clandestine meeting. But, he knew that in some way he had contributed to the general well-being of all of his Trackers. He recollected how the missions had increased and they became more difficult. It was a special time in his life. One example of that was the memory of waking up at first light one morning. The team had made their camp near a watering hole. He and Dick were watching as a great white heron came in silently and landed next to the water and stood there in the sun. This was an amazingly rare sight in the jungle. It then took off. He and Dick just looked at one another knowing that they had shared something incredibly rare in a lifetime. He still used it to still his spirit when under stress as the moment captured such serenity and freedom. It would create an aura of peace throughout his soul.

As tempted as he was to simply ignore the message and to reply that this was not the person the Trackers were looking for at all, but someone else entirely—he couldn't do that. For he was their Officer, and their friend, and whenever he was needed by them—they took first importance. Now he was needed again—and needed more than ever before. In the years that had intervened being a Vietnam Veteran had been tough. The public had welcomed these warriors home by spitting on them. There were no ticker tape parades for these Vets—no joy in the streets. For the first time in the country's history, it was perceived that America had lost this War. That wasn't the truth—the truth was very different. The public, spurred on by the media and other proponents of "Liberalism" had condemned not only the War—but the warriors themselves. The Vietnam War had become an object of disdain by mavens of the broadcast world. These self-serving critics had decided that they now had the power to mold public opinion in whatever way they chose. This War was an excellent vehicle to use to "flex their muscles."

Those who accepted America's call to arms were no less heroic than their fathers who fought in World War II. It wasn't the soldiers' fault that this War had become an icon of what was wrong with politics and in the social environment of the late 1960s and early 1970s. The public had no alternative to the slanted misinformation that they ingested during their dinners news on television. The media and liberal politicians of the day were so strong in their disapproval of the War, that the citizens found their target for dissatisfaction with the soldiers instead of those who had sent them. Here were young men who were in combat because they followed their consciences and did their duty. Instead of having this responsibility praised, they were derided and condemned by the "folks back home".

The Officer was well aware of what had been the reward of his men when they had completed their tours of duty. He thought of the injustice of his men fighting, bleeding and dying for an uncaring and hedonistic society. There was a terrible irony in all of this. He thought too of the brilliant leadership of General William Childs Westmoreland and how the General was denied his victory and place in America's History by the tactics of politicians and the media.

Seek On!

All of this and more went through the Officer's mind as he looked at the message, which started by saying, "Welcome Home, Combat Tracker." And as he looked at it again, he thought how fitting an expression that was. In many ways, the Trackers had not been able to "come home". They were here physically, but a part of them was locked in a time past called the Vietnam War. And it had seemed to him that a clock had stopped in a place called Viet Nam.

Mentally shaking his thoughts, the Officer thought of all the good things, the great men and the Labs. He was suddenly in fits of laughter as he thought of certain incidents which involved the very creative minds of his Team. One time, they had been tracking through an area with a lot of bomb craters. The Team and their infantry support element were engaged with the enemy. They pulled back to return to a more fortified position. When he looked around, two of his men were missing! He and his team were unable to get back to the area because the fire was too heavy. They had to call in artillery just to get out of the situation alive. After about four hours, things had settled enough so they could try to get back to their two missing men. The last one hundred feet had to be "belly-crawled" and each crater had to be checked. Finally, he heard something—and peeked over the crater rim where the sound had been heard. There were the two missing team members singing Christmas Carols and having a "spot of tea"! The Lieutenant could have killed them himself!

There were less humorous times, too. There was a trail which took the team through a village. He remembered that the rear guard opened fire on a woman sitting in a rocking chair on a porch. He had been stunned by the idea that the man had killed a "defenseless woman". When he questioned the "tail end Charlie" about why he had done it, the soldier replied that the woman had a grenade. The team checked—and found the grenade and a tunnel inside the house that concealed a cache of weapons. But, it was still a shocking event.

In remembering all of this, he also made up his mind to become a part of the reuniting of the Trackers. He made a determination to help bring the Family together again. For, that

Susan Merritt

is what the Trackers were—one Family. Didn't matter if they served in 1972 or 1967, they were all members of the same clan. And the very least that they deserved was an honorable homecoming after all those years. He applied his new found maxim, "If God brings you to it, He will bring you through it." It was time to come home.

CHAPTER THIRTEEN

An Old Dog Teaching New Tricks

One of the Teams was called in to search an area for antagonist activity. The infantry element that had requested the Tracker Team had been in sporadic contact throughout the night. The enemy was playing the usual "hit and run" games in order to frustrate the American unit and do the most damage it could, being a much smaller force against a larger and well stocked opponent. The CO (Commanding Officer) of the infantry platoon asked that the Team be brought in at first daylight. The Team would be choppered in at "0 dark hundred" so that they would be ready to go with the first light. The Tracker Lab was up for night work, but "Night Vision Goggles" had not been invented for humans at that time, so teams were sent in just before daylight for the fastest start on a new mission.

The line commander briefed the Tracker Team on the Mission, and this unit CO had known enough about how the Trackers operated to be sure that his troops did not "foul" the track. The Visual Tracker was deployed to search part of a tree line and several rice paddy dikes with a Coverman. They were to look for signs of the enemy's withdrawal; blood trails, footprints, disturbed foliage and dirt, in general—finding things that are out of the normal in the environment. The rest of the Team remained at the "holding area" with the infantrymen.

In this case, a Scout Dog and his Handler were added to the Team's searching effort. The Dogs and their Handlers were waiting for word from the Visual Tracker. The job of the Tracker team left behind was to explain to the Infantry troops why it was necessary that they did not "help" with the search. Since many of the line soldiers were not used to working with Trackers, they were not aware of the importance of keeping the track clean. Many missions for the Trackers ended at the start when they could not find the enemy's trail. Too many times, the infantry soldiers would be trying to find signs on their own, or simply milling around while waiting for orders to go forward.

In a situation like this, all the troops involved are anxious, they want to pursue the enemy. The Trackers have to keep their "edge" to be able to search effectively. It is the choreography of war. The line soldiers listened to what the Tracker team was explaining to them, and curbed their movements. It was another part of the Trackers' mission—to teach about their specialty.

One of the men in the infantry platoon found a door covered by bamboo, grass and other vegetation. The Lieutenant wanted to know if there was anyone on the other side of the door. He asked that both the Scout and Tracker dog check the area out for evidence of the enemy. Both the Tracker Dog Handler and the Scout Dog Handler tried to explain to the Officer that it was not reasonable for anyone to expect either of the dogs to be able to make that kind of detection. There had been too many people who had already walked through the immediate area—and as those soldiers were still in the area, the dogs would not be able to tell which track or people they were supposed to find.

The Lieutenant rejected the explanations and ordered the Dogs and Handlers to "sniff" the area at once. The Scout Dog went first, and "nosed" around the door and surrounding area. He showed little interest, and no alert. The Tracker Lab was put on to the same exercise. The Lab's reaction was the same as the Scout Dog's.

The Tracker Handler turned to tell the Lieutenant that this was not the way the dogs should be used. Before he could complete his thought, the door was torn into pieces by the piercing rounds from a full clip of an AK47. The rounds missed both the Tracker Handler and the Lab, but the RTO who had been standing in front of them was not so lucky. At the end of this mission, the score was still in the Americans' favor as there had been two VC in the hole. The enemy was allowed to surrender

Seek On!

and they were taken back to the base camp for interrogation. The troops' reaction was that even though there had been a "good result"—one more GI was heading home ahead of schedule. To the Trackers, the worst of it was that they were sure the line Officer would misuse Trackers, Scouts and their dogs again. He had "gotten results."

Meanwhile, CTT #7 had been working in II Corps with a Blue Team (a "fortified" Aero-rifle platoon of the 1/9th Cav). The Division had assigned a combat photographer to document the Provisional teams and he was on this particular mission with his trusty 8mm motion picture camera. The track was very hot and the team was closing on the enemy quickly with Sambo on point. The dog was eagerly working up the trail when he encountered a small trickle of water that crossed over the path. The dog suddenly stopped moving forward. Ignoring the obvious track direction, he veered sharply to the right pursuing the source of the water. Was he thirsty and looking for a drink, or was it something else? That trickle of water went up a steep slope that widened with the ascent. The area was rocky and covered with thick foliage and it was painfully obvious that no human had walked here, so what was Sambo doing on this strange deviation? The handler, photographer and team struggled, low-crawled, and scraped themselves through the briars and brambles and over the rocks and finally came to an open area. There was a makeshift dam and pond—the water source had been found. Opposite the dam and across the pond was a treed grove. An enemy encampment filled the grove and there were cooking fires and stacked weapons. The team froze in their concealed positions. They had not been employing noise discipline during their approach. There was no thought that this a discovery of this magnitude could have existed in their wildest imaginings. The Lieutenant from the Blue Team came forward to the Team's position. The still-burning fires and the stacked weapons were counted and this had been a large NVA enemy force that had been caught totally off balance. When they realized that, "something" was coming in from a direction that they had left unprotected because they had thought it was impossible to breach. They had fled in terror. The area was marked for a B52 strike and the Blue Team, CTT and photographer quietly withdrew from the area before the NVA could react to their presence. Upon their return to home, LZ 2 Bits, the combat photographer packed his gear and left. He said that, "Trackers are crazy as bat shit and I am never going out with them again!"

This was again a statement of the Tracker Lab's value to the team. Had they pursued the evident choice and continued on the trail, they could have been massacred. The Lab had started the track on a "ground scent"—easily following the earlier movement of the enemy. The scent that made him change direction was borne on the water flowing from the camp and down the streambed. The scent was more potent in the water, and it directed the Lab to the real source.

The Tracker teams were succeeding and it was a tribute to those who had trained them and to their own implementation of the "keys" that they had been given. Human visual trackers might have been able to read the enemy's track and follow it to its end. That was what the enemy had counted on. The acute sense of smell that the dog possessed—and that the handler could read—prevented a tragedy on that day. It also was a very lucky experience for the Team and their Blues. Normally, had they been on a trail the enemy would have been waiting for them. By reacting to the dog's actions, even with the loss of "noise discipline," they still retained the element of surprise. One maxim was adhered to by the Tracker teams—*never* allow the enemy to dictate the terms of the engagement. They would always find ways to utilize the unexpected appearance of a Team to best advantage.

In another similar situation, the Team found the conclusion of the track to be a "spider hole." The Team Leader decided that they were not going to take a chance with the probability of having the team ambushed from the hideaway and there was no way to ask the holed up enemy if they would like to give themselves up. The answer was to throw a grenade into the hole, which they did. They were not ready to have the grenade come flying back out at them, which it did! At least the Team Leader had the presence of mind to smash that thing right back—and this time, it went off as it was supposed to do. Trackers were not the best explosive experts.

In fact, even when they were at play, there was just something about things that went "bang" that didn't work right with the boys. One of the team groups had a basketball hoop in the area. The establishment of the hoop was legend in the area. It seems that some of the boys were digging the hole and found it tedious because the ground was really hard. They had gotten down to about eighteen inches or so and one of them came up with the idea of blasting out the rest of the hole! One of the team obtained some C-4, blasting caps and a fuse from "somewhere." They set everything in place and lit the fuse. They stood back, certain that this was the answer to the excavation problems. Nothing happened! One of the guys walked toward the hole to look into it and just before he got there, BANG! It finally went off covering him in dirt, dust and scaring the bejesus out of him. Everyone else just stared as if in a trance for at least several minutes. It became one of the stories that made the rounds.

The reasons for calling the Tracker Teams in were diverse. Any infantry element who suspected enemy activity, or who needed to reestablish contact with the enemy, could request the Trackers. Still there were other ways that sightings of the enemy would require the Trackers' skills.

At first light, the Team was inserted into a LZ on top of a large hill—a mountain by Vietnamese standards. To one side of the clearing was a group of troopers. They had no gear or weapons and were partially clad. Obviously distressed, some were crying and on their knees praying the Rosary. One Tracker turned to another Team member and said, "This isn't going to be a good day."

A gaggle of slicks approached the LZ. One by one, the helicopters came in inserting fresh troops and picked up the remnants of the company that had been here the previous day. The Army in its infinite wisdom was "sanitizing the battlefield" by substituting the uninitiated (fresh troops) for the initiated (battle worn). As they say, "out with the old in with the new."

Susan Merritt

Other things were happening in the area and the high ground of the LZ provided a vista. Several miles away and down the valley to the side of the mountain the Team saw a low flying "Bird Dog"—a slow flying Cessna single engine fixed wing observation aircraft. The Bird Dog had white smoke rockets mounted under its wing and was firing the rockets marking the area for a bombing run. With its mission complete, the Bird Dog left and the F-4 Phantoms arrived. They responded to the white smoke on the ground and began their bombing runs. They dropped fragmentary and napalm ordinance and finished by strafing the area with their nose-mounted twenty-millimeter explosive projectile Vulcan Gatlin guns. For a finale the Phantoms did Victory Rolls, than put on their after burners and flew back to from whence they came. They put on quite a show of firepower and the observers on the high ground were thankful they were not on the receiving end. The unusual thing about this was the speed of the aircraft. They flew "supersonic." The Team saw the bombs drop and the Vulcan's fire but heard nothing until the F-4s flew overhead. With their passing, they heard the ear-shattering sonic boom and then the sound of the exploding ordinance and guns. They had seen what the Phantoms were doing and then heard the "audio" after the fact. It was an incongruous and surreal experience.

 The new replacements had now arrived at the LZ and it was show time. The Team followed a trail off the top of the hill and descended into the valley with the newly inserted company following. The area had been fouled by activity the day before so it was not an optimal tracking mission. The dog was put on point. At the very least, he could serve in a scouting function. Down the hill the Team went. At midpoint in the descent, the dog began to alert. He started to give slight indication to the right, but strong to the left and forward. The handler came to a point in the trail that was covered an expanse of commo (communication) wire approximately three feet in width. The dog gave a very strong alert to the left. The Team did a recon and coming in on the high side of the incline found fortified bunkers. First one, then two, then three and on they went girdling the hill. There were no trails connecting the bunkers that indicated they were connected by tunnels. Undetected by the enemy, the Team backed out and returned to the trail. The dog was cast, proceeded down the trail and gave a strong alert forward. A friendly KIA was discovered. The dog was cast again but showed no interest in the area beyond the KIA. The Team halted as the relief company caught up and their Captain arrived for a briefing. The friendly was body bagged. The Captain asked, "Where's the enemy?" The handler responded, "Immediately back up the trail, Sir. Go to the commo wire and hang a right." "How many are there?" he asked. Based on the multi-strands of commo wire, the probed bunkers and the earlier air strikes a distance away the answer was "Large." The Captain asked, "Are they down this trail and in the valley?" The handler said, "The dog says no" The Captain said "Good, we're walking down there" Discretion is the better part of valor and the Team and company walked down the hill. The Captain was not going to let his company get ground up by a vastly superior and dug in enemy force. When the Team arrived in the valley, a slick flew in with chow and iced beer that was exchanged for the trooper in the body bag.

Then there were the problems with the supporting groups that called the teams in. On one mission, one of the teams assigned to the Cav was called in by a Company of the Black Knights (5th U. S. Army Cavalry). The outfit was hard-core and very cautious. They would not advance into enemy territory without artillery prepping the area forward of their advance. This is not advantageous to a Tracker team as the element of surprise is lost, as artillery certainly does not make for stealth. After being briefed by the company Captain, the track was established and the dog and handler were put on point. It was a hot track and the Team was a good half mile in front of the support element in no time. The area was triple canopy with the tallest of the foliage being two hundred foot tall teak trees. Just then, at that place, the "surprise" happened. The handler felt a strong concussion overhead and heard a "ripping" sound. The overwhelming noise of torn limbs and branches was torturing to his ears. The handler froze and a multi-pound piece of shrapnel buzz-sawed through the trees and landed directly in front of him—almost at his feet. He thought, "So, this is what a 105mm looks like after it goes off!" The team's advance was halted and with shrapnel in hand, the handler marched back to the support group. Passing through their point element, he asked, "Where's the F. O. (Forward Observer)?" Somewhere in the back of that line of one hundred plus men was the artillery officer responsible for the handler's near death experience. Finding the guilty party, they locked eyes, and the handler threw the piece of shrapnel at his feet. The F. O. said, "I guess that means 'Walk it out'?"

There was an "accidental find" when an A. R. A. (Aerial Rocket Artillery) run had been completed by a group of gunships. The gunships were headed back to their base and flying at an altitude that would render them harmless from ground fire. The Hueys were in formation when one of the crews spotted activity on the ground. The chopper pilots decided that since the suspicious movements were in a valley area, one of the ships would double back and take a closer look from a lower altitude. The lone ship was able to sneak up on the enemy element on the ground. The enemy was gathered in an open area surrounded by hills. Because of that, the noise from the "flock" of gunships was reverberating around the natural "bowl" of land. This particular Huey had left over ordnance and sighted on the enemy element. He fired on them. They knew that they had hit their adversaries, but not the details of the encounter, as they were still too high to accurately be able to identify them or the exact results of the strike.

The Combat Tracker Team was called in by HQ to work with an infantry platoon of Blues. The area where the gunships had spotted the enemy was in a wide valley surrounded by hills. Within the valley was the BonSon River that flooded the plain and enabled rice paddies to be farmed. There was a series of paddies and dikes to facilitate the rice crop.

The Trackers and their Blue Team were being inserted near the area where the aerial attack had taken place earlier. As they neared the insertion point, they saw an expanse of elephant grass. They noticed a burned area in the shape of a helicopter

Seek On!

surrounded by smaller burned areas the size of humans. The chopper and the remains of the crew had been removed but their ghostly images remained. It was a very sobering observation.

This particular plain ended at the foothills of the borderland between Cambodia and Vietnam. Normally, it was not an area of high activity so the Trackers had not worked it. However, this time, it was hot. The ground activity, which had been seen by the gunship, was set against one side of the valley near the encompassing foothills.

As soon as the Team and the Blues had been inserted, the Tracker Lab flew up the trail. The Handler was having a very difficult time keeping up with him. The dog was on a long lead. The Coverman was the only other member of the Team with the Lab and Handler, and they were tearing up the trail. All of a sudden, the dog veered hard to the right off to the side of the trail. He was obviously excited, but no actual alert was given. This was one of the times that underscored the necessity of the Handler being able to "think dog." The Lab could not tell the Handler in words what was going on, but something was definitely happening. The Handler was observing the Tracker dog's minute movements and expressions and had to ascertain what the dog was doing and why. He was asking himself about the unusual actions of the dog. It took mere moments for the Handler to halt the dog who than sat at the end of his extended long lead. The Handler then examined the area. He spotted a half-dollar sized hole directly in front of them in the surface of the trail. He began to probe the hole to see what had made his Lab react so strongly but without the "alert" that would have indicated enemy presence. He continued his examination of the surface of the trail where he had caught sight of the hole. He realized what the dog had been trying to "tell" him was that this was a six-foot deep pit filled with punji sticks. Punji sticks were sharpened wooden "spears," usually made out of bamboo, which were placed in a hole in the ground and covered with a natural latticework of branches. The hardcore VC would then put earth on top of the branches. They would make the entire hidden trap virtually invisible. When this was stepped on, the light cover of camouflaged material would give way, and the soldier would be impaled by the spears. These had been smeared with human excrement to insure infection developing from the puncture wounds. It was this scent that had made the Tracker Lab react. A Tracker Team that might have been operating as Visual might never have caught the "clue" by itself. The same was sometimes true regarding landmines. The tracker dogs were not trained specifically to detect explosives. However, canine handlers and trainers had a scientific theory about landmine detection. Since landmines had to be set underground, it was not possible to replace the soil around them with the same compacted density. The jungle climate was ideal for mold to grow—and frequently, the dogs would smell the difference in the area and be able to detect a mine. Another theory was the person placing the mine left a concentration of human scent that the dog detected. On the other hand, you could attribute the dog's detection abilities to the "X Factor."

In this instance, the Tracker Lab had saved his Handler and Coverman by being able to scent the punji pit. The Blues and the Tracker Team went on with their recon of the area; the dog gave a strong alert forward and discovered two enemy KIA. These had been killed by the earlier gunship attack. The KIA was dressed in civilian attire but wore a leather belt and brass buckle emblazoned with the Communist star. Next to him was an American issue M1 carbine with selector switch making the weapon capable of full auto fire. This was a classic example of US weapons getting into the wrong hands. The KIA was definitely VC and now the CTT and Blues knew what they were dealing with. Other enemy personnel were found as well, and these were KIA.

When a Team was on a Mission, they were usually so quiet and fast, that they were literally able to catch the enemy asleep before being detected. Once this happened, it was such a shock to the enemy troops that they were unable to think or react aggressively. They had no way of knowing whether the Trackers were in front of a platoon, a company or a larger support element or if air strikes were on the way. Many times, they would throw down their weapons a run for their lives. They could not comprehend this strategy that was unlike any other that they faced with the Americans and their Allies. The Trackers called it "Blowing holes through the enemy areas." It was very descriptive, very apt and the reason why there was a bounty on Tracker Teams.

Of course, some of the missions had surprising results. On one occasion after a Team had found a large enemy encampment, they gathered all of the documents and other usual things. This time, one of the enemy had brought a hand-operated sewing machine with them. One of the Team members became the CTT seamstress as G-2 did not have any use for a sewing machine!

There were other light moments. One of the Teams was about to board a chopper for a Mission. They were climbing in when they saw two familiar faces running towards the helipad waving at them to hold up. On closer inspection, they were all stunned. They could not believe it, but there were two of their Kiwi Instructors from BJWS. They had "borrowed American kit" (fitted themselves out with American military uniforms) and had come to give their "Yanks" some support. They all went out on a successful Mission. It seems that the Kiwis had flown in as American soldiers determined to see their "old pals." They had not been ordered to that area in Vietnam. No, these great guys had gone A. W. O. L.—not for some entertaining diversion—but to see their former students and be a part of this with them. They had missed them. The only time that the ersatz Americans had been in danger of being caught was by the sheerest coincidence on their flight in from "elsewhere" there just happened to be another Kiwi on their plane. It was not just any New Zealander, no, it was Major F. Huia Woods on his way into Viet Nam. The Major looked them over as if they looked familiar to him. Our two heroes lowered themselves in their very uncomfortable seats and pulled their hats as low as they could and feigned Afro-American jive talk! They were very, very glad that they were just young enough and that they had not been closer to the Major in the past! Wearing American uniforms was the saving grace for them in this case as they allowed the

Officers to deplane first and after taking several deep breaths got a case of the giggles over this latest escapade. They returned to their assignments and the story made the rounds for a long time. Nevertheless, all of their own team of NZSAS guys were very glad to know that their former trainees were alive and well and doing a super job.

CHAPTER FOURTEEN

Reflections New Zealand 2000

James, the veteran New Zealand SAS warrior, was emotional as he read the e-mail message. Father Bruce had just brought the Kiwi the invitation from his former British Jungle Warfare School students. Father Bruce was a Priest of the Old Catholic Church. He had grown up in the United States, and after serving his country, had immigrated to New Zealand. He was very active in the U. S. Veterans' group in his adopted land. Currently, he was the Adjutant Quarter-Master of the General Leonard F. Wing, United States Veterans of New Zealand Post 01. In his involvement with former military people, he was frequently on the "Internet" searching for records, people and documents for his vets. In the course of his "surfing", he and the new Combat Tracker Team website crew had made a connection. He was fascinated by what the Trackers had been all about, and when he contacted them, he was asked if he knew any of the NZ SAS. He asked why. They explained that there was a huge gap in the US veterans' knowledge about their own history, deployment and what had happened to their instructors from the UK side of things. At that time, the newly reuniting group was unaware of the school at Fort Gordon, Georgia. Finding their roots became very important to putting everything together for the veteran Trackers for both personal and governmental reasons. They explained about their original instruction at BJWS in Malaysia and how they wanted to find their New Zealand Instructors to thank them for passing on the training that they had needed to save their lives. They did not mention the "Kiwi shit house" of lasting fame.

He did, indeed. A very good friend of his was none other than the Trackers' zealous instructor who had taken a ride in a tree for their benefit. Father Bruce enthusiastically volunteered to be the "go between" for the Kiwi instructors and their former trainees. The communication lines were now opened and there was begun a flow of messages back and forth. It seemed as if the time in between "then" and "now" faded away.

The Trackers asked their former instructors to please join them at the International Tracker Reunion in June 2000. It was this invitation which the instructor had in his hand at that very moment. And the emotions it brought were intense, indeed. He remembered his own beginnings in the Army with his time in the National Service and how he knew he wanted more than just that. He remembered the grueling "Selection" process of the NZSAS—an absolutely killer period of two weeks that drove all but those with the very highest potential to "fall out". And, there were no second chances. If a guy didn't make just one of the runs in time, he went back to his regular unit that day. He harkened back to the times when he'd had to carry one of his mates "fireman style" for miles to work on a lesson that hadn't been done just right. There were so many memories of a lifetime given to the service of his country and Queen. And yet, he had never forgotten those American kids that came in determined to do whatever they threw at them. And, they took it in—and did it! What courage those lads had! And more than one had been a great pal back then—and there was still a place in the heart where they lived. Too often in a military life, those people loved and cared for were left behind when duty called and there were so many gaps where there should be events and occasions where they all should have been together. But, when one takes the path, that is part of the price. And yet, how good it would be to see those Yanks again.

The Australian SAS and New Zealand SAS had heritage that went back to the same roots as the Special Air Service 22 Regiment (SAS22R) itself. During World War II, a certain British Commando Captain and fellows started a training "centre" in Melbourne. The Captain was the same "Mad" Mike Calvert who had also determined the Malay and Borneo Campaign strategies and had helped to re-establish the SAS as part of that effort. In 1940, British instructors were called upon to train "Independent Companies" of New Zealand and Australian troops to become a "stay behind" force on the Island of Timor. Timor was located 500 miles from the Coast of Australia, and the Allies were quite sure that the Japanese would take it to mount attacks on New Zealand and Australia. These "Commandos", as they would be renamed in 1943, were to stay behind enemy lines on Timor, to fight the Japanese from within. A book has been written about the experiences of this group. Captain Spencer Chapman wrote the history down in a volume called, *"The Jungle Is Neutral"*. One of the more interesting facts presented in it, is the statement that these Commando trainees were taught "Tracking" techniques. The other history of the New Zealand and Australian involvement in Commando work on Timor was written by Christopher C. H. Wray, and is entitled, *"Timor 1942. Australian Commandos At War With the Japanese."*[32] How ironic that the heirs of this specialty were the instructors for the U. S. Combat Tracker Teams.

The Kiwi instructor recollected more of his own training at Hereford in England. One indelible memory was the "Clock Tower" at the SAS training "Centre" which had the names of KIA members of the Regiment on it. He also remembered the NZSAS Lieutenant, Albie Kiwi, who had been an Instructor at BJWS and had gone on to a leadership position in the Australian Paratroops. The former Lieutenant was in touch with one of his "Yank" students "Frenchy" La Farlette for years until his untimely and tragic death in a training exercise. La Farlette had maintained contact with Kiwi's family over the years. As luck would have it, the NZSAS and the tribal family that claimed Albie decided to bring his remains home from Australia just as the Trackers were reuniting. It gave the early Trackers, espe-

---

[32] Timor 1942. Australian Commandos at War with the Japanese", written by Christopher C. H. Wray, Published by Mandarin Publishers, Australia—ISBN #1 86330046 5

cially Frenchy and those closest to Albie in that time, to be able to say farewell and for the Combat Trackers as a united group to render a tribute to Albie. This would not have been possible only months before as the veteran Trackers had not found one another. The Tracker Family had connections back and forth through the military history of all the countries involved and the time had come to reunite.

It was this sense of "Family" that compelled the former instructor to attend the Reunion. He had thought about his young American Tracker trainees for years, and it was a common thread in the conversations of the Kiwi Instructors whenever they would get together. Imagine seeing them after all these years. He laughed to himself about the infamous "Kiwi Shit-House". This was Lieutenant Albie Kiwi's latrine built on a rise. And, as everyone knows, certain substances "roll downhill". When one of the trainees was slow in their daily P. T., he had the honor of running back and forth along the waste run that flowed from the edifice at the top of the hill. This was arduous punishment, indeed. However, it occurred to the laughing Kiwi that he might have joined up with a certain unnamed Yank student in a stealth exercise that involved some C4 and left said K. S. H. in ruins! He certainly hoped his old friend would be there. There were lots of things to talk about!

And, he'd have to remind certain men about the ultimate insult! His team was justly proud of their accomplishments and abilities. They had earned their place in the elite service and they wore the parachute with blue wings on their right shoulders with satisfaction. They also had their blood-red berets in those days emblazoned with the sword, wings and banner with the words, "Who Dares, Wins". They had just returned from combat and they did tend to swagger, justifiably, they believed. Now, for the Yank students, the issue became "How to get to these guys?" The usual harassment of blaring "The Battle of New Orleans" repetitiously just wouldn't work as most of the trainers were Kiwi, with a lot of Maori and James himself, a Prince of Tonga, so that wasn't going to get to them. He and his mates did tell their young protégées that their squadron was just about the stealthiest and that their bashas just couldn't be compromised. That was the wrong thing to say to their well-trained students! The boys had their goal and decided that hitting them in their strongest points was the best way to go. At about 0200 after an evening of over-indulgence, the operation had been launched by the Yanks as they snaked their way into the Kiwis' billet. Applying what they had been taught by the Kiwis themselves, the boys moved in with total noise discipline, low profile and no consideration of the time taken—"just don't wake the enemy in the process!" It must have taken them at least twenty minutes just to get the door open. Once in the building, they sneaked from rack to rack tying boot laces in un-doable knots and bollixing their kits at will. To traverse the small building took them more than two hours and they exfiltrated out the other end as quietly as they had entered. The next morning, James remembered the total shock as the instructors woke up to discover the sacrilege that had taken place in their home! They were all enraged and as soon as they could find something to wear, they went out to vent their wrath and there would be hell to pay! But, none of the innocent American lambs admitted responsibility. After all, how could they? The unspeakable had been done by students from a different section! Now, that was a "two-for". The vaunted Kiwis had been taken down a notch or two and their Yank students would pay for something they didn't do. So, "Who Dares, Wins"! Oh, yes, thought James, I really must get to that reunion. Too many years have passed already.

All these things and more were whirling through the Instructor's mind. There was absolutely nothing that would stop him from attending the Reunion with his Trackers. He made immediate plans to go to St. Louis. He notified the Trackers via Father Bruce that he would see them all in two weeks when the Reunion would be held.

The Instructor told the other surviving BJWS Staff members who lived throughout New Zealand that he would represent them in this "gathering of the Family". They were all excited to know how their "Yanks" had fared in Vietnam. The NZSAS group was interested in the outcome of this experiment as well.

Susan Merritt

They needed to hear that the training they had given the Americans had been realistic and had thoroughly prepared them for their combat. One of the hardest things that the instructors had to do was to maintain a steady pressure on their young students. It wasn't in their nature to be cruel or unnecessarily hard that way. The Instructors knew, though, from their own experience what a high cost there was if these troops weren't properly prepared. They really enjoyed the students and were constant in their thoughts of them when the new Trackers had gone off to the War. They took everything in their war training and threw it at the kids. They only had months to give them what they had learned over years—but they were determined to do it. It was also one of the reasons that the bond of Family had lasted so long. The American students could never thank them enough for "arming" them with all that they needed to survive in their jobs and the Kiwis and *all* of the instructors at BJWS, were they K9 or JWS cadre, were so proud of and concerned for "their Yanks" and the raw courage that the "kids" had shown, that they had never forgotten and had always wanted to "unbreak the circle".

One of the instructor's best friends was another Kiwi instructor and he remembered how he and his friend went AWOL to find his former students. The suspense of not knowing how they were faring was more that the miscreant New Zealanders could tolerate. They had to see for themselves. It wasn't a difficult thing for these superbly trained and seasoned Vets to find a way to go anywhere. He chuckled as he remembered sitting in the plane in American uniforms when Major Huia Woods entered the cabin. They sure as hell hadn't expected that. They had laughed about that for years and couldn't wait to share that one with his American mates.

All these thoughts were rushing through the Instructor's heart as well as his mind. He simply had to go to the "States" and reconnect with his Family. The other Kiwi NZSAS former instructors all supplied him with questions to be answered on his return. They had all developed a place in their concerns for these former students. There were certain names that stood out in their memories and they wanted to know how it had all turned out for them. Men who were warriors of this caliber were not unlike the knights of the tales told of the Middle Ages. Their world was a small one, indeed. This applied to the #2 WDTU veteran Trackers as well as other JWS cadre members who had taught the teams. There are too few who can attain the standards of excellence to become specialists of this stature. There is an honor code that may or may not have been spoken. There was a respect to be given to an enemy in war that would permit a total wiping out of the opposing force, but a strict prohibition of any form of desecration of the fallen. This way of life was shared by the masters of warfare of every culture and it meant that these ultimate soldiers also had a depth of "heart" that equaled the intensity of their ferocity. It was this great emotional pool that was opened to those who were peers—and their American Combat Tracker Teams fit that description. Time and distance made no difference in those feelings. They were life bonds as surely as if they had been tattooed on all. And now it was as if they were all coming home together after all those years.

Unlike the other wars that the United States had committed the military, the Vietnam War was set up in a totally different way. For most soldiers, there was a twelve-month tour of duty in Vietnam. The Marines had a thirteen-month time frame. This precluded the previous tradition of units training together and then being deployed together. Vietnam was a "modern" war and the current game plan of combat time was reduced to a period of time rather than a flow of a given unit starting and finishing at the same time. The Team concept was very unusual. This was one of the commonalities that the Combat Trackers had shared with their former mentors in the SAS 22 R and the NZ and Australian SAS as well as the #2 W. D. T. U. It was also another of the reasons that the feeling of familial bonds applied to all of these specialists.

This is also what the United States military establishment ignored during the War in Vietnam. They didn't reinforce a bond between small groups of combat unit soldiers. It was supposed to be methods where bodies could be "plugged in" where needed, but it didn't address the spirit of the men who were called on to do this. The Trackers had remained in their Team units, even if the overall appellation became "Infantry Platoon Combat Tracker" (IPCT) or "Infantry Detachment Combat Tracker" (IDCT). The Authorization and Organization Order for the Trackers came in February 1968 and designated the Teams as above. The Teams were not taken apart during their deployment unless one of the guys decided that he couldn't work as a Tracker anymore. It didn't happen often, but when it did, the man was gone immediately and sent to a regular line unit. The Teams worked together and stayed together for their entire enlistment time period. They lived, ate, partied, fought and worked together closer than most people in any fraternal relationship. It became easy for one of the guys to finish another's statement! And, the men in the Tracker Platoon or Detachment were still organized as Teams within that overall name.

After BJWS graduated its last American class, the Kiwi Teams and other British specialists who had split up to become Instructor Cadre had been reunited for Commando and Tracker Team duties in the Vietnam War. New Zealand and Australia were potent allies for the American military in combat. The NZSAS Teams went to distant parts to serve their country after the Vietnam War was over. They remained in their teams for the most part. The #2 WDTU went off to help in Northern Ireland. They also went as a group. The Combat Tracker Teams of the Vietnam War were dumped back into society or placed in totally different specialties and units if they remained in the Army. They were prohibited from speaking about their training, service or anything "Tracker". Most were sent to different assignments, breaking up the teams and making sure that the contact between them was severed. For that alone, the Trackers should have been awarded full benefits for post-traumatic stress disorder.

However, there was no breaking of the forged bonds, and that is what was inspiring all of the Trackers and their allied Instructors, fellow ANZAC Trackers, British Royal Army Veterinary #2 War Dog Training Unit, to come together again—because they were all a part of one Family and only the passage to the "final journey" would separate them again. And, even then ...

CHAPTER FIFTEEN

Major Rewards

Some of the Teams were "walking on water" by the time several months had passed in terms of accomplishments. A lot of the kinks had been ironed out as that was the only way to survive. There was no way to accurately count the number of lives saved by them, nor was there a way to accredit them with enemy KIAs. They were responsible for enemy casualties through their efforts, but the statistics went to the unit that called them in. After all, they were the "specialists"; a requested asset to be brought in for specific purpose. The issue was whether they supported the Infantry, or was the Infantry supporting the CTT. There were still serious problems with some of the teams assigned to certain Divisions or Brigades. There had been so many traumas at the 25th Infantry Division that it would take a complete renewal to bring things under control. There were some at higher levels who were becoming aware of the difficulties the teams were facing and some changes were being made to help pave the way. There were Officers and Senior NCOs that were going into the field with their Teams so that they could assess what was needed on a first-hand basis. But this was not universal and there were still Teams paying the price for things that were not in their control.

The Teams had developed many new tactics as a result of their experiences in the field. Since theirs was a completely new specialty; the boys were the practitioners and innovators. Some of them would spend many long hours in discussions of what had gone right and what had gone wrong to make sure that things would work in the future. There had been new challenges with every track in the beginning, but as time passed, they had become adept at being able to anticipate actions based on what had occurred historically. Since there was no higher echelon that was generic or easily accessible to the individual teams, these tactics discussions and solutions were held by the Team members—with their LTs and Sr. NCOICs if they were trusted and without if they were not. Another thing that some of the Teams did was to "vet" potential newbies as to whether or not he would be a "good fit" with a Team. A newly arrived Tracker had to be acceptable to the Team or he was rejected. If one of the Team members was "off", not up to doing his job "right", the Team would insist on a stand down. Their business was dead serious and there wasn't room for anyone to be less than they should be. This also brings to mind the suicide pact that some of the teams entered. They were very aware that their enemy had a particular hatred for them and there were those who had decided death was preferable to capture. They had seen too much of the vengeance that the opposition was capable of inflicting on those who were of special interest to them.

In late 1967, one of the CTT #6 had been called in to a mission by the 2/47th Mechanized Infantry (2/47th Mech). They had seen three or four individual enemy personnel run into the jungle and decided to call in for a Tracker team because the Trackers had run several successful missions for them in the past. When the team arrived, Mike Landers, the Team Leader, was briefed by the Battalion Intel Officer and the Battalion Commander about the mission at hand. George McDonald, the Visual Tracker, picked up the sign of the enemy and since they were moving into the jungle, the Team Leader kept the VT on the lead of the track. They were traveling forward in a staggered single file on the trail with the Landers acting as coverman for the VT. Before long, they found three booby traps (hand grenades) strung across the trail. The traps seemed old, but the sign was fresh. The support element was about 100 meters to the rear of the team. As they rounded a bend in the trail, they heard gun fire—but it didn't give the impression of being directed at them. Not taking any chances, they remained in a prone position on the jungle floor until the gunfire stopped and then recovered and moved on. McDonald, the VT, spotted a bunker to the front of them, so they moved to the right to out flank it, but it was empty. As they approached it, AK-47 fire came from the Team Leader's right and he instinctively dropped to a prone position again as did the VT. Landers and McDonald returned fire. They then moved back as their training had taught to allow the support unit forward into the bunker complex they had just discovered. This was the proper modus operandi for an optimal Tracker mission—finding the object of the track and bringing in the support to take care of the problem. Meanwhile, as this was happening, Troop B of the Third of the Fifth Cavalry (3/5 Cav) reported they had engaged four enemy soldiers on the opposite side of the jungle area. They had killed three but the fourth had escaped into the jungle. He was later recaptured by the 3/5 Cav Troop B. The 2/47th CO had been able to secure the area and the troops started to search the bunkers that the Trackers had found. At the same time, the 3/5 Cav was moving into the other end of the bunker complex but no one knew that it was one huge encampment at this point. The team's mission was successfully completed and they had called in for extraction and were flying back to their LZ at Bear Cat. They later learned that the two US elements had found the largest weapons cache in Viet Nam to that date. In fact, it became the second largest weapons cache discovery of the entire war and the first time that certain artillery pieces had ever been found. The largest cache ever uncovered was in Cambodia in 1970 by a Special Forces team.[33]

In their home LZs, the Trackers were self-sufficient group and they had some friends among immediate neighbors, but they were too "scary" for most of the troops around them. They had become like Siamese quintuplets with their individual teams—you couldn't go through laying your lives on the line in the most perilous situations day after day totally interdependent on one

---

[33] Mike Landers, Team Leader CTT #6, BJWS Graduate, attached to the 9th Infantry with VT George McDonald

another and not continue the bond in off time. They dealt with a hair's breadth proximity to death on a constant basis that became the norm rather than the exception. Even a breath too loud could have brought a rain of death down on them. The Lab's Handler had learned to "look into the dog's mind" and then translate the info back to the rest of the Team. All of the guys were totally cross-trained by now—and many of the handlers had become interchangeable with the other positions of the team—"just in case". These men were changed forever in ways that others couldn't fathom. They also had developed a tremendous depth of experience in the field and in their specialty.

Another team was working in a double canopy area. The trail came to an open meadow and crossed directly to a tree line on the other side. The normal Standard Operating Procedure (SOP) for this situation would have been to box around the open area and then pick up the trail. Also, by not going through an open area, another cardinal rule wouldn't be broken—"Thou shall not unnecessarily expose thyself to enemy fire." However, on this particular occasion, the Tracker dog was also very good at wind scenting ("scouting" in K9 terms) and the handler was about to discover another of the dog's talents. There was a wind advantage across this meadow and the dog indicated that there was no immediate human presence in the opposing tree line. The decision was made to go directly across the meadow and the dog and handler took off at a full run. The waist high elephant grass covering the area made it impossible for the handler to see the dog. At midpoint in the meadow the dog's long lead made a sharp upward motion. Obviously, he had jumped over something and the handler stopped abruptly. There, directly in front of him was a thin steel wire. It was attached to a stake and strung across the trail to the pin of a grenade. The grenade was affixed to a stake on the opposing side. The VT came forward and disarmed the booby trap. As all of this was going on, the dog came back to observe the activity and sat down. He looked at his team and turned his head slightly as if to say, "Why did we stop? You mean you didn't know that damn wire was there?" The handler now knew this veteran Brit dog had been trained to

Seek On!

avoid tripwires. But how had he done it at a full run? Chalk it up to the "X Factor".

During that summer, CTT #7 had worked with a company of the 7th Cav. They had a mission off of Highway 19 with the "Gary Owen" troopers in support. The team was pursuing a relatively large enemy force, probably company size and they knew that they were being followed. They did their utmost to slow their hunters. They placed punji stakes in the trail which was covered by waist-high elephant grass. Merritt was on point with Sambo on his long lead, arrogant and cocksure. Suddenly the lead went left to right in a tight motion. The dog was doing a serpentine around the punji stakes but by the time the handler figured it out, it was too late. There were two puncture wounds in his leg and another "lesson learnt": Always have visual contact with the dog and don't work too fast! The handler wanted to continue, but the company Captain insisted on a medevac. The only transport out that was available was the 7th Cav Six Ship (Command Helicopter) and it came in for the wounded handler. A group escorted the handler to an LZ. Before the mishap, the handler had been on point and his weapon had been on "full auto". He neglected to switch the weapon to "safe" and it inadvertently discharged. Fortunately, no one was hit—including the CO's bird! That would have been one hell of a way to express a guy's thanks for the ride! It was off to the hospital for the handler and the ensuing blood infection arrived on time. He recovered quickly and it was time to "Saddle up" again.

While Merritt was out on "Sick Call", Sambo was handled by his coverman Bill Reed. The track was continued for several days. The bad guys had tried the punji trick again and Sambo caught one in the chest. That dog was aggressive as hell and continued to work. The enemy tried to leave ambush parties behind, but the dog alerted and they were "foiled". The NVA left their dead behind in shallow graves. One grave yielded a tall Oriental man who was definitely not a Vietnamese and it was speculated that he was a Chinese advisor. The enemy began to discard their weapons to lighten their load in an effort to get to sanctuary. It was a very successful mission for the Trackers.

Susan Merritt

The Trackers had become the new experts. While their British, ANZAC and Far East Asian Instructors had years of experience, they did so in long mission increments. The first Teams were faced with their learning curve early in their deployment. They had been given all of the "tools" at BJWS. They had to become totally pragmatic at this point. CTT had been developed by the Brits as a counter insurgency tool which normally dealt with a small number of adversaries. Although that application also held true in Vietnam, the Teams were just as likely to encounter a well trained and armed enemy in significant numbers. They had to devise specific reactions to a plethora of field incidents—as the Brits would say, "On Your Toes Lively". It became routine to be able to run into an NVA camp or staging area. The Team had to quickly ascertain the enemy's response. This was an example of what the British Commander had meant in his welcome speech at BJWS. They remembered that, "The trouble with the U. S. Army was the same problem as that of the German and Russian Armies. They were used to a regular Army mindset, and when introduced to a guerilla or terrorist attack, not able to react swiftly enough." It was the same with the NVA and the South Vietnamese hard core VC Regulars which were full time military. The VC who were involved militarily as guerilla units were not bound by the same discipline and organization of the others. These were part-time terrorists or guerillas, and part-time farmers or "normal" citizens of South Vietnam. The CTT had adapted some of the enemy's tactics and were using them with success. They could "out guerilla the guerilla" and also deal with the regulars.

Therefore, when the Tracker Team would seemingly appear out of thin air in an NVA camp, VC regular base or HQ, the reaction was pandemonium. There wasn't an absolute in the enemy reactions—but there was always confusion and fear. The formerly relaxed enemy troops dropped weapons, food, everything and ran more often than not. They didn't know what or who was behind the Tracker Team that had just come into their sight accompanied by their "Devil Dogs". The Vietnamese were also especially superstitious of black dogs. The fleeing soldiers couldn't anticipate whether there was a platoon or company following the Trackers. They were terrified of hearing the "wap—wap—wap" sound of incoming Gun Ships or of the sight of fighter planes coming toward them. Had the Trackers not been able to "out think" the enemy, they would have been in grave peril—both from the enemy and their support group.

When the Trackers were encountering the guerillas (VC irregulars) a different knowledge of the enemy's thinking was called for. Especially in this circumstance, the knowledge of guerilla thinking which had been imparted to the Teams in training was a priceless gift. The British had succeeded in defeating both the regular and guerilla intentions during the Malay and Borneo Campaigns. Their hard-won ability to "think guerila" had bought the survival of many Americans and their allies. The training had instilled a familiarity with the land where the Trackers served. They were not intimidated by the enemy, whom they thought of as interlopers on their "Trackers' turf". While the regular Army units employed standard warfare tactics, the VC used unorthodox methods. The punji pits, booby traps, and other ways of maiming the forces of South Vietnam took a great toll on the ARVN and their Allies. When the Trackers were employed, they were schooled in the guerilla's tactics and were able to put themselves in the enemy's minds to counter them. They consistently used the "element of surprise". They always tried to maintain control of the situation rather than allowing the enemy to dictate the terms.

The key to the Teams' survival was the cohesion within the group. It was the secret to their success. It was partially due to the shared training which they had received, and also due to the natural kinship that evolved between the men. It enabled a given Team to prevail with or without the Lab. It all depended on what worked best for the group on any particular mission. No matter what components were added or subtracted, it was the unity of the entity that brought off their assignments. They could operate equally well in any of the war zones in Vietnam. They could have been deployed in any terrain in the world. It was their ability to flow seamlessly with each other in the missions that became the basis for their success and their survival.

Susan Merritt

On one mission, four men went into "Indian Country" together—but as a Visual team. There had been some Intel that this particular area was "hot" and they were going in to ascertain what was going on. Sergeant Neil Couch was the Sr. NCOIC on the Mission. The VT and Coverman were on point working the track on the staggered single file followed by Couch and another tracker. The two young men on point walked right into an ambush and were killed. Couch reacted quickly, maneuvered behind the enemy and eliminated them. It was a personal issue for Neil to avenge his slain men. Tracker teams were one entity—hurt one part and everyone felt the pain—and so would the enemy.

One of the former Sr. NCOs tells of a situation where a rear-echelon administrative Officer had come out on an assignment from Saigon. He was to locate any "stray" dogs and have them destroyed. He entered the Tracker's domain in error. One of the handlers had been walking his Lab off lead after a long working day. As the handler and Tracker Lab walked back to their billet area, the somewhat officious bureaucrat demanded that the handler turn his dog over because he wasn't on a leash. The handler looked at the perfectly groomed and properly attired messenger and told the officer that he should immediately perform an impossible physical act on his own body. Needless to say, the officer was dumbstruck at the Tracker's crude request. Furious, he marched off to HQ to bring the Tracker up on charges who, after all, was a lowly enlisted man. When he entered the HQ spluttering and threatening, he was finally able to gasp out what had transpired. The HQ staff started to laugh uproariously. The administrative officer couldn't believe their reaction. He was even more astonished when the men at HQ told him that he was lucky to be alive as it must have been a good mission day for the Tracker to have been so kind.

Another time in another place, one of the Trackers was enjoying some well earned rest, sitting back with feet up, smoking a cigarette and just letting it all hang out when a Major in a jeep with a driver stopped in front of him. The officer got out and walked over to him and the Tracker lazily looked up and then back at the vista that he had been taking pleasure in watching not paying any attention to the "personage" who had alighted from his "chariot". The Major, who was dressed in a well pressed uniform and polished boots was incensed at the lack of response, barked, "Do you see who I am, soldier?" At first, our veteran Tracker didn't really get what this pompous asshole was getting at, after all, he hadn't passed the importance register! When the realization came to him that the officer wanted some recognition of his status, our boy replied, "Yep." The Major became infuriated at this lack of respect, how could that grungy-looking combat rat dare to sit there, smoking his filthy cigarette and ignoring an officer as if he didn't exist? The Officer then committed the ultimate folly; he started to move his hand toward his holstered 1911 A1. It was as if to play the hero in some old-fashioned movie or something. The Tracker, however, was far from amused and finally rewarded the latter-day Patton wannabe with the recognition he so desired! He looked at the Major and stated firmly, "If you pull that out of your holster, I'm gonna stick it up your ass!" That just about drove the officer over the edge—but the man had the sense of self-preservation to want to find out if he was dealing with the Devil or what. "Who the hell are you and who are you with, soldier?" Our Tracker didn't even look up at him, he simply said, "I am a Tracker." The enraged officer never said another word; he was shaking with anger, but turned and got back in his jeep. The Tracker could see him gesturing to his driver—knowing damn well that he was telling the driver that he'd better not ever say a word about this to anyone! But both officer and driver knew for a surety that the threat hadn't been an idle one—and if he reads these words today, he'll remember that Southern Tracker.

The work that the Teams did balanced out and far outweighed their arrogance. Day after day, the teams were probing enemy territory. The statistics were on the documents of the Divisional and Brigade records and the lives that were saved would never be counted, but that wasn't the point. The success of the teams was all they cared about. They had wanted to be an equalizing force and they had accomplished this in a very short time from the days that they finished their training—no matter where it had been done. The primary requirements for trainees were high IQs, great physical abilities, good to excellent eyesight, courage and to be one step ahead of the stockade!

A Team was called in with a Blue Team for support. The VT established the track and the dog and handler went on point. After working the track for a short period of time, there was a bend in the train and the dog gave a strong alert indicating that human presence was directly in front of them. The handler halted and the Team Leader came forward and asked, "Why did you stop?" "Because the dog alerted!" responded the handler. That particular Team Leader didn't have much faith in the dog and less in the handler and commanded, "Walk it in! That's a direct order!" The handler told the dog to "Seek on!"—the command to continue a track. The dog took a few steps forward, turned abruptly, and ran at full speed between the handler's legs. The handler was almost knocked to the ground by the Lab's unexpected movement. After quickly straightening things out and reversing direction, he was dragged to the end of the supporting column by his fleeing animal. The Team Leader came running after them, furious that they had defied his direct order. He asked, "What is that dog telling us?" The handler replied, "The dog isn't going to go around that bend in the trail, Sir." Reluctantly, the Team Leader in coordination with the Blue Team "popped smoke" (colored smoke grenades used to mark position of those on the ground) and called in ARA. The Team and the Blues backed out from the area that would be hit and the ARA made their run. The air reeked of explosives. The group then proceeded forward to observe the effects. Around that bed in the trail was a dish-shaped open area covered in three-foot high elephant grass. The grass was beaten down in places and the ambush positions were obvious. The bastards had been just waiting for the troopers to come around that bend into the kill zone. The threat had been thwarted and the Team went back on point to track the fleeing enemy, albeit cautiously. The handler found something of interest on the trail—an approximately two inch square piece of human flesh with attached hair. One of the

Seek On!

enemy had been partially scalped by the Air Rocket Artillery intervention. The track was pursued until dusk with no further results. The Blues were rarely left in the field at night and it was time for extraction. The Team certainly wasn't complaining about that. Back at LZ 2 Bits the Trackers were happy at not being ambushed that day, but disappointed at not bringing the track to a conclusion. They went to a common area at the LZ where the Aero-rifle infantry and fly boys of all description met for some warm beer. There they were greeted by the Warrant Officers and crews who flew the Reds (ARA helicopters). They had been on site earlier in the day and followed the Tracker team's progress from altitude. They had been able to establish the direction of the fleeing enemy. Flying at altitude and miles ahead of the ground troops, they spotted the NVA in the open. All hell broke loose and two hundred plus enemy were killed. Could a CTT have done it themselves? No! But, when working with the right support, all things were possible.

The boys were defining enemy activities that enabled Intel to plan for future action. They were running down individual enemy units after ambushes or other interactions and not allowing them to "melt into the jungle". The Tracker teams were claiming the jungle as *their* territory.

CHAPTER SIXTEEN

Passing the Torch

The Provisional Teams were nearing the end of their current extensions in-country. They had been through the arduous training at JWS and had taken the "lessons learnt" from their instructors and turned them into a platform from which to create a distinctly different variation on a theme. Like the other small specialty entities, the Trackers were a world unto themselves and misfits in the regular military machine. They were also so successful that their idiosyncrasies were accepted and they were given a wide berth but with a great deal of respect and/or fear. Most of the boys hated to fly in the helicopters ("slicks", "ships", "birds" or "choppers") and thought that the pilots were nuts, but those same pilots wouldn't have traded places for all the gold in the world. Everyone knew that "them Trackers are crazy".

Replacements were coming in from JWS every two months or so. General Westmoreland had accomplished his goals to some degree in that the contract with JWS had been extended for another year and plans had been made for a Tracker School to be established in CONUS at Fort Gordon. The effort to obtain the British input had been successful and Major Huia Woods along with three 22 Special Air Service non-commissioned officers were going to help plan the facility for the Visual tracking and marry-up training and Captain Donald Hall-Smith, RAVC, would be representing the canine aspect. Fort Gordon was the home of the Army's Military Police Advanced Individual Training at that time and there were more than a few who felt that this was not a harmonious place to train. Tracker by its nature was far from a "spit-shine" outfit and didn't lend itself to garrison duty. It was specific to combat infantry use and definitely not Military Police procedure. Having filthy trainees oozing in from wretched days in the field simply didn't mix with the Provost Marshall's interpretation of proper military appearance. The only thing in common with the Military Police was their canine component. But even there, the Tracker application was very different as were their training methods. The MPs' sentry dogs were trained to patrol and attack by rote and heavy-handed command. "Heavy-handed" didn't correspond to the Tracker training where a handler "listened" and "learned" from his dog and "attack" just wasn't the Lab's forte. The dogs were not only different breeds (Labrador retriever vs. German Shepherd) but were also separated by very different applications. Tracker was anathema to the hosts of the school. However, that was still in the future. At this point in time, Major Woods, Captain Hall-Smith and their group were in America to make recommendations. And the scuttlebutt has it that they did not stay as long as had been planned and departed rather abruptly.

Meanwhile, some of the original graduates of JWS had already gone on to the "land of the Great PX" and some had left the Army altogether. Those first graduates who had been in Malaysia at the end of 1966 and had witnessed the three training deaths were very affected by that experience and some had gone into other infantry units in 'Nam rather than continue as Trackers. Some had been "held over" and added to the classes that started in the beginning of 1967. Things had been chaotic for CTTs #1—#5. They were the real pioneers and had experienced the most difficulties in bringing in the new specialty. There was a lack of preparation and readiness in the affiliated divisions. There were also insufficient numbers of personnel in positions of leadership for those early Teams. Great credit has to be given to then Lieutenants Don Best, Ron Hudson, Ron Reed, Jim Myrick and Sr. NCOICs Don Eveland, Roger Cool, Chris Hodge, and Dan Tharp for their leadership. It was an outstanding effort. This group had been among the earliest classes sent back to 'Nam and deployed as Trackers. By the time the next cycle of Teams #6—#8 had come out of Malaysia at the end of May into the early part of June 1967, there was a lot more continuity to their training and they were sent off feeling more prepared and confident than the first class. There were some good leaders in those Teams as well who deserve mention; Lt. Paul Richeson for CTT #6 and Ron Hudson for the short time he led CTT #8; the Sr. NCOICs who were the true leadership of CTTs #7 and #8- Joe "Nick" Nicholson #7 and Neil Couch #8 and Gary Ward #6 Sr. NCOIC. Teams #1—#8 had been trained by non-American personnel only and their Visual training and the marry-up of Visual and K9 was actually being done for the first time historically. There had never been a Combat Tracker Team created precisely like this, it was devised by the Brits for American needs. The first cycles, therefore, were not just the groundbreakers, but also the guinea pigs. By the time CTTs #9—14 finished the first contract, the program had begun to be "Americanized"—instead of a Visual cadre made of only British and Anzac personnel, there were newly trained Americans who had become proficient enough to be a part of the education process. Their fine leadership for this period also bears noting: then Lieutenants Steve Williams; Harold Bell; Tony Witter; and Don Hendricks. Their Sr. NCOICs were Grant Golden, Moses "Pappy" Nahinu, and Ted Kirmse. The initial fourteen teams had accomplished more than they knew as most of their statistics were compiled by the affiliated Divisions or Regiments and not by the Teams themselves. The new CTTs had established a new specialty; found and fixed the "elusive enemy" time and again; brought in information details that had saved untold numbers of troops; and been responsible for finding the second largest weapons cache of the war. All of this progression was to work toward a functioning Tracker specialty and training program for the future in the United States Army. It was also at this time that an actual written training manual was completed. Before October 1967, it was a matter of trial and error.

There were two other KIAs in this Provisional time, both in CTT #9. The Team was attached to the 101st Airborne "Screaming Eagles". John Harding lost his life on 8 October 1967 and

Gene Smoot gave the ultimate sacrifice on 5 January 1968. Bodie was the only Lab KIA in this time and Dagger, who was Marty Olhiser's dog in CTT #3, was killed in an incident that has never been reasonably explained. While no death is acceptable, the attrition rate for men who had not the slightest idea that they would be running down the "elusive enemy" a year before, was amazingly small.

The Provisional teams had become proficient and they were able to teach the "newbies" how to take that first step—going on that mission which could be a "baptism by fire". The training was superb and the confidence that it instilled was amazing, but when it came to taking the "show on the road", there was an enormous amount of courage needed. The veteran Trackers would include a new Tracker on a Mission because by the time Fall and Winter 1967 rolled around, there were a lot of slots to fill. That first time that a man went in with his team was a defining moment in his life. As a matter of record, as terrified as each and every one of them must have been, they acquitted themselves with honor.

Many of these veteran Trackers weren't even twenty-one years old at the time that their first tours ended. The cost of their adventures was etched in their faces to the degree that none of them was ever questioned for proof of age in a drinking establishment after they started their jobs for Uncle Sam. There were some injuries that were life changing and some of those who were wounded so badly reached in to that same spirit that had led them to finish the school at JWS in the first place, and rehabilitate themselves back into a productive life—and in some cases remain in the Army. The "friendly fire" incidents were always the ones the boys worried about most.

In the early fall of 1967, CTTs #7 and #8 had been working not only in their II Corps AO, but were probing points in I (pronounced "Eye" Corps) Corps in anticipations of the 1st Cavalry Division's move up north. Poncho Alvarez y Navarez had done his best to cross train Merritt as a Visual Tracker. The Teams were hard pressed for personnel and to fill positions, VTs and covermen began working as handlers. A mission call came in and it was CTT #7's turn. A decision was made to work without the dog. Moore and Alvarez y Navarez selected John Dupla, a recently arrived replacement, to join them on this mission, but were still one man short. Merritt volunteered. The Team would be working with a company of the 12th Cavalry. The plan was to "beat the bush"—to work up a valley and scare the bad guys into a blocking force that was waiting to light them up. At least, that was the plan.

With insertion, a trail was found and the Team was put on point. The trail showed no definitive sign of enemy activity. On a small intersecting side trail, a camp was discovered. It contained bamboo hooches, belchers, frames to display maps and various training aides—the entire place was better that LZ 2 Bits and at least company sized! But, no one had been there for some time and it was back to the main trail. Soon the trail just petered out—no spoor, no sign, a dry hole. However, they were committed to work up that valley. The Team came off the point and was then replaced by some of the 12th Cav troopers. They came to a gully with a high, almost vertical incline to the right and a heavily-foliated ascending slope to the left. The bottom of the gully was covered with small river rocks. One of the Trackers took a look at the area in front of him and his Sixth Sense jarred him. The thought had no more than registered when all hell broke loose. Merritt was hit in the left arm and knocked to the ground along with his M16. The ambushed group crawled a short distance up the ascending slope, Merritt sans weapon. Fortunately, it was retrieved by a trooper next to him. He rolled over onto his back and looked up at the ridge of the gully and assessed their situation. If some NVA came down that ridge firing at those below, or threw a grenade in, it would be "Ha! Ha! All dead!" The gully incline was alive with small arms and machinegun fire as the rounds hit the dirt.

Someone recognized the sounds of American weapons and yelled, "Cease Fire! Cease Fire!" The response was, "Gary Owen!" They had walked right into the blocking force, a company of the 7th Cavalry. All of the action had taken place in a matter of minutes.

The medic came forward to treat the wounded. Merritt's arm was laid open to the bone and the wound was dressed. The medic then asked him to remove his gear and stand. His left side, from the waist down, was covered in blood. He then removed his jacket. A nice hole in his flank was discovered, and the medic just said, "Million Dollar." John Dupla had been hit in the shoulder—great way for breaking in the new guy—and Poncho Alvarez y Navarez was hit in the ankle. For once, James P. "Poor Moore" Moore was unscathed. The wounded were escorted to a clearing and awaited medevac. The chopper arrived and the wounded were loaded aboard the blood-soaked deck of the ship. It seemed that others had also experienced a real bad day.

As the ship lifted out of the LZ and attained some altitude, Merritt looked down and there on a trail were two prone, spread-eagled NVA. They were wearing full gear and had AK47s. Merritt, expecting the bastards to jump to their feet and start shooting, alerted the Crew Chief. The Chief just smiled and made a universal signal by making a motion with his hand from the left to right side of his neck. Those NVA weren't going to do anything—they were dead.

In retrospect, what had happened that day? The blocking force of ninety to one hundred men was spread out on line with assigned fields of fire. That formation would represent a considerable distance. Perhaps one of their flanks opened fire on the friendlies while the opposing flank killed the two NVA? That's speculation and the issue will remain a mystery. It was war—and shit happens.

Then there was George Battles who had served with such distinction with CTT #13. A great guy and good buddy to everyone, a super Tracker and an asset in the field. He had just rotated out and life was going to be wonderful! Then there was a car accident and George was dead. His team was devastated. Shit happens.

There was a number of original Trackers who returned to the specialty or extended to continue; Bobby Baldwin, Ron Grove, Al Provost, Larry Snitgen, Marty Bongiorno, Tom McCart,

Charles Cherry, Al Horner, Roy Burchfield, Jon Wilde, Mike Landers, George McDonald, Joe "Nick" Nicholson, Neil Couch, Ben Miller, Jim Chaney, DeWitt Roberts, and Chuck Steward. Some of these also became Tracker instructors; Ron Hudson, Jim Myrick, Bob Gorham, Dan Tharp, George Thomas, James P. "Poor Moore" Moore all instructed at JWS for the Army. Some of them instructed at the Dog Training Detachment at Ben Hoa where an "in country" Tracker training center was set up as well as the Tracker School at Fort Gordon in Georgia.

Many of the boys finished up and were sent to CONUS to await their honorable discharges and go on from there. When they got back to the bases in the US, they were usually put in various "slots" that had absolutely nothing to do with Tracker. For instance, while Merritt was recuperating, he was issued a new MOS—he became a clerk typist. This is interesting—his "hunt and peck" method left much to be desired so the Army gave him a pool of civilians to do the work. His discharge papers and initial DD214 (Abbreviated DOD form that details the overview of a military career for whatever time period a person served)had no indication that he had ever been a Tracker, gone to BJWS, or anything related to his time with the program. He had become a REMF who somehow had combat awards. Perhaps that was the Army's reward for his service?

In fact, they were all warned not to discuss their time as Combat Trackers nor did their records reflect what they had done. They were billeted in different bases with no thought to keeping them with fellow team members. They were not allowed to wear the Tracker patch, shoulder tab or anything pertaining. This had been the most important and memorable part of their service, and they were told to "forget about it". And more, they had expected to be able to have some time to "decompress"—hopefully with at least some other Trackers who were the only ones who would understand what they had experienced—to ease themselves back into "normal" life. To the contrary, it seemed that steps had been taken to keep them separated from their former unit guys. It was a very traumatic and unnecessary severance for men who had been closer than brothers. It was done to preserve the British government's "neutrality" pledge from the time of the Geneva Conference in 1954 and it was a grievous wrong done to these men who fought with extreme valor and were never recognized for their honorable service. There were very few who had the capabilities to complete the training to become Trackers. These were men who had warrior skills next to none and an honor that kept them from abusing their unusual power and autonomy to wield it. They were boys who came into to the war who left as men tied to their teams with bonds of blood, sweat and tears and then had those relationships torn apart with total disregard. They were then thrust into a world that had been home when they left and was beyond understanding when they returned. Most had gone to Churches or Synagogues as kids when they went in and remembered being blessed for their desire to help their fellow man and when they came back, those same institutions where they had once felt a home for their souls, had become places of condemnation. The newspapers and TV stations that sent them off with praise showed crowds spitting at them as they returned. And, to top it off, they couldn't even talk to the guys they were closest to—their Team. What the hell had happened here?

And yet, the new Trackers took their places and tracked on. They had new complications and different things to surmount, but they were Trackers—and they followed in the first ones' footsteps and did it well! It never was an issue about where a Tracker was trained, with whom he was trained or whether he was trained at all. A Tracker was a rare breed and it would seem that a man who could attain the position had to be born with the potential. And the men who followed the Provisional teams proved themselves worthy of the name in every respect.

CHAPTER SEVENTEEN

Together Again

The veteran Trackers and their "extended family" were finally coming "home". The first Reunion that Mike Landers had put together with his guys from CTT #6—Perry Callaway, Gary Ward and others, plus some of the guys from CTT #7 and 8—Steve Cradick, John Dupla, Tom Presley and John Dotson, had brought about a kaleidoscopic range of emotion in everyone who had attended. Although almost of all them had experienced "aftershocks" from that first convocation, they were all determined to continue the "reconnection". It wasn't an easy thing to do. They all had trepidations about this Millennium Reunion. The prevailing thought was that this would be a time to finally find out what had happened to their Teams; and what had happened to CTT after they left; and how had this all come to pass; and did it really happen? The appearance of James, an instructor from BJWS, and two from the #2WDTU; Tony Rossell and Ray "Jock" Hardie, and the Instructors from Fort Gordon and the DTD, as well as Officers of the original teams, made the occasion a truly memorable time and a soul-satisfying one for most. Too many of the Trackers had given up hope that they would ever know anything about the most intense days of their lives. To a man, their time as a Combat Tracker had a place of importance in their personal histories that was of such importance that it was a thing apart from everything else they had ever done. The former team members would sometimes not recognize one another without the name tags—but then! It was as if the days, months and years fell away. The Team members not only went over old missions, but were finally able to know what had trans-

Seek On!

pired in the lives of these—their "brothers". Some of them had not been with the others since their last mission. Once a team member had been "wounded" or rotated out, communication would usually be severed. The cohesion that had been the communal life blood of the team re-emerged on contact.

The occupations ran the gamut, some had stayed in the Army and others had gone to college after their service. Many were vocationally or avocationally helping people. It was a need that they seemed to share. There was one feeling that had brought them back together, though. Something had been unfulfilled in their hearts and minds from that time. There was a place in each one that belonged to the other Trackers. It was a family that had been ripped apart by some horrendous trauma and reunited after years. It had that great an impact. And the reality was cemented by their old JWS cadre members and other instructors walking around and talking with them. Absolutely unbelievable for those who had been a part of those first Provisional teams. In fact, they hadn't believed that there were Trackers some of the times during their lives!

One of the other highlights of that first get together was finding out more information about fellow teams, instructors, officers and the Labs. The Trackers were fortunate. While they don't have absolute records on all of the Labs, there is good evidence that unless they were terminally ill, the Labs probably retired in CONUS. It is a fascinating history of how these Labs were "sneaked out". We know of certain persons in positions of command who, when required to bring in "evidence" of a KIA Lab, wrote the Lab off as having been destroyed in an enemy action. Meanwhile, the Tracker dogs were flying away with new masters who happened to be Officers in the Army. In Lewis Sorley's biography of General Creighton Abrams, he even shows a picture of a Lab that the General "purloined" from the Trackers.[34] "Booga Bear", who had served with the First Cav in

---

34 THUNDERBOLT, From the Battle of the Bulge to Vietnam and Beyond: General Creighton Abrams and the Army of His Times", by Lewis Sorley. Published by BRASSEY'S, 1998

the 62nd IPCT, had gone to the Embassy in Saigon. His former Handler was in a new duty station in Germany when a Lieutenant General called him to let him know that the General had his Lab. There was also another happy ending for one of the Tracker Labs. There were other times too. One of the Team's VT told of a mission that had been sent in to find a Flight Surgeon who had been taken captive by the NVA. The Trackers had been called too late. The Flight Surgeon and his captors had left the engagement area long before the Trackers were called in. The Team tried to follow and secure the release of the doctor but the distance involved and the time that had been lost was too much. The VT who told the story at the Reunion still got emotional when he remembered the abortive mission. He said that when the War was declared over, he watched as the American and Allied P. O. W.s were released. He could barely express his feelings when he spoke of seeing the doctor at the historic release.

Probably no recollection of Tracker experiences spoke of the hearts and minds of the guys better than that experienced in 1994. John Dupla, Frank Merritt and Mark Bowen (who had served with the 76th IDCT affiliated with the 199th LIB—Redcatchers), and were attending the VDHA (Vietnam Dog Handlers Association) Reunion in Washington, D. C. They were wearing either insignia or some other Tracker designations. They were locating some of the Trackers' names on The Vietnam Veterans' Memorial Wall. A quadriplegic vet approached them in his wheelchair. The disabled vet asked them, were they really Trackers? They affirmed that they were. He then asked if they had been one of the last teams "in-country", and they replied that, no, they had been with the first teams in. The vet wanted to know if the Trackers could find some of the members of the 557th IPCT who had been attached to the 101st Airborne. It seems that this vet had been on one of the last L. R. R. P. missions for the 101st when they were ambushed. He was barely alive and the other members of his unit were dead. A Tracker team had been sent out to try to find out what had happened to the L. R. R. P.s. When they arrived at the ambush scene, they quickly checked all of the men in the fallen unit for any sign of life. They realized that this soldier was still alive, and called for a medevac. The young, severely wounded soldier had survived, and gone through many operations and rehabilitation in the Army Hospital system. He was finally discharged and sent to his parents' home in Connecticut. The Tracker Team who had found the injured soldier was in the process of "being stood down". As if by "magic", the young man was greeted by the Tracker Lab who had been waiting for him at his home. This disabled vet had been trying for years to find the Trackers who had saved his life. And, yes, that Tracker Lab who had gone AWOL to cool himself in the stream had retired in Colorado with a former Officer of the Air Cav.

Another thing that was discussed by all of the reunited Trackers was the feeling that no one seemed to have heard of them or their service in that War. As a group, it was decided that if fifty thought that way, those who had been unable to get to this first gathering would have the same thoughts. There was some documentation at that time regarding the IPCTs and IDCTs. The early records were still rare due to the classified label that had been tagged on everything Tracker. One of the projects as a result of the Reunion was to find out more about where Trackers had been placed in the history of the Vietnam War. We wrote to General William Childs Westmoreland U. S. A. (Ret.). The General was gracious enough to reply. He did indeed remember "his" Trackers. In a quote from his letter, the General stated that "I believe and fully appreciate that the 'Trackers' did commendable work in Vietnam, however, there are many veterans unaware of their performance." Those of us who "publish" the website and the Newsletter for the Trackers went to work immediately to get "the word" out to the guys.

The General was also good enough to point the Trackers in the direction of obtaining more documentation on the soldiers and their service. In a search of available electronic records from the Center for Army Lessons Learned, (CALL) we found some other examples of the verdict of Tracker. In a Report on the Progress of the War written by General Westmoreland and Admiral U. S. G. Sharp (CINCPAC), they wrote of the accomplishments of the newly introduced Tracker Teams. The report had been issued on 30 June, 1968. In one of the theses in the Archives of the College of Command and General Staff, a Major Kelch also attested to the positive contribution of the Trackers during the Vietnam War. This was a "balm" for the Teams and their extended "family" of JWS trainers; R. A. V. C. #2WDTU, NZSAS and all those who had made Tracker possible. This was a rewarding find for the Trackers. Here was proof at the highest levels, that they had contributed "commendably" in the War.

It has been gratifying to find that some of the best attributes of the Tracker specialty didn't just disappear. They are being used today, incorporated within U. S. Special Operations and of course, the SAS 22 Regiment. This knowledge means a great deal to the Trackers. Knowing that parts of the specialty still goes on, continues to save the "troops", and is responsible for rescuing captured friendly personnel is tantamount to receiving a great award. Now that many members of the Teams are together and still gathering more of their own, they shared something else, a feeling of pride in their service to their Country as the Combat Tracker Teams of the Vietnam War.

There is a Not-for-profit Corporation that was chartered in Louisiana and moved up to Pennsylvania with Frank and Sue Merritt. This enabled the veteran Trackers a framework for whatever they wanted to do or become as a group. The Board of Directors for the Corporation, (Frank Merritt, Chet Ellingson III, Dick, Don Hendricks, Dave Layne, Mitch Scott and Sue Merritt), is there for legal purposes only. There are no honoraria to be given, no money to be had. It is a donation of care and an honor to do this for the guys. We have a very socially unacceptable nickname for ourselves that won't be repeated here—but it's certainly in keeping with the spirit of the Trackers. There are no "governing bodies" of the Trackers—everything is decided by the group as a whole. There are no dues, fees or costs for any Tracker whatsoever. Once a year, there is an auction set up and run by Sergeant Major Chuck Steward—a multi-toured Tracker and one of the mainstays of the group—or a "passing of the hat" at the Reunion for the costs of the website and administrative expenses for mailing or whatever. The website is over 400 pages at this point and is open to the public. It may be seen at *http://www.combattrackerteam.org*. If the reader knows of anyone who served as a Tracker during the Viet Nam War, please have them go to the site and if they choose to do so, get in touch. We know that there are many Viet Nam vets who are still in so much pain from that time that they cannot or will not involve themselves in anything dealing with it. We respect that. We are here for our own with open arms if they wish to come home to the family.

There is now an authorized United States Army Combat Tracker Team Memorial at Sacrifice Field, Fort Benning, GA. It lists our Teams, our fallen, both human and canine, and rests on Army ground. At the tenth Combat Tracker Reunion in June 2009, there was a special event planned: the formerly unknown and unsung Combat Tracker Teams presented a memorial Wreath at a Ceremony held for them at the Tomb of the Unknowns at Arlington National Cemetery. And, in this time of "asymmetric warfare", who knows, you may just see a Labrador retriever or other breed "out there" somewhere and know that indeed, the torch was passed.

There is a need for this specialty, more so now than in the Viet Nam War where it was first used in its reconfigured state by the very men who specialized in it. It is unlikely that we will see a war where lines of troops are facing their opponents in symmetric combat. Our military is too strong for an enemy to contemplate that form of warfare. There will be further development of terrorist/guerrilla tactics on the part of any oppositional force as they have studied our military history and believe that is our weak link. Our special operations forces should be as robust as possible and Combat Tracker Teams would be an asset of importance. This current and future combat is not and will not be a "law enforcement" issue, but once again a matter of the British counter insurgency/ anti-guerrilla two-fold model: "Hearts and Minds"—where our teams live with indigenous in villages that are fortified and supplied to ensure the well-being and stability of the people; and Operational teams to take the action to the enemy. Those of the Trackers who have remained current in the specialty have field tested and proven the theory of what the dog and team can do with the remains of IEDs. They have followed the scent of the bomb-maker to his hiding place. This was done in both testing and in the field. It is not only possible—it should be put into effect as soon as possible. The number of personnel who can create an IED is finite. Using the scent abilities of the canine, specific members of cells can be followed in both urban and rural areas.

Unlike other operational groups that use tracking as a tool to accomplish their mission, the mission of the CTT IS tracking—specifically. Just not an arrow in the quiver, it is the arrow. Tracker teams must be trained up as teams and continued to be deployed and billeted as teams. These Teams should not be open to individual rotation, but considered as one unit. Tracker should have no affiliation with military police. Combat Tracker is a very aggressive specialty that has no commonality with anything other than infantry. It should be used when needed and with the assets available today. Given the proper support, CTTs would be a potent "antidote" to many of the terrorist tactics in use today. Since there are records and surviving veteran Trackers, it could be done correctly and not tossed away when time would prove its worth.

In 1998, this effort was started with three goals: Find every veteran Tracker; Find every instructor to reunite with them and thank them; Bring the CTT specialty to today's military. Two out of three ain't bad.

The saga continues—"TRACK ON!"

APPENDIX

In the following charts, you will find the veteran US Army Combat Trackers who have become reunited to date. If you know of any others, please contact us at the Tracker website: *http://www.combattrackerteam.org* as we'd love to welcome them home.

The charts have various "codes": L indicates that the Tracker has been located; CO—a Commanding Officer; NCOIC—Non-Commissioned Officer In Charge; Sr. NCO—Senior Non-Commissioned Officer; an Asterisk * indicates multi-tours; KIA is Killed In Action; BJWS—trained at British Jungle Warfare School, Malaysia; (Scout)—A Scout Dog and Handler attached to a Tracker Team; Mine—Mine and Tunnel Dog and Handler Team attached to a Tracker Team.

The darkened bar has the Tracker Team designation and the Affiliated Division.

Here are my heroes:

	25TH INFANTRY DIVISION		
CTT #1	NAME	YEARS	25th INF. DIV.
L CO	BEST, DONALD	'66-'67	BJWS
L .SR.NCO*	EVELAND, DONALD	'66-'67	BJWS
*	ADAMS, RAY "POP"	'67	BJWS
L	ANGLIN, WILLIAM "JERRY"	'66-'67	BJWS
L	AUDET, DANIEL	'66-'67	BJWS
	BARRETT, ROBERT	'66'-67	BJWS
	BUTLER, ROGER W.	'66'-67	BJWS
	CUMMINGS, CARROLL D.	'66'-67	BJWS
	EATON, WILLIAM E.	'66'-67	BJWS
	FOSTERVOLD, RICHARD	'66-'67	BJWS

Susan Merritt

L	HADZIMA, LARRY	'66-'67	BJWS
	HARLER, ASHLEY W.	'66-'67	BJWS
L	HARTWELL, WILLIAM	'66-'67	BJWS
L	KATZFEY, PETER	'66-'67	BJWS
L	LEON, GEORGE	'66-'67	BJWS
L	LETTS, MEARL "HANK"	'66-'67	BJWS
	MEUNIER, RODNEY	'66-'67	BJWS
L	PATRICK, JOHN	'66-'67	BJWS
L	SISCO, MIKE	'66-'67	BJWS
	WITT, DENNY	'66-'67	BJWS

CTT #2	NAME	YEARS	25th INF. DIV.
L CO	HUDSON, RON	'66-'67	BJWS
KIA 1967	BREDE, ROBERT	'67	BJWS
KIA 1967	BOYER, JAMES ROGER	'67	BJWS
KIA 1967	HOWARD, MARK T. SR.	'67	BJWS
KIA 1967	JOHNSON, ARNOLD E.	'67	BJWS
KIA 1967	KOON, GEORGE K.	'67	BJWS
L	LAYNE, DAVID	'66-'67	BJWS
	MONARKO, PAUL	'67-'68	OJT
L	QUINN, JERRY	'66-'67	BJWS

CTT #12	NAME	YEARS	25th INF. DIV.
L *	BALDWIN, BOBBY	'67-'68	BJWS
*	GROVE, RONALD	'67-'68	BJWS
L	HOWARD, WILLIE	'67-'67	BJWS
	KARWOSKI, FRANCIS	'66-'67	BJWS
L	MOCKI, JOE	'67-'68	BJWS
*	PROVOST, ALFRED	'67-'68	BJWS
L	ROBERTS, DEWITT	'67-'69	BJWS
	SCHLECTER, GLEN	'66-'67	BJWS
	WALTERS, (?)	'66-'67	BJWS
	WIGGENS, (?)	'66-'67	BJWS

66th IPCT	NAME	YEARS	25th INF. DIV.
	ADDIS, STEVE	'68-'69	
L	AGUIRRE, INOCENTE	'69-'70	OJT
	AKI, WARREN	'69-'70	
KIA 1969	ANDERSON, WILLIAM A.	'68-'69	
	ARMSTRONG, BRIAN J.	'70'-'71	FT. BENNING
	ARNOLD, JOHN E.	'70-'71	
L	AUER, THOMAS A.	'69-'70	
L	BAILEY, ROBERT L.	'69-'70	
L *	BALDWIN, BOBBY J.	'67-'68	BJWS
L	BALYS, SAUL	'68-'69	
	BEILFUS, MICHAEL H.	'68-'69	
	BENJAMIN, HENRY JR.	'70-'71	

		BRISTOL, GLENN F.	'70-'71	FT. BENNING
L		BUTTS, ROGER L.	'68-'69	
L		BYBEE, HARRY	'69-'72	
L		CALVERT, JOHN	'69-'70	
L		CAREY, ED	1969	FT. BENNING
		CEDILLIO (?)		
L	*	CHANEY, JAMES	'69-'71	FT. GORDON
L	*	CLARK, GARY	'70-'71	FT. GORDON
L		COLHOUN, CHARLES	'67-'68	BJWS
		DENNINGTON, MICHAEL	'68-'69	
KIA 1970		DUNNING, WILLIAM M.	1970	
		EASTER, WILLIAM	'70-'71	
		ENGLAND, WILLIAM		
L		ENNIS, WALTER	'68-'69	BJWS
		FOGLESONG, BERNARD J.	'70-'71	
		FRANZEN, RON	'67-'68	OJT
		GALEHOUSE, (?) Lt.	'68-'69	
*		GORHAM, ROBERT SSG		BJWS
		GREENHOWE, WALTER	'70-'71	
*		GROVE, RONALD	'67-'68	BJWS
		GURNEY, GARY	'70-'71	
L		HALE, RICHARD		
L		HAWKINS, ALBERT. I.JR.	'69-'70	
L		HEATH, DAN	'67-'68	BJWS
L	*	HESLIN, JOHN (Scout)	1970	FT. BENNING
L		HICKEY, GREGORY E.	'69-'70	
		HICKS, RAY	'70-'71	
L		HIPP, MARK	1970	FT. GORDON
		HOPPER, (?)	'69-'70	
		HUGHES, DARRELL	'70-'71	
L	*	JACKSON, ROBERT C.	'70-'71	FT. GORDON
L		JERNIGAN, JOSEPH	'67-'68	BJWS
L		JOHNSON, DENNIS	'68-'69	BJWS
L		KAST, DAVID	'68-'69	
		KOSATAN, DAVID	'69-'70	
L	*	LANDERS, MIKE	'68-'70	BJWS
		LANE, MICHAEL	'69-'70	
L		LEYBA, ART	'67-'68	BJWS
L		LOUDER, PAUL	'68-'69	BJWS
		LYNN, RUSSELL Lt.	'68-'69	
		MacDONALD, ALASTAIR T.	'69-'70	
L		MANN, MICHAEL J.	'69-'70	BJWS
KIA 1968		MARRUFO, RODNEY	'67-'68	BJWS
		McFARLAND, DAVID	'67-'68	BJWS
L		McGEHEE, PATRICK	1969	BJWS
L		MOCKI, JOE	'67-'68	BJWS
		MONTOUR, DEAN H.	'70-'71	FT. BENNING

L	MORGAN, WARREN	'69-'70	
L	MURPHY, CHARLES	'67-'68	BJWS
*	NABORS, GARY D.	1970	BJWS
L	NORTHRUP, ROBERT	'69-'70	
	O'GRADY, DENNIS	'68-'69	
KIA 1968	PARRISH, BILLY JOE	'67-'68	BJWS
	PAYNE, CHARLES	'68-'69	
*	PROVOST, AL	'67-'68	BJWS
	PURCELL, CLIFFORD Lt.	'70-'71	
L	REYENGER, ROBERT S.	'70-'71	
L	ROBERTS, DEWITT	'67-'69	BJWS
L	ROBERTS, MICHAEL A.	'69-'70	
	SCHAEFFER, WILLIAM	'67-'68	BJWS
L	SEABROOK, BRUCE A.	'70-'71	
L	SHIRAH, HENRY N.	'68-'69	BJWS
	SMITH, HOWARD D.	'68-'69	BJWS
*	SMITH, MITCHELL	'67-'71	BJWS
*	SMITH, THEODORE SFC.	'67-'68	
L	STAMPER, WILLIAM	'70-'71	
	STEWARD, LARRY L.	'70-'71	
L	SUITOR, JERRY	'68-'69	
	TANCREDI, TONY	'70-'71	
	THEELER, ROBERT	'68-'69	
L	THRUSH, LOY E. JR.	'69-'70	
	TUTTLE. (?) Lt.	'67-'68	BJWS
	VENTERS, RAY	'69-'70	
	WILE, DAVID G.	'69-'70	
	WOODBURY, JOSEPH	'67-'68	BJWS
	WORSWICK, WINTON D.	'70-'71	
	LAB NAME	**YEARS**	**25th INF. DIV.**
	BINGO	'67-'71	BJWS
KIA 1967	BODIE	1967	BJWS
	MAJOR	1967	BJWS
	RODDY	1967-'69	BJWS
	BUTCH	1968-'70	BJWS
KIA 1969	BLACK	1968-'69	BJWS
	REBEL	1968-'70	BJWS
	SAMBO McWAGGS	1969-'70	
	4TH INFANTRY DIVISION		
CTT #3	**NAME**	**YEARS**	**4thINF.DIV**
L	HILLARD, JAMES R	'67-'68	BJWS
	JOHNSON, BENJAMIN	'67-'68	BJWS
KIA 1967	LUMSDEN, WILLIAM	1967	BJWS
L	McINTOSH, JAMES "Preacher"	'67-'68	BJWS
	MORGAN, JOHN	'67-'68	BJWS

L CO	MYRICK, JAMES S.	'67-'68	BJWS
	PAYNE, BROWN 1st Lt	'67-'68	BJWS
L	REED, WAYNE	'67-'68	BJWS
L	SEEVERS, GERALD "Jerry"	'67-'68	BJWS
	SHEER, MICHAEL	'67-'68	BJWS
	SIMPSON, WALTER	'67-'68	BJWS
L *	SNITGEN, LARRY	'67-'68	BJWS
L	THARP, DANIEL	'67-'68	BJWS
L	VUGRIN, WILLIAM	'67-'68	BJWS
CTT #4	**NAME**	**YEARS**	**4th INF. DIV.**
L	BLIBEL, SAM	'67-'68	BJWS
*	BONGIORNO, MARTIN	'67-'68	BJWS
L	CARROLL, JOHN	'67-'68	BJWS
L	DACUS, JAMES H	'67-'68	BJWS
L	ERVIN, DANIEL F.	'67-'68	BJWS
SR.NCO	GROUP(E), TED M.	'67-'68	BJWS
L	INKLAAR, DAVID	'67-'68	BJWS
L *	McCART, TOM	'67-'69	BJWS
	NEWMAN, DANIEL F.	'67-'68	BJWS
L	OLHISER, MARTY	'67-'68	BJWS
	SILVIA (SP), JAMES (?)		
L	THOMAS, GEORGE S.	'67-'68	BJWS
L	VAN DYKE, JULIAN	'67-'68	BJWS
L	WIERENGA, JAN	'67-'68	BJWS
CTT #10	**NAME**	**YEARS**	**196th BDE.**
L CO	BELL, HAROLD	'67-'68	BJWS
SR.NCO	GOLDEN, GRANT S.	'67-'68	BJWS
L	ALBERD, ROBERT	'67-'68	BJWS
L	NEAR, KENT	'67-'68	BJWS
L	BEYLE, EUGENE	'67-'68	BJWS
	DINKINS, WILLIS	'67-'68	BJWS
	DUBLE, HOWARD R.	'67-'68	BJWS
	MARTIN, FREDDY	'67-'68	BJWS
L	MARTIN, RUSSELL "SLUG"	'68-'69	
L	MATSUMOTO, ROY S.	'67-'68	BJWS
L	SENIUK, MICHAEL	'68-'69	
L	TAYLOR, LAVON	'67	BJWS
L	TOLSON, STEVE	'67-'68	BJWS
	PHILLIPS, ROBERT	'67-'68	BJWS
L	WOOD, JOHN	'67-'68	BJWS
64thIPCT	**NAME**	**YEARS**	**4th INF. DIV.**
L CO	RANKIN, RICHARD	'68-'69	BJWS
CO	POLLY, JAMES	'69-'70	
L CO	HOSTETLER, HAROLD R.	'69-'70	

L		ALBERTSON, GREG	'68-'69	BJWS
		AMINHDANG (KIT CARSON)	'69-'70	
		BACON (?)	'69-'70	
KIA 1970		BLAIR, CHARLES D.	1970	
		BLOCKER, WILLIAM	'69-'70	
		BOLAND, JIMMY	'69-70	
		BOWERS, RAY	1968	
		CLARK (?)	'69-'70	
L		COLTER, KEVIN J.	'70-'71	FT. GORDON
	*	CRAMER, THOMAS	1971	
L	*	DAVIS, ALAN D.	'69-'70	OJT
		DODSON, (?)	'68-'69	
		DOOD, LARRY	'68-'69	
		DUNG (KIT CARSON SCOUT)	'69-'70	
		EASON, SHARP	'69-'70	
		EITNER, JIM	'68-'69	
		ENGSTROM, RONALD	'69-'70	
L		FOWLER, GARY D.	'67-'68	BJWS
		GALLOWAY, GREGG	1971	
L		GARCIA, JOE E. II	'69-'70	
L		GOLLIHUGH, JOHNNIE	'68-'69	
L	*	GROSS, FREDRICK	1970	FT. GORDON
L	*	GUERRA, MICHAEL R.	'70-'71	FT. GORDON
L		GUITERREZ, RODOLFO R.	'67-'68	BJWS
L		HADDER, GEORGE "RENO"	'68-'69	BJWS
L		HARMON, MILTON	1971	
L		HAWKINS, IKE	'68-'69	
		HAYES, HOMER L.	'69-'70	
	*	HENDERSON, CHAS.	1971	
		HERZOG, RALPH	'68-'69	
L		HICKS, JESSE C.	'68-'69	
		HOHM, MICHAEL	'69-'70	
		HOLSTROM, HAROLD	1971	
		JANNEY, (?)	'69-'70	
L		KIZYMA, LUBKO	'69-'70	
L	*	KASPER, JAMES R. "BOBBY"	'70-'71	FT. GORDON
L		KLINE, KEN	'69-'70	
		LARGE (?)	'69-'70	
		LOCKMAN, TERRY	'69-'70	
		LOEFFELBEIN, T.	'69-'70	
		LONGO (?)	'69-'70	
		LUGO (?)	'69-'70	
		MARTINEZ, DANIEL	'69-'70	
L	*	MAYKUTH, FRANK J.	1971	
L	*	McCART, TOM	'68-'69	BJWS

		McKINNEY, MICHAEL	'69-'70	
L	*	McLAMB, HAROLD D.	1970	FT. GORDON
L	*	McLEMORE, THOMAS	1970	FT. GORDON
L		MILLER, RICHARD D.	'67-'68	BJWS
		MINOR (?)	'69-'70	
L		MORAN, HENRY W.	'67-'68	BJWS
	*	NABORS, GARY D.	'67-'68	BJWS
		NEWICKI, PETER	'69-'70	
L		OSBORNE, RAYMOND B.	'67-'68	BJWS
		PAULUS, (?)	'68-'69	
		PARSONS, (?)	'68-'69	
		ROBINSON, ROB	'68-'69	
L		ROLES, REGINALD G.	'68-'69	
		ROSE, DONALD	'69-'70	
		SCHINDLER (?)	'69-'70	
		SCHROEDER, ELDON	'70-'71	
		SCOTT, LARRY	'68-'69	BJWS
		SHARP, JASON	'69-'70	
		SHUKER, WILLIAM J.	'69-'70	
		TARVIN, HARRY	'69-'70	
		THIEL, JIM	'68-'69	
L		VAN DYKE, JULIAN	'68-'69	
		VAN STEENBERG. WILLIAM J.	'68-'69	BJWS
		VUICH, RONALD	'69-'70	
		WALKER, H. "REB"	'68-'69	
L		WILLIAMSON, GLADE	'69-'70	
		WILSON (?)	'69-'70	
		WITNER, JAMES M.	'68-'69	BJWS
	*	WOODBURY, DONALD E.		
		WOODHOUSE (?)	'69-'70	
		YOUNGBLOOD (?)	'69-'70	

	LAB NAME	YEARS	4th INF. DIV.
	BUTCH	1967-'69	BJWS
Died 1967	DAGGER	1967	BJWS
	DARKIE	1967	BJWS
	GOLDIE	1967-'69	BJWS
	JET	1970	BJWS
	LINDA	1969-'70	
	OMAR	1969-'70	
	OSCAR	1969-'70	
	SAM	1967-'69	BJWS
	SKIPPER	1967-'70	BJWS
	SMIGGER	1967	BJWS
	TWIGGER		
	ZIP	1967	BJWS

	1ST INFANTRY DIVISION		
CTT #5	**NAME**	**YEARS**	**1st INF. DIV.**
L CO	REED, RON G.	'67-'68	BJWS
L NCO	HODGE, CHRISTOPHER C.	'67-'68	BJWS
L	CARPENTER, GILBERT N.	'67	BJWS
L *	CHERRY, CHARLES	'67-'68	BJWS
L SR.NCO	COOL, ROGER	'67-'68	BJWS
L	BIANCARDI, DAVID	'67-'68	BJWS
	BREEDEN, ROGER L.	'67-'68	BJWS
	GRESS, TIMOTHY G.	'67-'68	BJWS
*	HORNER, ALFRED	'67-'68	BJWS
L	JOHNS, FRANKLIN C.	'67-'68	BJWS
L	O'BANNON, JACKIE E.	'67-'68	BJWS
L	REED, JOHN P.	'67-'68	BJWS
	ROBINSON, JOHN	'67-'68	BJWS
L	STONE, JAMES P.	'67-'68	BJWS
	WHITE, (?)	'67-'68	BJWS
	WILLIAMS, JAMES H.	'67-'68	BJWS
L	VANOVER, MICHAEL C.	'67-'68	BJWS
CTT #13	**NAME**	**YEARS**	**1st INF. DIV.**
L CO	HENDRICKS, DON	'67-'68	BJWS
L SR.NCO	KIRMSE, THEODORE D.	'67-'68	BJWS
	BATTLES, GEORGE D.	'67-'68	BJWS
L *	BURCHFIELD, ROY O.	'67-'68	BJWS
L	BURKE, RICHARD F.	'67-'68	BJWS
L	COX, WILLIE C.	'67-'68	BJWS
L	DODD, THOMAS	'67-'68	BJWS
L	HAYNES, ALFRED W. JR	'67-'68	BJWS
	SCOTT, JERRY W	'67-'68	BJWS
L	SHAW, NORMAN G.	'67-'68	BJWS
L	TESDALL, STEVEN J.	'67-'68	BJWS
L	TIMMINS, RICHARD D.	'67-'68	BJWS
*	WILDE, JON C.	'67-'68	BJWS
61st IPCT	**NAME**	**YEARS**	**1st INF. DIV.**
L CO	CANCHOLA, SAL	'68-'69	BJWS
L *	CAPUTO, LOUIS	'69-'70	FT GORDON
L	AUER, TOM	'69-'70	BJWS
L *	BATES, JERRY W.	'67-'68	BJWS
L	BLAIR, DOUG	'68-'69	BJWS
KIA 1969	BULLWINKEL, ALDEN J.	1969	BJWS
L *	BURCHFIELD, ROY O.	'68-'69	BJWS
L *	CHERRY, CHARLES	'68-'69	BJWS
L	COX, WILLIE C.	'67-'68	BJWS

Seek On!

L *	DAVIS, ALAN D.	'69-'70	OJT
	DICKEY, WILLIE	'68-'69	BJWS
L	DUDLEY, JEARALD	'68-'69	BJWS
L	ENO, MYRON L.	'68-'69	OJT
L	FERRARO, RONALD	'67-'68	OJT
	FINLEY, CHARLES W.	'68-'69	BJWS
L	FOLLAND, DAVID R.	'68-'69	BJWS
L	GIGUERE, LEONARD	'67-'68	BJWS
L	GOIN, JAMES	'68-'69	BJWS
L	GRADY, WILLIAM E. JR	'67-'68	BJWS
CO	HARRIS, DANIEL	'68-'69	
L	HAUSER, THOMAS C.	'68-'69	BJWS
	HOBBS, STEVE	'68-'69	BJWS
L	HORNBERGER, THEODORE E.	'68-'69	BJWS
L *	HORTON, MIKE	'69-'70	FT GORDON
L	LANTING, JOHN W.	'68-'69	BJWS
	JOHNSON, CARL	'68-'69	
	LIEDY, CARL E.	'68-'69	BJWS
L	LILE, DENZIL	'68-'69	BJWS
L *	LUKE, LEROY T. JR	'69-'70	
Vet Tech	MALONEY, JOHN	'69-'70	
	McCARTHY, JAMES J.	'69-'70	
KIA 1968	MEYER, LEO ROLAND	1968	BJWS
L	MILLER, ROBERT	'69-'70	
*	MONTFORD, JAKE	'69-'70	FT GORDON
L	POLEN, STEVE	'69	
L *	PRITCHETT, JERRY	'67-'68	BJWS
L	RICHARDSON, TERRY	'68-69	BJWS
L	ROBISON, JERRY .L	'67-'69	BJWS
L	ROPER, IVORY L.	'69-'70	OJT
	ROSELIO, ESPADA LUIS	'67-'68	BJWS
	SCARDINA, MICHAEL	'69-'70	
	SEPULVEDA, ROBERT	'68-'69	BJWS
L	SCOTT, JOHN Lt.	'69	
L	SILFIES, RANDY O.	'69-'70	
L *	SNYDER, DENNIS "Shorty"	'69-'70	BJWS
L	SPECHT, GARY	'69-'70	
L *	STEWARD, CHARLES E.	'67-'68	BJWS
L	WAGAMAN, JOHN	'68-'69	BJWS
L *	WHEELER, ED	'67-'68	BJWS
L	WHITE, L. ERIC "Rick"	'68	BJWS
*	WILDE, JON C.	'68-'69	BJWS
L	WILLIAMS, GERALD S.	'69-'70	OJT
	WILSON, ROBERT I.		
L	WILSON, O'DELL	'69-'70	DTD
L	WOHLBRANDT, DONALD	'68-'69	BJWS
CO	YOUNG, RICHARD A.	'69	

Susan Merritt

	LAB NAME	YEARS	1st INF. DIV.
KIA 1970	SAM	1967-'70	BJWS
Died 1969	JOEY	1967-'69	BJWS
	BRUCE	1967-'69	BJWS
	BLACKIE (* a.k.a. DEVIL)	1967-'69	BJWS
	SMIGGER	1968-'69	BJWS
	9TH INFANTRY DIVISION		
CTT#6	NAME	YEARS	9th INF. DIV.
L	CALLAWAY, PERRY	'67-'68	BJWS
L	COON, GARY	'67-'68	BJWS
L	FERRARO, DON	'67-'68	OJT
L	GAYDARIK, STEPHEN	'67-'68	BJWS
*	HORNER, AL	'67	BJWS
	KUFFELL, EUGENE	'67-'68	BJWS
L *	LANDERS, MIKE	'67-'68	BJWS
L *	McDONALD, GEORGE "Mac"	'67-'68	BJWS
L CO	RICHESON, PAUL Lt.	'67-'68	BJWS
L SR.NCO	WARD, GARY	1967	BJWS
CTT #14	NAME	YEARS	9th INF. DIV.
	FRIIS, JAMES	'67-'68	BJWS
	GATTINGER, GARY	'67-'68	BJWS
	GELL, LARRY	'67-'68	BJWS
L	HAWKINS, STEPHEN D.	'67-'68	BJWS
L	HUGHES, BILL	'67-'68	BJWS
	MANLEY, EDGAR, JR.	'67-'68	BJWS
	MANZANARES, BART.	'67-'68	BJWS
	RICHARDS, LARRY D.	'67-'68	BJWS
	SEDILLO, ALBERT	'67-'68	BJWS
	SIMPSON, JOHN R.	'67-'68	BJWS
	SMITH, DONALD H.	'67-'68	BJWS
	THIBAULT, KENNETH	'67-'68	BJWS
L	UPTON, BILLY	'67-'68	BJWS
	VAZQUEZ, PORFIRO	'67-'68	BJWS
L	WATSON, JOSEPH L.	'67-'68	BJWS
65thIPCT	NAME	YEARS	9th INF. DIV.
L	BEATTY, AL	'68-'69	BJWS
L	BLILE, SAM	'68-'69	
L *	BURKE, MICHAEL O.I.C.	'68-'69	
L	CATALDO, SAL		
L	CLARK, WILEY	'68-'69	BJWS
L	CRUMP, BERT W.	'69-'70	FT. GORDON
	CURRY, JOHN		
L	EITEL, RON Sgt.	'68-'69	BJWS

Seek On!

*	GORHAM, ROBERT SSG		BJWS
L	GOSS, KENNETH	'67-'68	BJWS
L	HARGRAVES, STEVE	1970	
L	HEFLIN, WARREN	'67-'68	BJWS
L	HESSENIUS, GEORG	'68-'69	
L	HUGGINS, MORRIS	'68-'69	BJWS
L	KAFKA, DOUG	'68-'69	
L	KEEN, ROBERT	'68-'69	
KIA 1969	KIEFHABER, ANDREW J.	1969	
L *	KONNO, EMERICK T.	1969	
L	KRISE, ROBERT	1969	
L *	LANDERS, MIKE	'68-'70	BJWS
	LEPACK, STANLEY		BJWS
	LEWIS, KERRY W.	'69-'70	
L	LOQUIST, GARY PSgt.	'68-'69	BJWS
	LOVIN, HUGH	'69-'70	OJT
L	MARNELL, ROGER	'68-'69	BJWS
L	MENDOZA, ROBERT J.	'69-'70	OJT
	MERCER, BRAD Lt.	'68-'69	BJWS
L	MORRIS, GARY	'68-'69	
	MURRAY, JOHN	'69-'70	OJT
	NAKAMURA, BRUCE A.	'69-'70	
	NASH, GERALD R.	'69-'70	
	PATTERSON, ROBERT	'69-'70	
L	QUIRK, RORY		
L	RICH, WILLIAM	'68-'69	
L	RICHARD, JESS	'68-'69	BJWS
	ROBINSON, NATHANIEL		
	SHAHA, ROBERT	'69-'70	OJT
L	SYNDRUM, ROBERT		BJWS
L	THOMAS, DAVID E.	'67-'68	BJWS
L	TOMLINSON, JAMES	'69-'70	BJWS
L	WARRICK, KENNETH	'68-'69'	BJWS
	WASHBURN, ROGER	'68-'69'	BJWS
L	WATSON, DAVID	'68-'69'	BJWS
	WOODS, SAMMY	'69-'70	
	LAB NAME	**YEARS**	**9th INF. DIV.**
KIA 1969	PRINCE	1967-'69	BJWS
	NIGGER	1967-'68	BJWS
	JET	1967-'69	BJWS
KIA 1970	JOE	1967-'70	BJWS

1ST CAVALRY DIVISION AIRMOBILE

CTT #7	NAME	YEARS	1st AIR CAV.
CO	HUNT, HOWARD	'67-'68	BJWS
L SR.NCO*	NICHOLSON, JOSEPH	'67-'68	BJWS
	MOORE, JAMES, SGT.	'67-'68	BJWS
L	CLEMINGS, RALPH	'67-'68	BJWS
L	DUPLA, JOHN	'67-'68	BJWS
L	LA FARLETTE, JAMES	'67-'68	BJWS
L	MAHONEY, LANCE	'67-'68	
L	MERRITT, FRANK	1967	BJWS
	NAVAREZ, JUAN	'67-'68	BJWS
L	PRESLEY, THOMAS G.	'67-'68	BJWS
L	REED, BILL	'67-'68	BJWS

CTT#8	NAME	YEARS	1st AIR CAV.
L CO*	HUDSON, RONALD	1967	BJWS
L SR.NCO	LAMB, HUGH E.	1967	BJWS
L SR.NCO*	COUCH, NEIL	'67-'68	BJWS
KIA 1967	BEUKE, DENNIS ARTHUR	1967	BJWS
	BROWN, KENNETH	'67-'68	BJWS
L	CRADICK, STEVE	'67-'68	BJWS
L	DOTSON, JOHN E.	'67-'68	BJWS
L	MAXHAM, REGGIE	'67-'68	BJWS
KIA 1967	MAHURIN, ELMER WAIN	1967	BJWS
L	NIGGERMEYER, TOM	'67-'68	BJWS

62nd IPCT	NAME	YEARS	1st AIR CAV.
L	ADAMS, JIMMY W.	1970	
*	ADAMS, RAY "POP"	'68-'69	BJWS
	ACOSTA, ANDY	'68-'69	
	ALONZO, D Sgt.		
	ALVAREZ, CARLOS	'70-'71	
	ANDERSON, (?)	'70-'71	
L CO	APPLEBY, DAVID	'71-'72	FT.BENNING
L	ARNADO, EDWARD	'68-'69	
	ARMSTRONG, PHILLIP	'70-'71	
L	BARTON, STEVE T.	'70-'71	FT. GORDON
	BATES, CLIFFORD	'70-'71	
L CO	BAUMER, RICHARD	'69-'70	FT. GORDON
L	BEHYMER, DAVID H.	'70-'71	
L	BECK, ROBERT M.	1968	OJT
L	BELL, JACK	'68-'69	FT. GORDON
L CO	BESECKER, KEN LT.	1970	
L	BODLE, DAVID	'70-'71	
	BREAUX, BARRY	'68-'69	
	BROWN, THOMAS R.	1970	

Seek On!

		BROWNE, GREGORY	'70-'71	
		BURR, JAMES	'70-'71	
L		BURWELL, LAWRENCE	'69-'70	FT. GORDON
		BUTORAC, ROGER	'71-'72	FT. GORDON
L		CASEY, WILLIAM C.	'69-'70	FT. GORDON
		CHURCH, JOHN	'70-'71	
		COOK, GARY	'69-'70	
		CRAIG, KEITH SSG	'69-'70	
		CROSKEY, BERNIE	'68-'69	
		CUNNINGHAM, JOHN	'68-'69	
		DEARING, JAMES R.	1971	
		DEROSIER, LARRY	'69-'70	BJWS
L		DION, ED	'68-'69	BJWS
KIA 1970		DRUM, THOMAS	1970	
L		EASTMAN, RON	'68-'69	
		EDWARDS, HAROLD	'68-'69	
L		ENDERS, DOUG	'67-'68	BJWS
		EUBANKS, (?)	'70-'71	
L		EVERHART, RAYMOND	'70-'71	
L		FAUST, ROBERT	'68-'69	
		FLOWERS, R Sgt.		
*		FRANKLIN, GEORGE	1971	BJWS
L		FRESCH, MARK	'69-'70	
L		FULMER, JAMES	'70-'71	
L		GERGEN, MICHAEL	'71-72	FT. GORDON
		GILL, STEVEN T.	'68-'69	
L	CO	GILMORE, GARLAND	'68-'69	BJWS
		GREEN, JAMES D.	1971	
L		HABEL, LEROY	'70-'71	
L		HAMMOND, ARTHUR "LYNN"	'68-'69	BJWS
		HARRIS, LARRY		
		HARTLEY, ROBERT	1968	
L		HARWOOD, R. DEAN	'70-'71	
L	*	HAUSMANN, CLEM	1971	
L		HILL, REX	'70-'71	
L		HINELY, CHARLES	'70-'71	FT. GORDON
L		HIPP, MARK	1971	FT. GORDON
		HOLBROOK, BURL	1971	
		HORNSBY, JON		
L	*	HUGHES, JOHN	'68-'69	
L		HUTCHINSON, JOHN D.	'68-'69	
L		HYLTON, DON	'68-'69	
L		JOHNSON, HOWARD	'68-'69	FT. GORDON
		JONES, JAMES E. "CLEM"	'69-'70	
		JONES, JAMES O. "SOUL"	'69-'70	
		KELLY, WILFORD	'68-'69	

L	KEPHART, JOSEPH W.	'67-'68	BJWS
	KOOIMAN, DENNIS	'68-'69	
L	LA FAVE, JOE	'70-'71	FT. GORDON
L	LAWLESS, LARRY	'70-'71	FT. GORDON
L	LUCE, NORMAN	'71-'72	
	LUGENBEHL, BILLY	'68-'69	
L *	LUKE, LEROY T. JR	'69-'70	
L	LUNDIN, GARY	'69-'70	OJT
	MAC INTURFF (?)	'69-'70	
	MANION, WILLIAM	1971	
KIA 1969	MARASCO, JOSEPH	1969	BJWS
L	MATHENY, C.W.	'70-'71	FT. GORDON
L	MATT, ESTEL	'70-'71	FT. GORDON
L	MAYNOR, JOHNNY	'70-'71	OJT
CO	MILLER, WILLIAM C.	'69-'70	
L *	MILLS, KAY	'70-'71	BJWS
L	MINOR, CARL	'70-'71	FT. GORDON
L	MORRIS, RAYMOND M.	'68-'69	BJWS
	NEWTON, MORRIS J.	1971	
L	NORTHRUP, BRUCE	?	
	NORWOOD (?) "ANIMAL"	'69-'70	
L	PASCUCCI, RUDY	'69-'70	
CO	PAYNE, HOWARD DAVID	1971	
	PAYNE, WILLIAM R.	'68-'69	FT. GORDON
	PETERSON, STEPHEN H.	'68-'69	FT. GORDON
L	PRINN, TERRY	'70-'71	
L	REED, WALTER M.	'67-'68	BJWS
KIA 1968	RIVERA, JAMES	1968	BJWS
L	ROSE, MARION "ALVIN"	'67-'69	BJWS
L	RUSSELL, DAVID	'70-'71	FT. GORDON
	SCHMITT, ROGER	'68-'69	
	SIMPSON, LEE F. JR	'69-'70	
L	SMITH, DENNIS	'68-'69	BJWS
L *	SNITGEN, LARRY	'70-'71	BJWS
L	SOKELAND, VIC	'68-'69	BJWS
L	SPIVEY, WILLIAM "Tex"	'70-'71	FT. GORDON
L	STEWART, GARY	'68-'69	
	STRONG, ARMAND	'70-'71	
L	TAKACH, STEVE	'70-'71	
L	TONELLI, BOB	'68-'69	BJWS
L	TREICHEL, CARL	'68-'69	BJWS
L	TROUTT, LARRY	'67-'68	BJWS
L *	TURNER, DONALD	'67-'68	BJWS
	VAN STEENBURG (?)	'69-'70	
L	VEST, HERB	'67-68	BJWS
	WALTERS, RUSSELL	'70-'71	
L	WALTZ, GEORGE A.	'67-'68	BJWS

L *	WARDEN, DANIEL	'68-'69	BJWS
L	WATSON, TERRY	'68-'69	
	WHITE, WILLIAM C.	'69-'70	
	LAB NAME	**YEARS**	**1st AIR CAV.**
	LUCKY	1967-'69	BJWS
	SAMBO	1967-'71	BJWS
KIA 1968	SHADOW	1967-'68	BJWS
	BRUCE	1967-'71	BJWS
	BLACK(IE)	1970-'71	
	BOOGA BEAR	1971-'72	
	BOY	1971	
	MACKEY	1970-'72	BJWS
	MAJOR	1970	BJWS
	NOBLE	1971-'72	
	OTIS	1970-'71	
KIA 1970	TENEQ	1968-'70	
	TRAVELER	1969-'70	
	101ST AIRBORNE DIVISION		
CTT #9	**NAME**	**YEARS**	**101st ABN.**
L	ASINO, RODNEY	'67-'68	BJWS
	BOYER, RICHARD	'67-'68	BJWS
L	CANNON, BILL	'67-'68	BJWS
L	FARMER, JOSEPH A.	'67-'68	BJWS
	HAHN, DAVID	'67-'68	BJWS
KIA 1967	HARDING, JOHN H.	1967	BJWS
L *	MILLER, BEN	'67-'68	BJWS
KIA 1968	SMOOT, ROBERT GENE	'67-'68	BJWS
SR.NCO	TEETERS, JOHNNY	'67-'68	BJWS
L CO	WILLIAMS, STEPHEN A.	'67-'68	BJWS
	WOMACK, CHARLIE L.	'67-'68	BJWS
557thIPCT	**NAME**	**YEARS**	**101st ABN.**
	ADAMS, JIMMY W.	'70-'71	FT. GORDON
	ANDERSON, JESSIE	'70-'71	FT. GORDON
	ARVELO, BOB "Chief"	1969	
	BENJAMIN, HENRY R.	'70-'71	FT. GORDON
	BENNET, CHARLES D.	'70-'71	FT. GORDON
L	BLAIR, JAMES R.	'70-'71	FT. GORDON
L	BRAMHAN, JAMES E.	'70-'71	FT. GORDON
L	BROTHERS, DOUG	'70-'71	FT. GORDON
L	BROWN, ART	'70-'71	FT. GORDON
L	BUDNEY, ED	'69-'70	FT. GORDON
L	BUFFINGTON, DON L.	'70-'71	FT. GORDON
L	CAMPBELL, DONALD R.	'70-'71	FT. GORDON
L	CAPRESECCO, JIM	'69-'70	FT. GORDON

L	*	CAPUTO, LOUIS	'70	FT. GORDON
		CARNAHAN, RON	'70-'71	FT. GORDON
L	*	CHANEY, JAMES	'70-'71	FT. GORDON
L	*	CLARK, GARY	'71	FT. GORDON
KIA 1970		CONNER, JACK WM.	1970	FT. GORDON
KIA 1969		CONNORS, JACK LEE	1969	FT. GORDON
L		DIVENS, GEORGE	1970	FT. GORDON
L	*	DUENAS, JUAN	'68-'69	BJWS
		ERICKSON, JOE "Snuffy"	'68-'69	BJWS
		GARCIA, (?) Sgt/	'68-'69	BJWS
L		GATER, BRAD	'68-'69	OJT
		HAIR, LARRY	'68-'69	
		HALSEY, JERRY "Shorty"	'68-'69	BJWS
		HANNAWAY, EGBERT	'70-'71	FT. GORDON
L		HANSON, FRANK. A	1969	
L		HARMON, MILTON A.	'70-'71	FT. GORDON
L	*	HESLIN, JOHN	'70-'71	FT BENNING
		HICKS, ED "Gunnar"	1969	
L		HINELY, CHARLES	'70-'71	
L	*	HORTON, MIKE	'70-'71	FT. GORDON
L	*	JACKSON, ROBERT C.	'70-'71	FT. GORDON
		JOHNSON, WALTER L.	'70-'71	
		KIMBROUGH, THOMAS	'68-'69	BJWS
KIA 1969		KING, ALEXANDER	'68-'69	BJWS
L		KNAPP, MAX	'68-'69	BJWS
KIA 1970		LAGODZINSKI, ROGER T	1970	BJWS
L		LABUDA, RAYMOND	'70-'71	FT. GORDON
		LEVEQUE, JOHN	'70-'71	FT. GORDON
		MACKEY, (?)	'68-'69	BJWS
L		MARKT, WAYNE	'68-'69	BJWS
		McCONNAHAY, STEVE	'68-'69	BJWS
L	*	McDONALD, GEORGE "MAC"	'68-'69	BJWS
L		MEEKS, JOHN W.	'70-'71	FT. GORDON
L	*	MENDOZA, ROBERT Sgt.	'70-'71	OJT
L	*	MILLER, BEN	'68-'69	BJWS
	*	MONTFORD, JAKE	'70	FT. GORDON
	CO	MOORE, (?) Lt	'68-'69	
L		MULHOLLAND, MICHAEL	'68-'69	BJWS
L		MUXLOW, TERRY	'69-'70	FT. GORDON
		MURRAY, HARVEY	'70-'71	FT. GORDON
		MYERS, GORDON	'70-'71	
		NEWBURY, ALONZO	'70-'71	FT. GORDON
L		NOTESTINE, RICHARD	'68-'69	FT. GORDON
		ONCHA, NICK	'70-'71	FT. GORDON
		PATTERSON, B. "Pat"	1969	FT. GORDON
L		PAUL, HENRY	'70-'71	FT. GORDON

L	PEREZ, JOSE "Pepe"	'68-'69	
L	PIXLEY, LARRY W.	'70-'71	FT. GORDON
L	PROCTOR, KEN	'70-'71	FT. GORDON
L *	PURSLEY, LLOYD	'70-'71	FT. GORDON
L	RADICE, LARRY	'70-'71	FT. GORDON
KIA 1971	RATCLIFF, BILL H.	'70-'71	FT. GORDON
L	REYENGER, ROBERT	'70-'71	FT. GORDON
	RHOADES, RON	'68-'69	BJWS
KIA 1969	ROBERTS, VIRGIL JESSIE	1969	
	ROZHON, JOSEPH	'70-'71	FT. GORDON
L	SANBORN, TITUS RAY	'70	FT. GORDON
	SAPP, MICHAEL Lt. CO	1969	
	SCHAEFFER, WILLIAM	'70-'71	FT. GORDON
	SCHAFER, TED	'70-'71	FT. GORDON
	SCOTT, ROBERT F.	'70-'71	FT. GORDON
	SHARPE, REGINALD	'70-'71	
	SMALLWOOD, (?)	'69	
KIA 1969	SMITH, LAWRENCE LEON	1969	
L	SMITH, DANIEL	'70-'71	FT. GORDON
L	SMITH, DONALD R.	'70-'71	FT. GORDON
*	SMITH, MITCHELL D.	'70-'71	BJWS
	SMITH, (?)	'68-'69	
L *	STEWARD, CHARLES E.	'70-'71	BJWS
	SWIFT, ROBERT	'68-'69	BJWS
L	TAYLOR, WENDELL	'70-'71	DTD
KIA 1971	TERESINSKI, JOSEPH A.	1971	
L	THOMAS, MERLE F. Sgt.	'69-'71	BJWS
L	TILLERY, DONALD	'70-'71	FT. GORDON
	VILLALOBOS, ALEX	'70-'71	
L	WADE, GEORGE SSgt.	'68-'69	BJWS
L	WILSON, TEXAS L.	'70-'71	FT. GORDON
L *	WOLFARTH, BRUCE	'68-'69	BJWS
	YATES, (?)	'68-'69	BJWS
CO	YOUNG, RICHARD A.	'70	
	YOUNGBLOOD, EMMETT	'70-'71	FT. GORDON
42nd SD	**NAME**	**YEARS**	**101st ABN.**
L	BODNAR, BILL	'70—	
47th SD	**NAME**	**YEARS**	**101st ABN.**
L	BURGHART, PETER	'70-'71	FT. GORDON
	LAB NAME	**YEARS**	**101st ABN.**
	MACKEY	'67-'70	BJWS
	TARKA	'67-'70	BJWS
	BRUCE	1970	BJWS

	DRACO	'69-'71	
	MOE	'69-'71	
	SMOKEY	'69-'71	
	THOR	'70-'71	
199TH LIGHT INFANTRY BRIGADE			
CTT #11	NAMES	YEARS	199th LT.INF. BDE.
L CO	WITTER, JAS A. "TONY"	'67-'68	BJWS
L SR.NCO *	NAHINU, MOSES K. "PAPPY"	'67-'68	BJWS
L	COHRAN, LARRY A.	'67-'68	BJWS
L	DEJEWSKI, JEFFERY "JEFF"	'67-'68	BJWS
L	GEORGE, WILLIAM P. "BILL"	'67-'68	BJWS
L	IYOTTE, LAWRENCE "CHIEF"	'67-'68	BJWS
KIA 1968	LACHNEY, FLOYD C.	'67-'68	BJWS
L	LAWSON, JAMES F. "JIM"	'67-'68	BJWS
L	SCOTT, MITCHELL D. "MITCH"	'67-'68	BJWS
L	SEYDELL, CLIVE L.	'67-'68	BJWS
76th IDCT	NAMES	YEARS	199th LT.INF. BDE.
L	ALBERTIE, DON	'68-'69	OJT
L	BOWEN, MARK	'68-'69	BJWS
	BROWN, DENNIS	'68-'69	BJWS
	BRUNSWICK, MICHAEL S.	'68-'69	
L	CARTER, WILLIAM	'68-'69	BJWS
L	COATES, GRANT	'68-'69	OJT
KIA 1969	COX, EDWARD ERLIN JR.	1969	
	COX, GEORGE R.	'69-'70	
	DENISON, GARY	'68-'69	BJWS
	DIXON, RICHARD	'69-'70	
	EVANS, LOUIS	'68-'69	
	FRANCE, RICHARD	'68-'69	
L	FREELAND, CHARLES I.	'68-'69	OJT
KIA 1968	FULLER, STANLEY CARL	1968	BJWS
	GRAHAM, LARRY	'68-'69	BJWS
	KEEN, JAMES	'69-'70	
	KELLY, WINFORD	'68-'69	BJWS
KIA 1970	LEVINS, FREDERICK R.	1970	
	MARTIN, JAMES A.	'68-'69	
	McDOWELL, STEVE	'69-'70	
L	MUIR, ERNIE	'68-'69	BJWS
L	POLLEY, DOUGLAS R.	'69-'70	FT. GORDON
L	ROLES, REGINALD G.	'68-'69	
L	SMITH, DANIEL	1970	
L	STANBAUGH, DAVID B.	'68-'69	
L	STOCKELL, WILLIAM J. "BILL"	'68-'69	BJWS

L		TURNER, JACK	'69-'70	FT. GORDON
L		VERHELLE, THOMAS J.	'68-'69	
L	*	WARDEN, DAN	'68-69	BJWS
L		WRIGHT, ALLEN W.	'69-'70	

	LAB NAME	YEARS	199th LT.INF. BDE.
	SHANE	1967-'70	BJWS
	INCE	1967	BJWS
	RIGGER	1968-'70	BJWS

23RD INFANTRY DIVISION			
63rd IPCT		NAME	YEARS	23rd INF. DIV
L	*	ADAMS, RAY	1971	
L		ADDY, RAY	'69-'70	FT. GORDON
L		AUGESON, JERRY	'70-'71	OJT
*		AYERS, DOUG	1971	
		BAILEY, BILLY F.	'70-'71	
		BALCH, EDWARD	'70-'71	
L		BARELA, DENNY	1971	FT. GORDON
L		BEACH, GEORGE	'69-'70	
L		BEREND, LARRY	'70-'71	
		BLAZAK, (?)	'68-'69	BJWS
L		BLOOM, RICKY	'70-'71	
		BOLLIN, SPENCER	'70-'71	FT. GORDON
L	*	BOWMAN, KENNETH L.	'70-'71	FT. GORDON
L	*	BRAMHAN, JAMES	1971	
		BRIGGS, (?)	'70-'71	FT. GORDON
L		BROWN, GRADY F.	'70-'71	FT. GORDON
		CARTER, STEPHEN M.	'70-'71	
L		CLUCAS, PAUL E.	'68-'69	BJWS
L		COBB, JAMES F.	1971	FT.GORDON
L		COONROD, DAVID Sgt.	'68-'69	BJWS
L		COLLEY, HOWARD	'68-'69	BJWS
		COLLINS (?)	'70-'71	
L		COOK, CHARLES BAILEY	'69-'70	
		CORBAN, GARY R.	'70-'71	
L		CORR, RONALD	1971	
		COSTELLO, RAY	'68-'69	BJWS
L		DEAN, MICHAEL	'70-'71	
		DERNICK, TERRANCE	'70-'71	
		DETTER, (?)	'70-'71	OJT
		EPP, PRESTON	'70-'71	
		EUSTICE, LAWRENCE	'68-'69	BJWS
		FARLEY, RAY	'68-'69	BJWS
L		FERGUSON, JOHN	1970	FT. GORDON
L		FISHER, GREG	'70-'71	OJT

L	FISKE, ROBERT B.	'68-'69	BJWS
L	FRACHISEUR, FRANK E.	'70-'71	OJT
L	FRANK, JOE	'68-'69	BJWS
L	GABBERT, GARY G.	1971	
L	GARCIA, ARNELLO	'70-'71	
	HAMEL, YVES	'70-'71	
	HARRIS, (?) Sgt.	'68-'69	BJWS
L	HOOKS, PHILLIP	'68-'69	BJWS
*	HOOT, WILLIAM A.	1971	
	HORNE, MICHAEL	'70-'71	
L	HUGHES, ROBERT	'70-'71	FT. GORDON
	HUFF, BILL	'70	FT. GORDON
	JAYNES, TERRANCE	'70-'71	
L	JENDRASZEWSKI, ED	'68-'69	BJWS
L	KADERLIK, THOMAS	'70-'71	
L	KEITH, MILDREN	'71-'72	
L	KIDD, RAYMOND		BJWS
	KING, ALBERT J.	'70-'71	
L	KONARSKE, ROBERT	1971	FT. GORDON
L	LEISGANG, THOMAS	'70-'71	FT. GORDON
L	LEMOINE, PERRY	'70-'71	FT. GORDON
	LOREY, ELMER	'70-'71	
	MAGEE. LLOYD "MAC"	'68-'69	BJWS
	MANBECK, HAROLD "DUTCH"	'70-'71	
	MARSHALL, PAUL	'70-'71	
L	MARTIN, JAMES A.	'68-'69	BJWS
L	MARTIN, RUSSELL "SLUG"	'69	
	MARTINDALE, (?) SSgt.	'68-'69	
L	MASON, FITCHIE	'68-'69	BJWS
L	MAYERS, RICKY	'71-'72	
L *	McLEMORE, THOMAS	'70-'71	FT. GORDON
	MEYERS, RICHARD	'69-'70	FT. GORDON
L	MILLER, ART "TINK"	'68-'70	
L	MORNE, MICHAEL	'70-'71	
	MURPHY, DAVID	'70-'71	
L	OBERMEYER, JAMES Lt.	'68-'69	
	OWEN, PHILLIP G.	'70-'71	
	PARKER, RONALD	1971	
	PARMLEY, RICHARD	'70-'71	
	PARRISH, RICHARD H.	'70-'71	
L	PATTERSON, RODNEY J.	'70-'71	FT. GORDON
	PRICE, VEEDEE	'70-'71	
L *	PURSLEY, LLOYD	1971	FT. GORDON
L	RADICE, LARRY	'70-'71	
L	RAUCH PHILLIP E.	'69-'70	
	REEVES, HENRY	'70-'71	
L *	REYNOLDS, LARRY	1971	FT. GORDON

Seek On!

		ROBERTS, (?)	'68-'69	
		ROGERS, MELVIN O.	'70-'71	
		RUCH, WAYNE	'70-'71	
		SATTLER, THOMAS A.	'70-'71	
L	*	SCHETROMPF, HOWARD	1971	BJWS
L		SENKUS, GARY L.	'70-'71	FT. GORDON
L		SENIUK, MIKE	'68-'69	BJWS
		SHELTON, LAWRENCE	'70-'71	
		SHERINGHAM, (?)	'68-'69	
		SIMS, PHIL	'68-'69	BJWS
		SNELL, JAMEW	'70-'71	
L	*	SNYDER, DENNIS (Shorty)	'69-'70	
L		SOUDER, GARY	'68-'69	BJWS
L		STAMBAUGH, DAVID B.	'68-'69	BJWS
L		TALBOT, ALAN	'70-'71	
		TERRES-VELEZ, JUAN	'70-'71	
		THOMPSON, HENRY	'70-'71	
L		THOMPSON, MICHAEL G.	'70-'71	
		TISDALE, PATRICK	'68-'69	
L		TRENT, CYRUS E.	'68-'69	BJWS
L		TUCKER, RICHARD E.	'68-'69	
		URBAN, FRANK	'70-'71	
		VOTAVA, TOM	'68-'69	
L		WALSH, JOE	'70-'71	DTD BIEN HOA
		WALTERS, ?		FT.GORDON
L		WEST, GEORGE	'69-'70	DTD BIEN HOA
L		WHITE, CLAYBOURNE	'70-'71	DTD BIEN HOA
		WHITE, THOMAS G.	'69-'70	
L		WHITMAN, NOEL	1971	
L		WILLIAMS, RAY	'70-'71	FT. GORDON
L		WOOD, JOHN	'67-'68	
*		WOODBURY, DONALD E.		
		WOODS, JAMES R.	'68-'69	
L		ZIGLER, PAUL	'70-'71	
63rd IPCT		**MINE & TUNNEL TEAMS**	**YEARS**	**23rd INF. DIV.**
		BALL, JOHN	'70-'71	TUNNEL
L		BANDLEY, JOHN	'70-'71	
L		BARDO. SAM	'70-'71	MINE
		CARTER, STEPHEN	1970	
L		COLVIN, DON	1971	TUNNEL
L		COOPER, TERRY	'70-'71	MINE & TUN.
L		DE LONG, ROBERT	1970	MINE
		DERNICK, TERRANCE	'70-'71	TUNNEL

	EPP, PRESTON	'70-'71	
	FLORIO, JOSPEH L.	'70-'71	
KIA 1970	GRIFFIN, WILLIAM D. II	1970	TUNNEL
KIA 1970	HATCHER, DAVID LEE	1970	MINE
	HOULIHAN, ROBERT	'70-'71	MINE
L	HOWELL, JESS	'70-'71	MINE
L	HUNDLEY, BRUCE	'70-'71	SCOUT
	KADERLIK, TOM	'70-'71	
L	LESLIE, CARL H. JR	'69-'70	MINE
L	LOUCH, GREGORY	'71-'72	
	LUTTRELL, JAMES W.	1971	
L	MURPHY, GERRY	'70-'71	MINE
KIA 1970	NUDENBERG, DAVID A.	1970	MINE
	OWEN, PHILIP	'70-'71	
L	REIBLE, ED	'70-'71	MINE
	SHIMABUKU, DANNY	'70-'71	SCOUT
L	SLOUGH, MONTY	'70-'71	MINE
L	STRINGER, SKIP	'71-'72	MINE
L	WILSON, MARK	'70-'71	MINE
L	WILSON, TOMMY RAY	'71-'72	MINE
	LAB NAME	**YEARS**	**23rd INF. DIV.**
	DARKIE	1967-'69	BJWS
	ZIP	1967-'69	BJWS
	INCE	1968-'71	BJWS
	ABBY	1970-'71	
	BLACKIE	1967-'69	BJWS
	BURCHES	1971	
	DUKE	1971	
	LUKE	1970-'72	
	MOE	1970	
	O'BRIAN	1971	
	OPAL	1971	
	OSCAR	1971	
	THOR	1970	
	WILLIE	1971	
	173RD AIRBORNE BRIGADE		
75th IDCT	**NAME**	**YEARS**	**173rd ABN.**
L	APMAN, EARL W. "SONNY"	'67-'68	BJWS
L	BAKER, ROBERT	'68-'69	BJWS
L *	BATES, JERRY W.	'69-'70	BJWS
	BERSUCH, JOHN	'68-'69	BJWS
	BROWN, DAVE	'69-'70	OJT
	BUTTS, MICHAEL A.	'67-'68	BJWS
L	CARRIERE, STEVE	'69-'70	

L	COLTER, KEVIN J.	'70-'71	FT. GORDON
L	CURTIS, FLOYD	'70-'72	FT. GORDON
	DIAZ, OSCAR	'69-'70	
	EATON, STACEY	'69-'70	
SR.NCO	EATON, WILLIAM E.	'69-'70	
L	GARCIA, LEONARD	'67-'68	BJWS
	GIBSON, ARCHIE L.	'67-'68	BJWS
	GRAVES, SCOTT	'69-'70	
L *	GUERRA, MICHAEL	'70-'71	FT. GORDON
L	HANSEN, GARY	'67-'68	BJWS
	HARMON, JAMES	'69-'70	
L	HERBERT, DAVID J.	'68-'69	FT. GORDON
L	HOBSON, SAM	'69-'70	OJT
	HOLLAND, TONY	'69-'70	
L	HOLROYD, MARTIN	1970	FT. GORDON
	HOWE, BILLY	'68-'69	BJWS
L	JOHNSON, HENRY	1969	
L *	KASPER, JAMES R. "BOBBY"	'70-'71	FT. GORDON
L	KING, DOUGLAS	'70-'71	FT. GORDON
L	KOECKES, HENRI N.	1968	BJWS
L	KRAUSE, STEVE	'69-'70	
KIA 1968	LAWTON, EDWARD W.	1968	BJWS
	LILLY, WAYNE	'69-'70	
L	MALAE, PETE	'68-'69	BJWS
L	MASSEY, NORMAN	'67-'68	BJWS
L *	MILLER, BEN L.	'70-'71	
Scout	MONTEZ, LOU	'69-'70	
L	NAKAGAWA, JIMMY M.	'67-'68	BJWS
L	NEMETH, CHARLES B.	'67-'68	BJWS
	NEWBOLD, JOHNNIE	'69-'70	
	NICHOLAS, LEROY J. "GINNY"	'67-'68	BJWS
	OTT, BRUCE	1970	FT. GORDON
L	PEREZ, HECTOR	'68-'69	BJWS
L	PETERSON, PETE	'68-'69	OJT
	PITTMAN, LYNN	'68-'69	BJWS
KIA 1970	RATLIFF, BILLY H.	1970	
	SASSER, "RED"	'69-'70	
L *	SCHETROMPF, HOWARD	'67-'68	BJWS
	SCOTT, ROBERT	'69-'70	
L	SECREST, WYNN	'68-'69	FT. GORDON
	SELHIME, EARNEST	'69-'70	
	SIMPSON, PAUL	'69-'70	
L	STEWART, JOHN R.	'67-'68	BJWS
	TATIANO, PERRY	'68-'69	
	TAYLOR, ALAN	'68-'69	BJWS
L	TIDWELL, RICK	'68-'69	BJWS

		TURNBULL, DOUGLAS	'70-'71	
L		VAUGHN, RICHARD Sgt.	'68-'69	BJWS
		WENK, FRED	'69-'70	
L		WHITTLE, MIKE	'70-'71	FT. GORDON
		WILLIAMS, CLIFTON W.	'67-'68	BJWS
		WOODS, STAN	'69-'70	
		LAB NAME	**YEARS**	**173rd ABN.**
		BRYN	1969	BJWS
		MOOSE	1967	BJWS
		SHANE	1970	BJWS
		5TH INFANTRY (MECH) & 82ND AIRBORNE		
77th IDCT		**NAMES**	**YEARS**	**5th ID/ 82nd ABN**
L	*	COUCH, NEIL	'69-70	BJWS
L	*	AYERS, DOUG	'70-71	
	*	BARNES, BILLY	'70-'71	
L	*	BEHMYER, DAVID H.	1971	
L		BONCZKOWSKI, ROBERT	'70-'71	
L	*	BOWMAN, KENNETH	'70-'71	FT. GORDON
L	*	BRAMHAN, JAMES E	1971	
		BUTLER, BOYD D. JR	'70-'71	
		CRAMER, THOMAS R.	'70-'71	
		DANIEL, JOHN	'70-'71	
		DEHLER, WILLIAM	1971	
		FLACK, MAX	'70-'71	
		FLYNN, JOHN	1971	
		FRIGO, RAYMOND	'70-'71	
L	*	GABBERT, GARY G.	1971	
		GALLOWAY, GREG	'70-'71	
		GOODMAN, DAVID P.	'70-'71	
		GREINDL, JOHN C.	'69-'70	
L	*	GROSS, FREDERICK	'70-'71	FT. GORDON
L	*	HAUSMANN, CLEM		FT. GORDON
		HENDERSON, CHARLES A.	'70-'71	
		HOOT, WILLIAM A.	1971	
		HUDSON, STEVEN D.	'70-'71	
		HUNROON, ROY G.	'70-'71	
L	*	KONO, EMERICK T.	1969	
L	*	KRISE, ROBERT	1969	
		JOHNSON, HAROLD	1971	
		KERSEY, FRANK	'70-'71	
		LILLY, EDWARD	'70-'71	
L	*	MAYKUTH, FRANK	'69-'71	FT. GORDON
		McDANIEL, EARNEST	'70-'71	

Seek On!

L	*	McLAMB, HAROLD D.	'70-'71	FT. GORDON
L	*	MORRIS, GARY	1969	
L	*	PATTERSON, ROBERT J.	'70-'71	
L	*	PRESLEY, THOMAS G.	1971	
L	*	PURSLEY, LLOYD	'70-'71	FT. GORDON
L		REYNOLDS, LARRY R.	1971	FT. GORDON
L		RICH, WILLIAM	1969	
		ROZHON, JOSEPH	'70-'71	
L	*	SCHETROMPF, HOWARD	'70-'71	BJWS
		SMITH, GLEN T.	'70-'71	
L		STEWART, ROBERT F. "DOC"	'70-'71	
		TIMS, ANDRE B.	'70-'71	
		WELLS, EUGENE JR.	'70-'71	
		WESTERN, FRANKLIN	'70-'71	
L		WILLIAMS, GARY LEE	'70-'72	FT. BENNING
		WILLIAMS, PATRICK L.	1971	
L		WILSON, TEXAS	'70-'71	
L		WOOD, JOHN JR.	'70-'71	
L		YOUNG, GREGG	'70-'71	FT. GORDON

	LAB NAME	YEARS	5th ID/ 82nd ABN
	DRACO	1971	
	SKIPPER	1970-'71	BJWS
	TOBY	1970-'71	
	KING (Shepherd Scout)	1970-'72	

1st FIELD FORCE—10TH CAVALRY				
78th IDCT		NAMES	YEARS	10th CAVALRY
	*	GADDIS, CECIL Sgt.	1971	
L	*	SYNDRUM, BOB Sgt.	1971	
	*	SMITH, ? Sgt.	1971	
L		BEILING, RONALD	1971	FT. GORDON
L		COLEMAN, JOHN J.	1971	FT. GORDON
L		ELLINGSON, CHET III	1971	FT. GORDON
L		GRAHAM, CLIFFORD	1971	FT. GORDON
L	Scout	HIGHFILL, ROGER	1971	FT. BENNING
L		MENDENHALL, WILLIAM	1971	FT. GORDON
L		NAGEL, JOHN	1971	FT. GORDON
L		NEWBERRY, MOODY	1971	FT. GORDON
L		NOVACICH, KEN	1971	FT. GORDON
L		O'KEEFE, TOM	1971	FT. GORDON
L		PINKERTON, VANCE	1971	FT. GORDON
		RESNER, DAVID	1971	FT. GORDON
L	Scout	THORNTON, LINWOOD	1971	FT. BENNING

	LAB NAME	YEARS	10th CAVALRY
	CINNAMON	1971	
	TARKA	1971	

COMBAT TRACKER TEAMS SERVING IN KOREA			
CTT	NAME	YEARS	2ND INF DIV
LSR.NCO *	NICHOLSON, JOE "NICK"	'68-'69	BJWS
Scout	BERG, BILL		FT. BENNING
Scout	BERRY, ROBERT		FT. BENNING
L	BIGGS, RICHARD L.	'68-'69	FT. GORDON
L Scout	BRUENING, KENNETH	'68-'69	FT. BENNING
L	COMSTOCK, FRED	'68	
L	FITZPATRICK, TOM	'68-'70	FT.GORDON
	GILLESPIE, BOB	'68-'69	
Scout	HEATHER, MICHAEL	'68-'69	FT. BENNING
L	HILLHOUSE, ARVILLE	'68-'69	FT. GORDON
	JARSOLAW, DANIEL A.	'68-'69	FT. GORDON
L	JOHNSON, BRUCE M.	'68-'69	FT. GORDON
	LANSING, WADE A.	'68-'69	FT. GORDON
L SR.NCO *	MATSUMOTO, ROY S.	'68-'89	BJWS
L	McNEAL, CARL E.	'68-'69	FT. GORDON
L *	MENDENHALL, WILLIAM H.	'68-'69	FT. GORDON
L	WHITAKER, MICHAEL K.	'68-'69	FT. GORDON
	SCHWARZ, RICHARD A.	'68-'69	FT. GORDON
L VetTech	STRAUSS, JAMES A.	'68-'69	FT. GORDON
L	YEOMANS, PATRICK A.	'68-'69	FT. GORDON
Scout	YOUNG, RUSSELL	'68-'69	FT. BENNING

INSTRUCTORS	
ADMINISTRATION	BJWS
WOODS, HUIA (MAJ) "British Education Officer"	SAS 22 R
DOWN, T.M.S. (CPT) COMMANDER—Cycle #4	SBS—RM
HALL-SMITH, D. (CPT) RAVC	R.A.V.C.
KIWI, ALBERT (LT)	NZ SAS OIC
SELLERS, RODGERS D. (MAJ) USARV	U.S. ARMY
WELCH, WILLIAM A. (CPT/MAJ) USARV L	U.S. ARMY
MAJORS, "PAPPY" (SFC) USARV (K-9)	U.S. ARMY
INSTRUCTORS – NZ SAS	BJWS—VISUAL
WYDUR, FRANK (SGT-NCOIC) NZ SAS L	BJWS-VISUAL
OAKLEY-BROWNE, HUGH (LT) NZ SAS L	BJWS-VISUAL
ILOLAHIA, KELLY (SGT) NZ SAS L	BJWS-VISUAL
KENO, RICKIE (SGT) NZ SAS	BJWS-VISUAL
MORUNGA, BEN (SGT) NZ SAS	BJWS-VISUAL
RAU, HENRY "Hank" (SGT) RNZINF L	BJWS-VISUAL

RIRINUI, "GORILLA", SNOOKS, (CPL) NZ SAS	BJWS-VISUAL
TE PAA, DAVID (CPL) NZ SAS	BJWS-VISUAL
CTT DOG HANDLER TRAINERS-RAVC	**#2 WDTU**
AYLWARD, MICK L	CANINE
HARDIE, RAY "JOCK" (SGT)	CANINE
HIGGS, JOHN (CPL) L	CANINE
JOHNSON, TREVOR	CANINE
PACKRISAMY, LOGANATHAN	CANINE
ROSSELL, TONY (MAJ) –Ret L	CANINE
YEANDLE, GEORGE—(B.E.M.) L	CANINE
ARAMUGAN (L.E.P)	CANINE
MUTHIAN, FRED (L.E.P)	CANINE
MAHALINGHAM (?), (L.E.P.)	CANINE
VERASAMY, (?)	CANINE
U.S. ARMY INSTRUCTORS	**FACILITY**
HUDSON, RONALD (LT)	BJWS-VISUAL
MALONE, CLYDE (LT)	BJWS-VISUAL
MYRICK, JAMES (LT)	BJWS-VISUAL
ADAMS, "POP" (SSG)	BJWS-VISUAL
ANWEILER, R. (SSG)	BJWS-VISUAL
GIBSON, ARCHIE L. (SSG)	BJWS-VISUAL
GORHAM, ROBERT (SSG)	BJWS-VISUAL
HODGE, CHRIS (SSG) L	BJWS-VISUAL
KOECKES, HENRI N. (SSG) L	BJWS-VISUAL
SMITH, R. (SSG)	BJWS-VISUAL
THARP, DAN (SSG) L	BJWS-VISUAL
THOMAS, GEORGE S. (SSG)	BJWS-VISUAL
WIERENGA, JAN (SSG) L	BJWS-VISUAL
CONUS FACILITY	
LARKIN, DAN (LTC) 1968—Program Director	FT. GORDON
CAMPBELL (CPT)—Administrative	FT. GORDON
RIBSL (CPT)—Administrative	FT. GORDON
HOFFMAN (SGM)—Administrative	FT. GORDON
SWINEY, TOMMY—Administrative	FT. GORDON
ADAMS, "POP" (SSG)	FT. GORDON
BAUMER, RICHARD (LT) 1970 L	FT. GORDON
BLESSING, BOB (SSG) L	FT. GORDON
CORHAN, LARRY (SGT) L	FT. GORDON
COUCH, NEIL (SGT) L	FT. GORDON
DUENAS, JUAN (SSG) L	FT. GORDON
ELLISON, RICK L	FT. GORDON
ERWIN (SP5)	FT. GORDON
GORHAM, ROBERT (SSG)	FT. GORDON

GRADY, PATRICK (SSG)	FT. GORDON
GROVE (SGT)	FT. GORDON
HOOKS, PHIL L	FT. GORDON
LANDERS, MIKE (SSG) L	FT. GORDON
LILE, DENZIL L	FT. GORDON
LOUDER, PAUL L	FT. GORDON
McLEMORE, THOMAS L	FT. GORDON
MILLER, BEN L	FT. GORDON
NABORS, GARY D.	FT. GORDON
NICHOLSON, JOSEPH (NICK) L	FT. GORDON
PAYNE, HOWARD DAVID III (LT) *KIA 1971*	FT. GORDON
PEREZ. JOSE (PEPE) L	FT. GORDON
REED, WAYNE L	FT. GORDON
ROBERTS, DeWITT L	FT. GORDON
SHAW, NORMAN L	FT. GORDON
SHRANK (SSG)	FT. GORDON
SNITGEN, LARRY (SSG) L	FT. GORDON
SMITH, R. (SSG)	FT. GORDON
STEWARD, CHARLES (SSG) L	FT. GORDON
STRINGER (SSG)	FT. GORDON
SWINEY, TOMMY	FT. GORDON
THARP, DANIEL L	FT. GORDON
THOMPSON, MICHAEL G. (SSG) L	FT. GORDON
WALTZ, GEORGE (SSG) L	FT. GORDON
WARD, GARY (SFC) L	FT. GORDON
WARD, JIM L	FT. GORDON
WOODBURY, DONALD E.	FT. GORDON
IN COUNTRY INSTRUCTORS	**DTD—30th I.D.**
CELINO, FRANCIS L	ADMINISTRATIVE
HOHL, DOUG	ADMINISTRATIVE
JOHNSON, RICK L	INSTRUCTOR
LAMB, HUGH (SFC) L	SR. INSTRUCTOR
MAJORS, "PAPPY" (SFC)	SR. INSTRUCTOR
MOORE, JAMES (SSG)	INSTRUCTOR
SHAW, NORMAN L	INSTRUCTOR
THARP, DAN (SSG) L	INSTRUCTOR
WIERENGA, JAN L	SR. INSTRUCTOR
VETERINARIANS & VET TECHS	**DIVISIONS**
BERENDS, LARRY—VET TECH. L	23rd INFANTRY
HADAD, MELVIN—D.V.M. L	25th INFANTRY
MALONEY, JOHN—VET TECH.	1st INFANTRY

TRACK LAYERS	SCHOOL
CLEMENT, CLIFF L	BJWS
DIXON	BJWS
ENDERS, DOUG L	BJWS
ERVIN, DAN	BJWS
HIMROD, BOB L	BJWS
INKELAAR, DAVID L	BJWS
KEEN, ROBERT L	BJWS
KREBS, RONALD	BJWS
PAULUS, RICHARD	BJWS
RIVERA, JAMES *KIA 1968*	BJWS
SMITH, LAWRENCE	BJWS
THOMAS, DAVID E. L	BJWS
TROUTT, LARRY L	BJWS
VICK	BJWS
WATSON, DAVID L	BJWS
WOODS, JAMES L	BJWS

CPSIA information can be obtained at www.ICGtesting.com
Printed in the USA
LVOW062259220413

330416LV00003B/185/P